MW01503298

THE

RVers

BIBLE

Explore the Great Outdoors Coast to Coast •

A Definitive Guide to Scenic Campgrounds and Accomodations
Across the United States.

Mike & Claire Davis

© Copyright 2024 by Mike & Claire Davis- All rights reserved.

This document is geared towards providing exact and reliable information in regards to the topic and issue covered. The publication is sold with the idea that the publisher is not required to render accounting, officially permitted, or otherwise, qualified services. If advice is necessary, legal or professional, a practiced individual in the profession should be ordered. - From a Declaration of Principles which was accepted and approved equally by a Committee of the American Bar Association and a Committee of Publishers and Associations. In no way is it legal to reproduce, duplicate, or transmit any part of this document in either electronic means or in printed format. Recording of this publication is strictly prohibited, and any storage of this document is not allowed unless with written permission from the publisher.

All rights reserved.

The information provided herein is stated to be truthful and consistent, in that any liability, in terms of inattention or otherwise, by any usage or abuse of any policies, processes, or directions contained within is the solitary and utter responsibility of the recipient reader. Under no circumstances will any legal responsibility or blame be held against the publisher for any reparation, damages, or monetary loss due to the information herein, either directly or indirectly.

Respective authors own all copyrights not held by the publisher. The information herein is offered for informational purposes solely and is universal as so. The presentation of the information is without contract or any type of guarantee assurance. The trademarks that are used are without any consent, and the publication of the trademark is without permission or backing by the trademark owner. All trademarks and brands within this book are for clarifying purposes only and are owned by the owners themselves, not affiliated with this document.

HOW TO USE THIS BOOK

When my wife and I started writing this book, it wasn't just about compiling a list of campgrounds; we wanted to share our experience from the many miles we've traveled on the road with our beloved RVs. Over the years, we've been fortunate enough to own four different campers, each with its own unique features. We began with a small Class B van, then upgraded to a more spacious Class C, moved on to a fifth-wheel for longer trips, and finally settled into a Class A motorhome, which has been our mobile home for several years. Each model taught us something new, and everything we've learned is captured in this book.

Whether you're an experienced traveler or a beginner, this book is designed to help everyone—from weekend warriors to seasoned RVers.

The book is organized by geographic location, making it easier for you to plan your next tour without having to browse through states in alphabetical order. If you're planning a cross-country trip, you'll find this setup particularly useful.

In each state, we've included a range of campground options. You'll find **classic campgrounds**, with important notes on services and activities, as well as some campgrounds in **national parks** for those who want to fully immerse themselves in nature. Additionally, we've added a few **boondocking** options for those who want to try this style of camping or simply want to include a budget-friendly stop during their trip.

The goal of this book is to provide you with a **comprehensive and accessible guide** that showcases both well-known destinations and hidden gems that we've discovered during our travels. We want to help you explore new places and give you the freedom to create your own journey, whether it's a night in a famous national park or a peaceful spot under the stars.

Extra Content: Beyond the Campgrounds

Along with the campgrounds, we've also included **seven bonus resources** covering everything from choosing the perfect RV for your needs to a logbook for recording all of your camping experiences. By scanning the QR code at the end of the book, you'll gain access to these extra resources, which will provide additional tips and insights to enhance your RV adventures. These bonuses give you a **complete view of the RVing world**, so you'll always be prepared for your next trip.

Our goal was to create a guide that is not only comprehensive but also affordable. RVing represents freedom, and that includes the freedom to explore without breaking the bank. Whether you're looking for a destination for your next weekend getaway or planning a trip across the United States, this guide will be your trusted companion.

THE ULTIMATE GUIDE TO RV CAMPING

This guide will walk you through the essential process of selecting the right RV, whether you're buying or renting. It breaks down the pros and cons of each approach, and we've included comprehensive advice on the different RV types—Class A, B, and C, as well as fifth-wheels and travel trailers. To make things even better, we've included a culinary section with practical RV kitchen tips and some of our favorite road-tested recipes. Plus, you'll find a selection of pre-planned scenic routes that offer unforgettable landscapes and points of interest, giving you even more ways to enhance your travels.

RV Camping Logbook

Track your RV experiences with our RV Camping Logbook. It's designed to help you document each destination, campground, activity, and memorable moment on your journey. It's a keepsake for reliving adventures and a resource for planning future trips.

Boondocking Guide

For those curious about boondocking or free camping, this guide gives you everything you need to get started. From finding the best sites to following boondocking rules, you'll be well-prepared to explore off-the-beaten-path locations.

RV Checklist

A successful RV trip starts with preparation, and our RV Checklist ensures you're ready for the road. It covers everything from essential gear to pre-trip vehicle checks, helping you avoid common oversights and make the most of your journey.

RV Solar Power Guide

Many RVers are embracing sustainable energy options. Our guide to RV solar power explains how to set up an efficient solar system, from understanding the basics to installing and optimizing your setup for travel.

Travel Planner

Planning your journey can be half the fun, and our Travel Planner makes it easy to map your itinerary, manage travel times, and select stops along the way. Tailor each leg of your trip to ensure an unforgettable experience from start to finish.

RV Coloring Book

For a bit of lighthearted fun, we've included an RV-themed coloring book, great for kids or anyone looking to unwind. With illustrations inspired by the RV lifestyle, it's perfect for adding some creativity to your trip.

RUSH TO THE END OF THE BOOK
AND DOWNLOAD YOUR BONUSES!

For us, planning our RV trips has always been part of the adventure itself. We see it as an exciting step that allows us to imagine the destinations, activities, and experiences we'll encounter along the way. Having a well-thought-out plan has often saved us from unexpected surprises and allowed us to enjoy the journey more freely.

As mentioned earlier, we've included many helpful tools among the digital bonuses, including a travel planner to help you keep track of all the details, from campgrounds to activities. It's a valuable resource to stay organized and stress-free throughout your trip.

To get started, here are a few practical tips that can make a significant difference in ensuring a smooth and memorable journey:

1. Consider Your Needs

Every RVer has different preferences and requirements. Before choosing your campgrounds, think about what's essential for your trip. Do you need large spaces for a bigger RV? Would you prefer a secluded, nature-filled campground or one with convenient access to services? In this book, we've provided details and real customer feedback for each campground to help you compare and find the ones that best suit your style of travel. Whether you're seeking adventure or relaxation, planning around your needs will enhance your overall experience.

Among the considerations are the types of campsites available, which we've included throughout the book:

- **Primitive Campsites**: Basic sites without water or electricity, and sometimes without flush toilets or showers.

- **Partial Hookup Campsites**: These include water and electric hookups but lack sewer connections, so you'll need to use a dump station.

- **Full Hookup Campsites**: These sites provide water, electricity, and sewer connections, and sometimes extras like cable TV and Wi-Fi.

In addition to campsites, you'll find recommended scenic routes tailored to each state—perfectly planned for you to experience some of the most stunning drives in the U.S.

2. Plan Your Budget

Even if budget constraints aren't an issue, it's wise to plan expenses in advance. By knowing what you'll spend on campgrounds, you can manage resources more effectively and set aside savings for future trips. This book classifies each campground by price range:

- **$**: Affordable campgrounds (under $30 per night)

- **$$**: Mid-range options ($30 to $60 per night)

- **$$$**: Premium campgrounds (above $60 per night)

This approach will help you make the most of your budget without financial surprises, letting you save where possible and allocate funds for other trip essentials.

3. Research Campground Availability

Once you've selected your campgrounds, the next step is booking. Some popular locations, especially during peak seasons, require advance reservations. Be sure to check availability online using platforms like Recreation.gov or the campground's official website. Some campgrounds operate on a first-come, first-served basis, so early arrival is crucial if you're visiting one of these.

For those who love returning to a favorite spot, many campgrounds offer seasonal reservations, allowing you to secure a site for an extended stay, which can be ideal for longer retreats.

4. Look Into Campsite Reviews

Before finalizing your selection, it's always wise to check the latest reviews. While the details we've provided in this book are reliable, online reviews can give you up-to-date insights about the conditions of the campgrounds, amenities, and the overall customer experience. This is especially important for understanding seasonal changes, cleanliness, and service quality.

5. Consider Road Conditions to the Campground

Some campgrounds, especially those in remote or mountainous areas, may have challenging road access. Be mindful of steep grades, gravel paths, or narrow clearances that could pose issues for larger RVs. Reviewing road conditions ahead of time—or consulting online forums and the campground itself—can be extremely helpful.

6. Join Loyalty Programs or RV Clubs

Many campgrounds offer discounts for members of RV clubs such as Good Sam, KOA, or Passport America. Checking for these memberships can help you save on reservations and unlock exclusive benefits, making your trip more affordable and enjoyable.

7. Check for Last-Minute Alerts

Before setting out, it's essential to check for any last-minute updates. Visit the campground's official site or use travel apps to stay informed about closures, weather alerts, or road construction. Staying connected with RV communities online can also provide real-time information from fellow travelers, helping you avoid unexpected issues and enjoy a smoother trip.

8. Follow the 3-3-3 Rule

To keep your travels relaxed, consider following the 3-3-3 rule:

- o Drive fewer than 300 miles in a day.
- o Arrive by 3 PM, ensuring plenty of daylight for setup.
- o Plan to stay at least three days at each location, giving you time to relax and explore without rushing.

By following these tips and tapping into the resources provided, you'll be well-prepared for an enjoyable journey that captures the true essence of RV travel.

Maine: The Wild and Scenic Northeast

Maine, with its rugged coastline, dense forests, and charming seaside towns, is a state that invites RVers to experience the beauty of the Northeast in all its glory. Known as "Vacationland," Maine is a haven for nature lovers, offering everything from majestic mountain ranges to picturesque fishing villages where the pace of life slows down. Whether you're exploring the rocky shores of Acadia National Park or camping in the quiet solitude of the Maine woods, this state offers a refreshing and peaceful escape.

The best season to RV in Maine is **late spring through early fall**, from **May to October**. **Summer** is the perfect time to enjoy the coastal areas, with warm, pleasant weather and endless outdoor activities like hiking, kayaking, and whale watching. **Fall** in Maine is truly magical, with cool, crisp air and the stunning display of autumn foliage painting the landscape in vibrant reds, oranges, and yellows. **The season to avoid** is **winter**, from **November to April**, as Maine's winters are harsh, with heavy snowfall and freezing temperatures that make RVing extremely challenging. However, if you're a winter sports enthusiast and prepared for the cold, Maine offers fantastic opportunities for snowmobiling and skiing.

What I love most about Maine is its sense of untouched wilderness. As you drive through the state, the dense pine forests and craggy coastline give you a sense of peace and solitude. Acadia National Park is a must-visit, with its dramatic cliffs, rocky beaches, and panoramic views from the top of Cadillac Mountain. For RVers who prefer a quieter experience, Maine's many state parks and campgrounds provide perfect places to escape into nature, whether you're camping along a tranquil lake or deep in the heart of the forest.

Maine's coastal charm is another draw for RVers. Towns like Bar Harbor, Camden, and Boothbay Harbor offer a quintessential New England experience, where you can enjoy fresh lobster rolls, explore historic lighthouses, and wander through quaint seaside streets. The state's campgrounds range from well-equipped RV resorts to more rustic, secluded spots where you can fall asleep to the sound of the waves crashing against the shore.

Maine is a destination that offers the best of both worlds for RVers: rugged outdoor adventure and serene, peaceful getaways. Whether you're waking up to the sight of the Atlantic Ocean or hiking through the quiet woods, Maine's natural beauty and charm will leave you feeling rejuvenated and connected to the world around you.

Searsport Shores Ocean Campground

216 West Main Street, Searsport, ME 04974

(207) 548-6059 — $$

Campground Description:

A scenic oceanfront campground offering stunning views of Penobscot Bay. It's perfect for nature lovers and adventurers, with easy access to kayaking, beachcombing, and hiking. Art programs and workshops add a creative touch to the experience.

Types of Sites Available:
- RV sites with water and electric hookups
- Tent camping sites
- Cabins for rent

Amenities:
- Boat ramp and kayak rentals
- Art studio and fiber arts program
- Hiking trails, playground

Activities:
- Kayaking, fishing, hiking
- Beachcombing, birdwatching

Unique Experiences: The campground combines outdoor beauty with creative workshops, offering a tranquil retreat by the ocean.

Feedback: Praised for its peaceful setting and variety of activities, it's a great spot for those seeking nature and art.

Paradise Park Resort Campground

50 Adelaide Road, Old Orchard Beach, ME 04064

(207) 934-4633 — $$

Campground Description:

A family-friendly campground located near the famous Old Orchard Beach. Paradise Park Resort provides easy access to the beach and pier, offering a fun seaside camping experience with modern amenities like pools, hot tubs, and a playground.

Types of Sites Available:
- RV sites with full hookups
- Tent camping sites
- Cabin rentals

Amenities:
- Swimming pool, hot tubs
- Dog park, playground
- Shuttle service to Old Orchard Beach Pier

Activities:
- Swimming, beachcombing
- Exploring Old Orchard Beach and Pier

Unique Experiences: Seaside camping just minutes from the beach, with resort-style amenities for a relaxing family vacation.

Feedback: Highly praised for its clean facilities and proximity to the beach, making it a favorite for summer vacations.

Patten Pond RV Resort

 1470 US-1, Ellsworth, ME 04605

📞 (207) 667-7600 —— $$

Campground Description:

Set on the shores of Patten Pond, this peaceful resort is ideal for those seeking both adventure and relaxation. Located near Acadia National Park, the resort offers a tranquil lakeside experience with activities like kayaking, swimming, and fishing.

Types of Sites Available:

- RV sites with full hookups
- Tent camping sites
- Cabin rentals

Amenities:

- Private beach, boat rentals
- Picnic areas, playground

Activities:

- Swimming, kayaking
- Exploring Acadia National Park
- Fishing for bass, trout, and perch
- Exploring Acadia National Park and Bar Harbor (a short drive away)

Unique Experiences: The resort offers a serene lakeside retreat, with easy access to Acadia National Park and Bar Harbor for day trips.

Feedback: Guests love the peaceful setting and convenient location near Acadia, making it a great destination for nature lovers.

Sandy Pines Campground

 277 Mills Rd, Kennebunkport, ME 04046

📞 (207) 967-2483 —— $$$

Campground Description:

A luxurious campground offering a blend of glamping and traditional camping. Nestled in the woods near Kennebunkport, Sandy Pines provides upscale accommodations such as glamping tents and cottages, alongside traditional RV and tent sites. The campground offers a wide range of amenities, making it perfect for those seeking comfort in nature.

Types of Sites Available:

- RV sites with full hookups
- Tent camping sites
- Glamping tents, cottages, Airstream rentals

Amenities:

- Heated saltwater pool
- General store, playground
- Bike rentals, nature trails

Activities:

- Swimming, hiking, biking
- Exploring Kennebunkport's beaches and shops

Unique Experiences: Combines luxury camping with outdoor adventure, offering upscale accommodations close to southern Maine's famous beaches.

Feedback: Praised for its upscale facilities and proximity to the beach, it's a top choice for glamping enthusiasts and families alike.

HIDDEN GEMS

Wells Beach Resort Campground
Address: 1000 Post Rd, Wells, ME 04090

Campground Description:
A family-friendly campground near the scenic Wells Beach, offering a relaxing environment with easy beach access.
Unique Experience: Enjoy a peaceful stay just minutes from the ocean and explore the nearby coastal towns.

Amenities:
• Full RV hookups
• Swimming pool

Activities:
• Beach visits
• Biking

Blueberry Pond Campground
Address: 218 Poland Range Rd, Pownal, ME 04069

Campground Description:
A tranquil wooded campground close to Freeport, ideal for those looking for a quiet and serene getaway.
Unique Experience: Relax in the peaceful countryside, just a short drive from Maine's scenic coastline.

Amenities:
• Restrooms and showers
• Full RV hookups

Activities:
• Hiking
• Wildlife watching

NATIONAL PARKS

Acadia National Park - Blackwoods Campground
Address: 194 McFarland Hill Dr, Bar Harbor, ME 04609

Campground Description:
A popular campground within Acadia National Park, offering easy access to the park's stunning ocean views and mountain trails.
Unique Experience: Camp in the heart of Acadia National Park and explore its iconic landscapes, from Cadillac Mountain to the rocky coastline.

Amenities:
• Restrooms
• Fire pits

Activities:
• Hiking
• Sightseeing

Camden Hills State Park
Address: 280 Belfast Rd, Camden, ME 04843

Campground Description:
This state park offers beautiful views of Camden Harbor and Penobscot Bay, with great hiking and camping opportunities.
Unique Experience: Hike up to Mount Battie and enjoy panoramic views of the Maine coastline.

Amenities:
• Restrooms and showers
• Picnic areas

Activities:
• Hiking
• Scenic drives

Boondocking

Katahdin Woods and Waters National Monument

Address: North Entrance, Sherman, ME 04776

Campground Description:
A remote and rugged area, perfect for boondocking and exploring Maine's wild beauty.

Unique Experience: Enjoy pristine wilderness views, with opportunities to hike, canoe, and stargaze in this untouched natural area.

Amenities:
• Primitive campsites
• Vault toilets

Activities:
• Hiking
• Wildlife watching

Bigelow Preserve

Address: 128 Sugarloaf Mountain Rd, Stratton, ME 04982

Campground Description:
Offering remote boondocking options in the shadow of Bigelow Mountain, perfect for those seeking solitude and adventure.

Unique Experience: Camp at the base of one of Maine's highest peaks, with access to challenging trails and spectacular views.

Amenities:
• Primitive campsites
• Fire rings

Activities:
• Hiking
• Fishing

Others Campgrounds

• Bar Harbor Campground (Bar Harbor, ME)
• Papoose Pond Resort & Campground (Waterford, ME)
• Loon's Haven Family Campground (Naples, ME)
• Hid'n Pines Family Campground (Old Orchard Beach, ME)
• Rangeley Lake State Park Campground (Rangeley, ME)
• Mt. Desert Narrows Camping Resort (Bar Harbor, ME)
• Megunticook Campground by the Sea (Rockport, ME)
• Lily Bay State Park Campground (Greenville, ME)
• Old Orchard Beach Campground (Old Orchard Beach, ME)
• Balsam Woods Campground (Abbot, ME)

Others Boondocking

• Deboullie Public Reserved Land
• Cupsuptic Lake Park & Campground (boondocking areas available)
• Nahmakanta Public Reserved Land
• Four Ponds Public Reserved Land
• Little Moose Public Reserved Land

Others National Park

• Acadia National Park - Seawall Campground

New Hampshire: A Scenic New England Escape

New Hampshire, with its majestic mountains, serene lakes, and picturesque small towns, is a quintessential New England destination for RVers. Known for its natural beauty and outdoor adventures, this state offers a peaceful retreat for those looking to explore the great outdoors. Whether you're hiking through the **White Mountains**, kayaking on **Lake Winnipesaukee**, or enjoying the vibrant fall foliage, New Hampshire is a place that makes every RV journey feel like an adventure.

The best season to RV in New Hampshire is **spring through fall**, from **May to October**. **Summer** is perfect for outdoor enthusiasts, with warm days ideal for hiking, boating, and camping in the state's many forests and parks. **Fall** is the crown jewel of New Hampshire, with the foliage turning the mountains and valleys into a stunning display of reds, oranges, and yellows. **Winter**, while offering excellent skiing and snowmobiling opportunities, can be harsh, particularly in the mountainous regions, making it less ideal for RVing unless you're fully equipped for cold-weather travel.

One of the highlights of RVing in New Hampshire is exploring the **White Mountains**, where towering peaks, cascading waterfalls, and endless hiking trails await. The **Kancamagus Highway**, a scenic byway that cuts through the heart of the White Mountains, offers breathtaking views and access to campgrounds surrounded by nature. For those seeking a lakeside retreat, **Lake Winnipesaukee** and the nearby **Squam Lake** provide stunning campgrounds with opportunities for swimming, boating, and fishing.

New Hampshire's small towns and historic sites add to its charm. You can explore the quaint town of **Portsmouth** on the coast, rich with colonial history, or visit **Concord**, the state capital, to experience New England's heritage firsthand. For RVers looking for a peaceful camping experience, New Hampshire's state parks, such as **Franconia Notch State Park** and **Crawford Notch State Park**, offer well-maintained campgrounds with stunning mountain views and outdoor activities.

What sets New Hampshire apart is the serenity of its landscapes. Whether you're waking up to the sight of mist rolling over a lake or watching the sunset behind the mountains, RVing in New Hampshire is a chance to slow down and connect with nature. The state's mix of rugged wilderness, scenic drives, and charming small towns makes it an unforgettable destination for RVers.

Danforth Bay Camping & RV Resort

196 Shawtown Rd, Freedom, NH 03836

(603) 539-2069   — $$

Campground Description:

Located in the scenic town of Freedom, New Hampshire, Danforth Bay Camping & RV Resort offers a family-friendly lakeside experience in the heart of the Lakes Region. With spacious RV sites, tent camping, and cabin rentals, guests can enjoy water activities, modern amenities, and organized events. Set against the backdrop of the White Mountains, this campground is perfect for those seeking outdoor adventure and relaxation.

Types of Sites Available:
- RV sites with full hookups
- Tent camping sites
- Cabin rentals
- Pull-through and back-in sites

Amenities:
- Free Wi-Fi, heated swimming pools, beach area
- Canoe, kayak, and paddleboard rentals
- Fire pits, dog park, fitness center

Activities:
- Kayaking, swimming, fishing
- Hiking and biking nearby
- Family-friendly games, arts & crafts, live music

Unique Experiences: Danforth Bay offers a perfect mix of lakeside relaxation and outdoor adventure with its proximity to the White Mountains and access to water-based activities on Danforth Bay.

Feedback: Praised for its well-maintained facilities and variety of activities for all ages, making it a top destination for family vacations in the Lakes Region.

Moose Hillock Campground

96 Batchelder Brook Rd, Warren, NH 03279

(603) 764-5294   — $$

Campground Description:

Nestled in the White Mountains of New Hampshire, Moose Hillock Campground offers a fun, family-friendly camping experience with spacious wooded sites and a tropical-themed swimming pool. Known for its impressive amenities and proximity to outdoor activities like hiking and fishing, this campground is perfect for nature lovers seeking a mix of adventure and relaxation.

Types of Sites Available:
- RV sites with full hookups
- Tent camping sites
- Cabin rentals

Amenities:
- Free Wi-Fi, tropical pool with slides
- Hiking trails, playground, fire pits
- Organized activities, dog park

Activities:
- Swimming in the tropical-themed pool
- Hiking in the White Mountain National Forest
- Fishing, exploring local attractions like Lost River Gorge

Unique Experiences: The tropical-themed pool and water slides offer a unique family experience, while the campground's location in the White Mountains provides endless outdoor adventure opportunities.

Feedback: Highly praised for its family-friendly environment, spacious sites, and the fun tropical pool, making it a favorite for summer vacations.

Twin Mountain / Mt. Washington KOA

📍 372 Rt. 115, Twin Mountain, NH 03595

📞 (603) 846-5559 — $$

Campground Description:

Located in the heart of New Hampshire's White Mountains, Twin Mountain / Mt. Washington KOA provides a peaceful camping experience with easy access to Mount Washington and other outdoor attractions. With RV sites, tent camping, and cabins, the campground serves as an excellent base for exploring the region's natural beauty.

Types of Sites Available:

- RV sites with full hookups
- Tent camping sites
- Cabin rentals

Amenities:

- Free Wi-Fi, seasonal pool
- Fishing access, playground, picnic areas
- Shuttle service to local attractions

Activities:

- Fishing, swimming, hiking in the White Mountains
- Visiting Mount Washington, Franconia Notch, and the Flume Gorge
- Stargazing and scenic drives

Unique Experiences: The campground's proximity to Mount Washington and Franconia Notch makes it a prime location for outdoor enthusiasts. The family-friendly amenities and organized events create a perfect blend of adventure and relaxation.

Feedback: Guests praise the campground for its cleanliness, friendly staff, and ideal location near top attractions in the White Mountains.

Mountain Lake Camping Resort

📍 485 Prospect St, Lancaster, NH 03584

📞 (603) 788-4509 — $$

Campground Description:

Mountain Lake Camping Resort, located in Lancaster, NH, offers a scenic lakeside camping experience with a variety of recreational activities. The campground features a private lake perfect for fishing, kayaking, and swimming, as well as modern amenities and proximity to local attractions like Mount Washington.

Types of Sites Available:

- RV sites with full hookups
- Tent camping sites
- Cabin rentals

Amenities:

- Free Wi-Fi, private lake access
- Canoe, kayak, and paddleboat rentals
- Fire pits, playground, swimming pool

Activities:

- Swimming, fishing, kayaking on the private lake
- Hiking and exploring the White Mountains
- Visiting local attractions such as Santa's Village and Mount Washington

Unique Experiences: The campground's private lake provides a serene environment for water activities, while its proximity to the White Mountains offers adventure for outdoor enthusiasts.

Feedback: Guests love the peaceful lakeside setting and variety of activities, making it a top choice for family vacations.

Silver Lake Park Campground

Address: 1762 Belmont Rd, Belmont, NH 03220

Campground Description:
A scenic lakeside campground offering a peaceful retreat with access to Silver Lake for swimming and fishing.

Unique Experience: Enjoy the serene beauty of the lake, perfect for families seeking a relaxing camping trip.

Amenities:
• Beach access
• Picnic areas

Activities:
• Swimming
• Fishing

Branch Brook Campground

Address: 97 Branch Brook Dr, Campton, NH 03223

Campground Description:
Nestled along the Pemigewasset River, this campground offers a family-friendly atmosphere with wooded campsites.

Unique Experience: Relax by the river while enjoying nature walks and outdoor activities in a quiet setting.

Amenities:
• Riverfront sites
• Pool

Activities:
• River fishing
• Nature trails

Franconia Notch State Park (Lafayette Place Campground)

Address: I-93, Franconia Notch State Park, Franconia, NH 03580

Campground Description:
Located in the heart of Franconia Notch, this campground offers easy access to hiking trails and stunning mountain views.

Unique Experience: Hike the iconic Flume Gorge and explore the scenic beauty of Franconia Notch.

Amenities:
• Restrooms
• Picnic tables

Activities:
• Hiking
• Sightseeing

Hampton Beach State Park

Address: 160 Ocean Blvd, Hampton, NH 03842

Campground Description:
A beachfront campground offering ocean views and direct access to the sandy shores of Hampton Beach.

Unique Experience: Camp right by the ocean, with the sound of waves as your backdrop.

Amenities:
• Full hookups
• Beach access

Activities:
• Swimming
• Beachcombing

Boondocking

White Mountain National Forest

Address: Multiple dispersed camping areas across the forest

Campground Description:
Offering dispersed camping in various locations, White Mountain National Forest is ideal for those seeking solitude and adventure.

Unique Experience: Camp among the towering pines and explore rugged mountain trails.

Amenities:
• Primitive campsites
• Fire pits (designated areas)

Activities:
• Hiking
• Wildlife viewing

Jericho Mountain State Park

Address: 298 Jericho Lake Rd, Berlin, NH 03570

Campground Description:
This expansive park offers dispersed camping with easy access to ATV trails and a quiet lake for outdoor activities.

Unique Experience: Enjoy off-roading and water activities in a remote, scenic location.

Amenities:
• Primitive campsites
• Boat launch

Activities:
• ATV riding
• Boating

Others Campgrounds

• Crawford Notch Campground (Bartlett, NH)
• Chocorua Camping Village KOA (Tamworth, NH)
• Jigger Johnson Campground (Conway, NH)
• Gunstock Mountain Resort (Gilford, NH)
• Cold Springs Camp Resort (Weare, NH)
• Lost River Valley Campground (North Woodstock, NH)
• Lake Francis State Park (Pittsburg, NH)
• Coleman State Park (Stewartstown, NH)
• White Lake State Park (Tamworth, NH)
• Greenfield State Park (Greenfield, NH)

Others Boondocking

• Kancamagus Highway (along Route 112)
• Bear Notch Road
• Sandwich Notch Road (near Waterville Valley)
• Tripoli Road Dispersed Camping
• Jericho Mountain ATV Trails (for off-road camping)

Vermont: The Green Mountain State for RVers Seeking Tranquility and Beauty

Vermont, with its rolling green hills, charming small towns, and picturesque landscapes, is a quintessential New England destination for RVers. Known for its peaceful atmosphere, covered bridges, and vibrant autumn foliage, Vermont offers a perfect blend of outdoor adventure and rural charm. Whether you're hiking through the **Green Mountains**, exploring the shores of **Lake Champlain**, or wandering through quaint villages, Vermont is a state where RVers can slow down and savor the beauty of nature.

The best season to RV in Vermont is **spring through fall**, from **May to October**. **Spring** brings blooming flowers and mild temperatures, making it an ideal time for hiking, biking, and exploring Vermont's scenic byways. **Summer** offers warm weather perfect for camping, kayaking, and enjoying the state's lakes and rivers. **Fall** is when Vermont truly shines, with its world-famous foliage transforming the state into a breathtaking landscape of reds, oranges, and yellows. **Winter** can be cold and snowy, particularly in the mountains, but it offers excellent skiing, snowshoeing, and a cozy, tranquil atmosphere for those prepared for colder conditions.

For RVers who love the outdoors, Vermont's **Green Mountains** are the heart of the state's natural beauty. The **Green Mountain National Forest** offers endless opportunities for hiking, camping, and wildlife watching, with campgrounds nestled among the trees and near scenic lakes and rivers. **Mount Mansfield**, the state's highest peak, provides stunning views and challenging trails for adventurers, while the more peaceful **Stowe** area offers a blend of mountain beauty and small-town charm.

Lake Champlain, which borders Vermont and New York, is another favorite destination for RVers. The lake offers plenty of water-based activities, from fishing and boating to swimming and paddleboarding. RV-friendly campgrounds along the lake's shore provide a relaxing atmosphere with stunning views of the water and the **Adirondack Mountains** in the distance. **Burlington**, Vermont's largest city, offers a vibrant arts scene, local breweries, and farm-to-table dining, all within easy reach of nearby campgrounds.

Vermont is also known for its charming small towns and villages, where covered bridges, historic buildings, and quaint shops offer a glimpse of classic New England life. RVers can explore towns like **Woodstock**, known for its beautiful village green, or **Bennington**, home to the famous **Bennington Battle Monument**. The **Vermont Country Store** and the many local farmers' markets are perfect for discovering local crafts, artisanal foods, and Vermont's famous maple syrup.

Vermont's campgrounds reflect the state's love for nature, offering a range of options from full-service RV parks to more rustic, nature-focused spots in state parks. Whether you're camping by a peaceful lake, in the shadow of the Green Mountains, or near one of the state's scenic byways, Vermont's campgrounds provide easy access to outdoor activities and serene surroundings.

For RVers looking to escape into nature, enjoy quiet, scenic drives, and experience the quintessential charm of New England, Vermont is the perfect destination. Whether you're hiking the mountains, paddling on a tranquil lake, or simply soaking in the vibrant fall colors, Vermont offers an unforgettable RV experience that celebrates the beauty of the natural world.

Lake Champagne Resort

53 Lake Champagne Dr, Randolph Center, VT 05061

(802) 728-5293 $$

Campground Description:

A peaceful, family-friendly lakeside resort in Vermont's Green Mountains, offering a relaxing blend of outdoor recreation and scenic views.

Types of Sites Available:

- RV sites with full hookups
- Tent sites
- Cabin rentals

Amenities:

- Swimming beach
- Free Wi-Fi
- Picnic areas and playground

Activities:

- Swimming, fishing, and boating on Lake Champagne
- Hiking and exploring nearby trails

Unique Experiences: Enjoy a serene lakeside retreat surrounded by Vermont's lush forests, perfect for swimming and hiking in beautiful natural surroundings.

Feedback: Guests praise the scenic setting, clean facilities, and variety of activities, making it a favorite for families seeking relaxation.

Woodford State Park Campground

142 State Park Rd, Woodford, VT 05201

(802) 447-7169 $

Campground Description:

A rustic, peaceful campground in Vermont's Green Mountains with access to Adams Reservoir, offering a back-to-nature experience for outdoor enthusiasts.

Types of Sites Available:

- Tent sites
- Lean-to shelters
- RV sites (no hookups)

Amenities:

- Canoe and kayak rentals
- Fishing and hiking trails
- Restrooms and showers

Activities:

- Canoeing, kayaking, and fishing in Adams Reservoir
- Hiking trails in the Green Mountain National Forest

Unique Experiences: A high-elevation campground with cooler temperatures and access to scenic hiking trails and wildlife viewing, perfect for those seeking tranquility in nature.

Feedback: Guests love the quiet, remote atmosphere and well-maintained trails, making it a top choice for those wanting a peaceful escape.

TABLE OF CONTENTS

Smugglers' Notch Campground

4109 Route 108 South, Jeffersonville, VT 05464

(802) 644-8183 — $$

Campground Description:

Set near the iconic Smugglers' Notch Pass, this campground offers a range of outdoor activities and family-friendly amenities in Vermont's Green Mountains.

Types of Sites Available:
- RV sites with full hookups
- Tent sites
- Cabin rentals

Amenities:
- Heated pool
- Playground
- Free Wi-Fi

Activities:
- Hiking, biking, and exploring Smugglers' Notch
- Swimming in the heated pool

Unique Experiences: Enjoy year-round activities, from summer hiking to winter skiing, with easy access to the stunning Smugglers' Notch Pass.

Feedback: Praised for its scenic location and variety of activities, this campground is a favorite for adventure seekers and families.

Pinewood Lodge Campground

190 Pinewood Rd, Plymouth, MA 02360

(508) 746-3548 — $$

Campground Description:

A tranquil, wooded campground in Massachusetts offering lakeside camping with plenty of outdoor recreation, ideal for families and nature lovers.

Types of Sites Available:
- RV sites with full hookups
- Tent sites
- Cabin rentals

Amenities:
- Beach and swimming area
- Fishing lake
- Hiking trails

Activities:
- Swimming, fishing, and boating on the lake
- Hiking in the surrounding woods

Unique Experiences: Relax by the lake or hike the scenic trails, offering a perfect escape into nature in a peaceful and family-friendly setting.

Feedback: Guests enjoy the serene lake setting, clean facilities, and relaxing atmosphere, making it a top choice for families looking for outdoor fun.

The Wilderness at Big Bear Lake

Address: 110 Woods Hill Rd, Stowe, VT 05672

Campground Description:
A peaceful, secluded campground nestled in the Vermont wilderness, perfect for families and outdoor enthusiasts.
Unique Experience: Enjoy camping in the tranquil woods near Big Bear Lake, with easy access to hiking and wildlife viewing.

Amenities:
• Restrooms
• Fire pits

Activities:
• Hiking
• Wildlife viewing

Little River State Park Campground

Address: 3444 Little River Rd, Waterbury, VT 05676

Campground Description:
A beautiful lakeside campground in the Green Mountains, offering a variety of outdoor activities.
Unique Experience: Camp along the Waterbury Reservoir, surrounded by forested mountains and offering prime fishing and hiking.

Amenities:
• Boat launch
• Restrooms

Activities:
• Fishing
• Hiking

Marsh-Billings-Rockefeller National Historical Park Campground

Address: 54 Elm St, Woodstock, VT 05091

Campground Description:
Located near the only National Park dedicated to conservation, offering a mix of history and nature.
Unique Experience: Stay near this historical park that celebrates the conservation legacy of Vermont, with nearby trails for scenic hikes.

Amenities:
• Picnic areas
• Restrooms

Activities:
• Historic tours
• Hiking

Mount Philo State Park Campground

Address: 5425 Mount Philo Rd, Charlotte, VT 05445

Campground Description:
A small, scenic campground with stunning views of the Champlain Valley and the Adirondack Mountains.
Unique Experience: Camp atop Mount Philo, with breathtaking panoramic views and access to hiking trails.

Amenities:
• Picnic areas
• Restrooms

Activities:
• Hiking
• Wildlife viewing

Boondocking

Green Mountain National Forest

Address: Vermont (various dispersed camping locations)

Campground Description:
Scenic dispersed camping throughout Vermont's Green Mountains, offering seclusion and wilderness exploration.

Unique Experience: Boondock in the heart of the Green Mountains, with access to miles of hiking trails and untouched nature.

Amenities:
• Primitive sites
• Scenic views

Activities:
• Hiking
• Wildlife watching

Groton State Forest

Address: Vermont (various dispersed camping locations)

Campground Description:
Dispersed camping within Vermont's largest state forest, perfect for those seeking solitude and nature immersion.

Unique Experience: Enjoy a remote, natural setting with opportunities for hiking, fishing, and stargazing in Groton's vast wilderness.

Amenities:
• Primitive sites
• Scenic views

Activities:
• Fishing
• Hiking

Others Campgrounds

• Button Bay State Park Campground (Vergennes, VT)
• Branbury State Park (Salisbury, VT)
• Emerald Lake State Park (East Dorset, VT)
• Gifford Woods State Park (Killington, VT)
• Grand Isle State Park (Grand Isle, VT)
• Half Moon Pond State Park (Hubbardton, VT)
• Molly Stark State Park (Wilmington, VT)
• Bomoseen State Park (Bomoseen, VT)
• Ricker Pond State Park (Groton, VT)
• Lake Carmi State Park (Franklin, VT)

Others Boondocking

• Kelley Stand Road (near Stratton, VT)
• Somerset Reservoir (near Wilmington, VT)
• Lincoln Gap (near Warren, VT)
• Elmore State Park (Elmore, VT - dispersed options nearby)
• Hazen's Notch State Forest (Lowell, VT)

Massachusetts: A New England Treasure

Massachusetts, with its rich history, charming coastal towns, and scenic countryside, is a state that offers endless possibilities for RVers. From the rugged beauty of Cape Cod's beaches to the rolling hills of the Berkshires, Massachusetts is a New England treasure that invites exploration. Whether you're drawn to the cultural and historical landmarks of Boston or seeking the tranquility of the state's many parks and forests, Massachusetts has something for every RVer.

The best season to RV in Massachusetts is **late spring through early fall**, from **May to October**. **Spring** brings blooming flowers and lush greenery, making it the perfect time to explore the state's countryside and coastal areas. **Fall**, however, is when Massachusetts truly shines, with its world-famous autumn foliage painting the landscape in vibrant shades of red, orange, and gold. **Summer** is ideal for beach lovers, especially on Cape Cod, Martha's Vineyard, and Nantucket, where you can enjoy long, sunny days by the ocean. **Winter** can be cold and snowy, particularly in the western and northern parts of the state, so it's best to avoid RVing during this time unless you're prepared for the harsh conditions.

One of the most iconic places for RVers to visit in Massachusetts is **Cape Cod**, where the sand dunes, lighthouses, and charming seaside towns create an unforgettable coastal experience. You can park your RV near the water and spend your days cycling the Cape Cod Rail Trail, fishing, or simply soaking in the beauty of the Atlantic Ocean. For history lovers, **Boston** is an absolute must. Though you may need to park your RV outside the city, Boston's historic Freedom Trail, museums, and cultural landmarks are worth the trip.

For those seeking nature and quiet, the **Berkshires** in western Massachusetts offer a peaceful retreat, with beautiful forests, hiking trails, and mountain vistas. The region is perfect for RVers who want to escape the hustle and bustle and enjoy the natural beauty of New England. State parks like **Myles Standish State Forest** and **Mohawk Trail State Forest** provide well-maintained campgrounds surrounded by nature, offering everything from hiking and fishing to peaceful nights under the stars.

Massachusetts is a state that combines the best of New England's natural beauty with a deep sense of history and culture. Whether you're visiting a quiet coastal village, exploring historic towns, or hiking in the forested hills, RVing through Massachusetts offers a rich and diverse experience that's perfect for any traveler.

Normandy Farms Family Camping Resort

📍 72 West Street, Foxborough, MA 02035

📞 (866) 673-2767 — $$$

Campground Description:

Normandy Farms, located between Boston and Cape Cod, offers a luxurious camping experience with RV sites, tent camping, and upscale cabins or yurts. With amenities like pools, fitness center, bike park, and nature trails, it's a favorite for families looking for adventure and relaxation.

Types of Sites Available:

- RV sites with full hookups
- Tent camping sites
- Cabin rentals, yurts, safari tents

Amenities:

- Indoor and outdoor pools, hot tubs
- Fitness center, wellness pavilion
- Dog park, fishing pond

Activities:

- Biking, hiking trails
- Fitness classes, wellness programs
- Swimming, disc golf

Unique Experiences: A luxury camping resort with modern amenities, perfect for exploring both Boston and Cape Cod.

Feedback: Praised for its well-maintained facilities, family-friendly atmosphere, and variety of activities.

Pine Acres Family Camping Resort

📍 203 Bechan Rd, Oakham, MA 01068

📞 (508) 882-9509 — $$

Campground Description:

Set along the shores of Lake Dean, Pine Acres offers a fun family-friendly experience with water activities like swimming, fishing, and boating. The resort features a pool, mini-golf, and nature trails, making it an ideal spot for outdoor enthusiasts and families.

Types of Sites Available:

- RV sites with full hookups
- Tent camping sites
- Cabin rentals

Amenities:

- Swimming pool with splash pad
- Mini-golf, playground, game room
- Boat and kayak rentals

Activities:

- Fishing, kayaking on Lake Dean
- Mini-golf, basketball, hiking
- Swimming, family-friendly games

Unique Experiences: A peaceful lakeside campground with a range of activities for water and outdoor lovers.

Feedback: Loved for its variety of activities and kid-friendly amenities, making it a top choice for family vacations.

Atlantic Oaks Campground

📍 3700 US-6, Eastham, MA 02642

📞 (508) 255-1437 — $$

Campground Description:

Located in the heart of Cape Cod, Atlantic Oaks Campground offers a convenient camping experience with easy access to the Cape Cod National Seashore and scenic bike trails. Known for its clean facilities and friendly atmosphere, it's a great base for exploring Cape Cod's beaches and attractions.

Types of Sites Available:

- RV sites with full hookups
- Tent camping sites

Amenities:

- Free Wi-Fi, restrooms, showers
- Playground, camp store
- Access to Cape Cod Rail Trail

Activities:

- Biking and hiking on the Cape Cod Rail Trail
- Exploring nearby beaches
- Picnicking, stargazing

Unique Experiences: A prime location for beachgoers and cyclists, offering direct access to Cape Cod's famous trails and shores.

Feedback: Highly praised for its location and cleanliness, making it a favorite for short stays and extended visits.

Sandy Pond Campground

📍 834 Bourne Rd, Plymouth, MA 02360

📞 (508) 759-9336 — $$

Campground Description:

Sandy Pond Campground, located by a freshwater pond in Plymouth, offers a serene setting for families and outdoor enthusiasts. With water-based activities like fishing, swimming, and kayaking, plus proximity to Plymouth and Cape Cod attractions, it's an ideal destination for relaxation and adventure.

Types of Sites Available:

- RV sites with full hookups
- Tent camping sites
- Cabin rentals

Amenities:

- Swimming beach on the pond
- Playground, hiking trails
- Boat and kayak rentals

Activities:

- Fishing, kayaking, boating
- Hiking, exploring Plymouth's historical sites
- Relaxing by the campfire

Unique Experiences: A peaceful lakeside retreat with access to both water activities and historical Plymouth landmarks.

Feedback: Praised for its relaxing environment and proximity to Plymouth's attractions, making it popular families.

Berry's Grove Campground

Address: 75 Berry Rd, Tyngsboro, MA 01879

Campground Description:
A peaceful family-friendly campground located along the Merrimack River, ideal for those looking to enjoy nature close to home.

Unique Experience: Relax by the river and take in the tranquil surroundings of Tyngsboro's wooded beauty.

Amenities:
• River access
• Picnic areas

Activities:
• Canoeing
• Fishing

Maurice's Campground

Address: 80 State Hwy Rte 6, Wellfleet, MA 02667

Campground Description:
Located on Cape Cod, this cozy campground offers a beachy escape with easy access to the ocean and the Cape Cod Rail Trail.

Unique Experience: Camp near the coast and explore the beauty of Cape Cod's famous beaches and scenic bike paths.

Amenities:
• Beach access
• Camp store

Activities:
• Biking
• Beachcombing

Nickerson State Park

Address: 3488 Main St, Brewster, MA 02631

Campground Description:
A beautiful state park on Cape Cod, offering wooded campsites near kettle ponds and plenty of outdoor activities.

Unique Experience: Explore the park's tranquil kettle ponds and miles of bike trails while enjoying a serene Cape Cod getaway.

Amenities:
• Bike paths
• Restrooms

Activities:
• Hiking
• Swimming

Wompatuck State Park

Address: 204 Union St, Hingham, MA 02043

Campground Description:
Located near Boston, this state park offers a variety of outdoor activities with wooded campsites and over 12 miles of biking trails.

Unique Experience: Discover the natural beauty of the South Shore, just minutes from the city, with easy access to scenic trails.

Amenities:
• Bike paths
• Picnic areas

Activities:
• Biking
• Hiking

Boondocking

Otter River State Forest

Address: 86 Winchendon Rd, Baldwinville, MA 01436

Campground Description:
A serene forested area offering rustic campsites and dispersed camping for those seeking a quiet wilderness retreat.

Unique Experience: Experience true solitude and natural beauty while camping under the canopy of Massachusetts' state forest.

Amenities:
• Primitive campsites
• Fire pits

Activities:
• Hiking
• Wildlife watching

Mount Greylock State Reservation

Address: 30 Rockwell Rd, Lanesborough, MA 01237

Campground Description:
The highest peak in Massachusetts offers stunning views and a perfect spot for dispersed camping in the scenic Berkshires.

Unique Experience: Camp at the base of Mount Greylock and enjoy breathtaking views from the summit.

Amenities:
• Primitive campsites
• Hiking trails

Activities:
• Hiking
• Stargazing

Others Campgrounds

• Adventure Bound Camping Resort (Cape Cod, MA)
• Pinewood Lodge Campground (Plymouth, MA)
• Prospect Lake Park (North Egremont, MA)
• Gateway to Cape Cod RV Campground (Rochester, MA)
• Bourne Scenic Park (Bourne, MA)
• Boston Minuteman Campground (Littleton, MA)
• Circle CG Farm Campground (Bellingham, MA)
• Sutton Falls Camping Area (Sutton, MA)
• Shady Acres Campground (Carver, MA)
• Lake Dennison Recreation Area (Winchendon, MA)

Others Boondocking

• October Mountain State Forest
• Myles Standish State Forest
• Savoy Mountain State Forest
• Beartown State Forest
• Freetown-Fall River State Forest

Others National Park

• Cape Cod National Seashore

Rhode Island: Coastal Charm and New England Beauty

Rhode Island, the smallest state in the U.S., may be small in size, but it offers RVers a wealth of coastal beauty, charming towns, and rich history. Known as the "Ocean State," Rhode Island is a perfect destination for those seeking a peaceful seaside escape with all the charm of New England. From the rocky shores and sandy beaches to the historic streets of **Newport**, this state invites RVers to slow down, relax, and soak in the coastal atmosphere.

The best season to RV in Rhode Island is **late spring through early fall**, from **May to October**. **Summer** is the prime time to visit, with warm temperatures perfect for beach days, sailing, and exploring the state's coastal towns. **Fall** is equally beautiful, offering cooler weather and the striking autumn colors that blanket the countryside. **Winter** in Rhode Island can be cold and windy, particularly along the coast, making it less ideal for RVing unless you're looking for a quiet off-season getaway and are prepared for the chillier weather.

For RVers, Rhode Island's coastline is the main attraction. The **Newport Cliff Walk** offers stunning views of the Atlantic Ocean and the famous Gilded Age mansions, making it a must-see for history and architecture lovers. You can camp near the coast and enjoy easy access to Newport's historic landmarks, charming downtown, and scenic waterfront. The state's numerous beaches, including **Narragansett Beach** and **Misquamicut State Beach**, provide excellent spots to relax, swim, and take in the beauty of the Atlantic Ocean.

In addition to its beaches, Rhode Island is rich in history. **Providence**, the state capital, offers a vibrant arts scene, colonial architecture, and plenty of historic sites to explore. The **Roger Williams National Memorial**, honoring the state's founder, and **Benefit Street**, known for its preserved 18th- and 19th-century homes, are just a few of the highlights for RVers interested in history.

If you're looking for a more nature-focused experience, Rhode Island's state parks offer quiet, scenic campgrounds. **Burlingame State Park**, located near **Charlestown**, is one of the largest in the state, offering lakeside camping and plenty of outdoor activities, including hiking, canoeing, and fishing. For those who want a more rustic experience, the park's peaceful woodlands provide a serene retreat.

Despite its small size, Rhode Island offers plenty of campgrounds and RV parks, often located near the coast, giving travelers the perfect balance of comfort and stunning ocean views. Whether you're enjoying a beachside campground or staying closer to one of the state's picturesque towns, Rhode Island offers a charming and relaxing escape.

For RVers looking to explore New England's coastal beauty, Rhode Island is the perfect destination. Its mix of historic charm, seaside activities, and natural beauty makes it a delightful spot to park your RV and enjoy the peaceful rhythm of the Ocean State.

Melville Ponds Campground

181 Bradford Ave, Portsmouth, RI 02871

(401) 682-2424 — $$

Campground Description:

Set among ponds and wooded areas in Portsmouth, this peaceful campground offers easy access to outdoor activities like hiking and fishing, and is close to Newport's historic attractions.

Types of Sites Available:

- RV sites with full hookups
- Tent camping sites

Amenities:

- Restrooms and showers
- Picnic areas
- Fishing ponds

Activities:

- Hiking and wildlife watching
- Fishing in the ponds
- Exploring Newport's historic landmarks

Unique Experiences: Guests enjoy the tranquil setting with opportunities for outdoor recreation and easy access to Rhode Island's coastal attractions.

Feedback: Praised for its peaceful atmosphere and scenic beauty, it's a great base for exploring the Newport area.

Wawaloam Campground

510 Gardiner Rd, West Kingston, RI 02892

(401) 294-3039 — $$

Campground Description:

This family-friendly campground features a water park, swimming pool, and organized activities, making it a perfect destination for families seeking fun and relaxation in a wooded setting.

Types of Sites Available:

- RV sites with full hookups
- Tent camping sites
- Cabin rentals

Amenities:

- Swimming pool and water park
- Mini-golf course
- Playground

Activities:

- Swimming at the pool and water park
- Mini-golf and outdoor games
- Attending campground events and movie nights

Unique Experiences: Wawaloam Campground's water park and variety of family activities make it a favorite for families looking to create lasting memories.

Feedback: Guests love the clean facilities and family-friendly atmosphere, with plenty of activities for kids.

Ashaway RV Resort

Campground Description:

This luxury RV resort offers top-tier amenities in a serene setting, ideal for families and couples looking to enjoy outdoor activities like swimming and hiking, with easy access to local beaches and attractions.

Types of Sites Available:

- RV sites with full hookups
- Cabin rentals

Amenities:

- Heated swimming pool
- Sports courts
- Playground

Activities:

- Swimming in the heated pool
- Playing basketball and volleyball
- Exploring local hiking trails and beaches

Unique Experiences: Ashaway RV Resort combines luxury and nature, offering a relaxing yet activity-filled stay near Rhode Island's coastline.

Feedback: Praised for its clean facilities and variety of activities, it's a top choice for families seeking a rela-

HIDDEN GEMS

NATIONAL PARKS

Fort Getty Park and Campground

Address: 1050 Fort Getty Rd, Jamestown, RI 02835

Campground Description:
A waterfront campground offering beautiful views of Narragansett Bay, perfect for RVs and tent campers alike.

Unique Experience: Enjoy peaceful seaside camping with stunning sunsets and access to historical Fort Getty.

Amenities:
• Restrooms
• Picnic areas

Activities:
• Fishing
• Beachcombing

Fishermen's Memorial State Park

Address: 1011 Point Judith Rd, Narragansett, RI 02882

Campground Description:
A well-maintained park offering coastal camping near the best fishing spots in Narragansett.

Unique Experience: Enjoy easy access to the beaches and fishing piers, making it a favorite for anglers and beach lovers.

Amenities:
• Full hookups
• Bathhouses

Activities:
• Fishing
• Beach walks

Holiday Acres Campground

Address: 591 Snake Hill Rd, Glocester, RI 02857

Campground Description:
A family-friendly campground set in the heart of Rhode Island's woods, offering plenty of outdoor recreation and relaxation.

Unique Experience: Immerse yourself in nature with hiking trails and a peaceful wooded atmosphere.

Amenities:
• Playground
• Swimming pool

Activities:
• Hiking
• Swimming

Fort Getty Campground

Address: 1050 Fort Getty Rd, Jamestown, RI 02835

Campground Description:
A historic, waterfront campground offering stunning views of the bay with plenty of nearby historical landmarks to explore.

Unique Experience: Discover Rhode Island's history while enjoying beautiful seaside sunsets and quiet, spacious campsites.

Amenities:
• Restrooms
• Boat launch

Activities:
• Kayaking
• Historical tours

Boondocking

George Washington State Campground

Address: Putnam Pike, Chepachet, RI 02814

Campground Description:
This primitive campground located within the George Washington Management Area offers rustic camping with scenic forest views.

Unique Experience: Enjoy peaceful, secluded camping surrounded by forests and hiking trails.

Amenities:
• Primitive sites
• Lake access

Activities:
• Fishing
• Hiking

East Beach Campground

Address: 250 East Beach Rd, Charlestown, RI 02813

Campground Description:
A remote campground right along the beach offering simple, primitive camping for those who love coastal wilderness.

Unique Experience: Camp steps from the ocean and wake up to the sound of waves, with excellent beach access.

Amenities:
• Primitive sites
• Beach access

Activities:
• Surf fishing
• Beach walks

Others Campgrounds

• Burlingame State Park Campground (Charlestown, RI)
• Oak Embers Campground (West Greenwich, RI)
• Whispering Pines Campground (Hope Valley, RI)
• Echo Lake Campground (Pascoag, RI)
• Timber Creek RV Resort (Westerly, RI)
• Worden Pond Family Campground (Wakefield, RI)
• George Washington Memorial Camping Area (Chepachet, RI)
• Westwood YMCA Campground (Coventry, RI)
• Charlestown Breachway Campground (Charlestown, RI)
• Fishermen's Memorial State Park (Narragansett, RI)

Others Boondocking

• Arcadia Management Area (Richmond, RI - dispersed camping allowed in certain areas)
• Beach Pond State Park (Exeter, RI - primitive camping spots)
• Woody Hill Management Area (Westerly, RI)
• Durfee Hill Management Area (Glocester, RI)
• Tillinghast Pond Management Area (West Greenwich, RI)

Connecticut: A Charming New England Escape

Connecticut may be one of the smaller states, but don't let its size fool you—this little corner of New England is packed with charm, history, and natural beauty. For RVers, Connecticut offers a peaceful retreat with scenic drives, coastal views, and picturesque small towns that look like they belong on a postcard. Whether you're exploring the rolling hills of the northwest or the quaint villages along the Long Island Sound, Connecticut has a way of making you feel like you've stepped into a slower, more relaxed pace of life.

The best season for RVing in Connecticut is **spring through fall**, from **April to October**. **Spring** brings blooming flowers and vibrant greenery, while **fall** offers one of the most spectacular displays of foliage you'll ever see. The changing leaves, with their shades of red, orange, and gold, make every drive feel like a scene from a movie. **Summer** is also a great time to visit, especially if you enjoy the coast, where you can spend your days relaxing on the beaches of Mystic or touring the historic seaports. **The season to avoid**, if possible, is **winter**, from **December to February**, when the cold weather and snow can make RVing challenging, particularly in the more rural areas where roads may be icy or closed.

Connecticut's appeal lies in its diversity. You can spend your morning hiking in the lush forests of the Litchfield Hills and your afternoon wandering through the maritime history of Mystic Seaport. And let's not forget about the food—whether it's fresh seafood along the coast or visiting one of the many farm-to-table restaurants that dot the countryside, Connecticut is a food lover's dream.

RVers will appreciate the well-maintained campgrounds and RV parks, many of which are located near the state's beautiful lakes and rivers. There's nothing quite like setting up camp under a canopy of trees, with the sounds of nature all around. The state's compact size also makes it easy to explore; within a few hours, you can be in a completely different landscape, whether it's a coastal town or a quiet forested area.

Connecticut is a perfect destination for those seeking relaxation with a touch of adventure. It's a place where the history is rich, the scenery is stunning, and the slower pace invites you to just sit back and enjoy the ride.

Mystic KOA Holiday

118 Pendleton Hill Rd, North Stonington, CT 06359

(860) 599-5101 — $$

Campground Description:

A family-friendly campground near Mystic, CT, with easy access to Mystic Seaport, Mystic Aquarium, and Rhode Island beaches. Ideal for families, offering modern amenities, planned activities, and various accommodation options.

Types of Sites Available:
- RV sites with full hookups
- Tent camping sites
- Deluxe cabins

Amenities:
- Pool, dog park, Wi-Fi
- Camp store, playground
- Bike rentals

Activities:
- Visiting Mystic Seaport and Aquarium
- Hiking, biking, and fishing
- Family-friendly activities

Unique Experiences: Perfect for exploring the rich history and beauty of the New England coast, with easy access to attractions and fun family activities.

Feedback: Great for families looking for a comfortable and convenient base to explore Mystic and nearby attractions.

Sun Outdoors Mystic

45 Campground Rd, Old Mystic, CT 06372

(860) 245-6038 — $$

Campground Description:

Located in Old Mystic, CT, this campground offers a peaceful retreat close to Mystic's historic sites and coastal beauty. Featuring spacious RV sites, cottages, and premium tent sites, Sun Outdoors Mystic is great for families, couples, and solo travelers.

Types of Sites Available:
- RV sites with full hookups
- Tent camping sites
- Cottages

Amenities:
- Pools, dog park, sports courts
- Clubhouse, picnic areas
- General store

Activities:
- Swimming and biking
- Exploring Mystic and Old Mystic
- Kayaking, fishing, and planned events

Unique Experiences: A serene woodland setting near Mystic's famous attractions, combining relaxation with local exploration.

Feedback: Perfect for families and couples wanting a mix of adventure and relaxation near Mystic.

Lake Compounce Campground

📍 185 Enterprise Dr, Bristol, CT 06010

📞 (860) 583-3300 — $$

Campground Description:

A fun family campground near Lake Compounce, North America's oldest amusement park, offering easy access to the park's rides and water park. Ideal for those seeking a mix of outdoor camping and thrilling amusement park experiences.

Types of Sites Available:

- RV sites with full hookups
- Tent camping sites
- Cabins

Amenities:

- Shuttle to Lake Compounce
- Wi-Fi, picnic areas, fire pits
- Playground and arcade

Activities:

- Visiting Lake Compounce Amusement Park
- Hiking, stargazing, family games
- Relaxing by the campfire

Unique Experiences: A unique mix of camping and amusement park excitement, perfect for family vacations filled with fun and relaxation.

Feedback: Great for families looking for action-packed vacations near Lake Compounce.

Cozy Hills Campground

📍 1311 Bantam Rd, Bantam, CT 06750

📞 (860) 567-2119 — $$

Campground Description:

A family-friendly campground in Bantam, CT, known for its warm community atmosphere and scenic surroundings. Offers RV, tent, and cabin accommodations, with planned activities for all ages.

Types of Sites Available:

- RV sites with full hookups
- Tent camping sites
- Cabins

Amenities:

- Pool, fishing pond
- Playground, arcade
- Weekend activities

Activities:

- Fishing, swimming, hiking
- Planned activities like arts & crafts, movie nights
- Exploring local nature preserves

Unique Experiences: A welcoming, community-oriented campground with plenty of activities for families, set in a peaceful forested area.

Feedback: Ideal for families looking for a fun and relaxing camping experience in the Connecticut countryside.

HIDDEN GEMS

Gentile's Campground

Address: 966 Torringford St, Plymouth, CT 06782

Campground Description:
Gentile's Campground is a family-friendly, wooded campground offering a peaceful retreat with spacious sites and a wide variety of outdoor activities.
Unique Experience: Enjoy a relaxed, family-oriented atmosphere with easy access to scenic nature trails.

Amenities:
• Swimming pool
• Playground

Activities:
• Hiking and nature walks
• Swimming and outdoor games

Branch Brook Campground

Address: 435 Watertown Rd, Thomaston, CT 06787

Campground Description:
Branch Brook Campground offers a quiet, riverside setting with easy access to outdoor activities like fishing and hiking in a relaxed, natural environment.
Unique Experience: Camp by the river and enjoy peaceful, scenic views of the Connecticut countryside.

Amenities:
• Fishing access
• Camp store

Activities:
• Fishing in the nearby brook
• Hiking local trails

NATIONAL PARKS

Hammonasset Beach State Park

Address: 1288 Boston Post Rd, Madison, CT 06443

Campground Description:
Hammonasset Beach State Park offers beachfront camping with access to Connecticut's longest shoreline, perfect for beach lovers and water sports enthusiasts.
Unique Experience: Camp steps away from the beach and enjoy panoramic views of Long Island Sound.

Amenities:
• Restrooms and showers
• Beach access

Activities:
• Swimming and sunbathing on the beach
• Biking along the scenic shore

Black Rock State Park

Address: 2065 Thomaston Rd, Watertown, CT 06795

Campground Description:
Black Rock State Park is nestled in the rolling hills of western Connecticut, offering a serene camping experience with access to hiking trails and scenic views.
Unique Experience: Camp in the foothills of the Berkshire Mountains and enjoy hikes with views of lush forests and rugged terrain.

Amenities:
• Restrooms and showers
• Fishing access

Activities:
• Hiking the trails in the park
• Fishing in the stocked ponds

Boondocking

Mohegan Sun Casino

Address: 1 Mohegan Sun Blvd, Uncasville, CT 06382

Campground Description:
Mohegan Sun Casino offers free, dry camping in their parking lot, providing easy access to the casino's entertainment and dining options.

Unique Experience: Enjoy the excitement of casino life with the convenience of free overnight camping.

Amenities:
• Dry camping
• 24-hour access to casino

Activities:
• Casino gaming and entertainment
• Dining at the on-site restaurants

Pachaug State Forest

Address: Pachaug State Forest, Griswold, CT

Campground Description:
Pachaug State Forest offers dispersed, off-grid camping in a tranquil forest setting, perfect for those seeking a peaceful and remote outdoor experience.

Unique Experience: Camp deep within Connecticut's largest state forest and explore endless miles of hiking and riding trails.

Amenities:
• Primitive campsites
• Scenic forest views

Activities:
• Hiking through forest trails
• Horseback riding and wildlife viewing

Others Campgrounds

• Aces High RV Park
• Riverdale Farm Campsites
• Nelson's Family Campground
• Odetah Camping Resort
• Laurel Ridge Campground
• Countryside Campground
• Salem Farms Campground
• Charlie Brown Campground
• Wolf's Den Family Campground
• Indianfield Campground

Others Boondocking

• Natchaug State Forest (dispersed camping)
• Shenipsit State Forest (dispersed camping)
• Tunxis State Forest (dispersed camping)
• Meshomasic State Forest (dispersed camping)
• Mohawk State Forest (dispersed camping)

New York: Beyond the City, a Natural Wonderland

New York may be known for the bustling streets of Manhattan, but for RVers, the state offers so much more beyond the city limits. From the stunning beauty of the **Adirondack Mountains** to the serene shores of the **Finger Lakes** and the rugged coastline of **Long Island**, New York is a state that surprises with its variety of landscapes and outdoor opportunities. Whether you're exploring the forests, mountains, or lakes, New York offers RVers an escape into nature just a few hours from one of the world's most famous cities.

The best season to RV in New York is **late spring through early fall**, from **May to October**. **Summer** is ideal for enjoying the state's many lakes, rivers, and hiking trails, while **fall** offers one of the most stunning displays of autumn foliage in the country, particularly in the **Adirondacks** and **Catskills**. **Winter**, though beautiful in the northern and mountainous regions, brings cold and snow, which can make RVing more challenging unless you're equipped for winter conditions. However, for those who love winter sports, New York's ski resorts and snow-covered landscapes offer a different kind of adventure.

The **Adirondack Park**, one of the largest protected areas in the United States, is a must-see for RVers seeking solitude and natural beauty. Here, you can camp near pristine lakes, hike towering peaks, and enjoy some of the best paddling and fishing in the Northeast. **Lake Placid**, with its Olympic history, offers both outdoor adventure and small-town charm, making it a great base for exploring the Adirondacks.

The **Finger Lakes** region is another highlight for RVers, with its rolling vineyards, clear lakes, and charming small towns. You can park your RV near one of the many lakes, enjoy wine tastings at local wineries, and explore the scenic byways that wind through this picturesque region. **Watkins Glen State Park**, famous for its beautiful gorge and waterfalls, is a perfect spot for camping and hiking.

For those looking for coastal beauty, **Long Island** offers a mix of sandy beaches, quaint seaside towns, and easy access to the vibrant culture of New York City. Campgrounds along the island's north and south shores provide a relaxing retreat, where you can enjoy the Atlantic Ocean or the quieter waters of the **Long Island Sound**.

New York's campgrounds are as diverse as its landscapes, ranging from full-service RV resorts to more rustic, wilderness spots in state parks. Whether you're camping in the mountains, by a lake, or near the coast, New York offers a variety of options for every type of RVer.

For RVers seeking a combination of outdoor adventure, scenic beauty, and cultural experiences, New York delivers far more than just the bright lights of the city. It's a state where you can escape into nature, yet still be close enough to enjoy world-class attractions, making it an ideal destination for those looking to experience the best of both worlds.

Brennan Beach RV Resort

📍 80 Brennan Beach Rd, Pulaski, NY 13142

📞 (315) 298-2242 — $$

Campground Description:

Located on the shores of Lake Ontario, Brennan Beach RV Resort offers a stunning lakeside experience with over a mile of sandy beach. This family-friendly resort provides a range of activities for all ages, including water sports, fishing, and boating. With spacious RV sites, tent camping, and vacation rentals, the resort is perfect for both short-term and extended stays.

Types of Sites Available:

- RV sites with full hookups
- Tent camping sites
- Vacation rental units

Amenities:

- Restrooms and showers
- Picnic areas
- Camp store
- Dog park

Activities:

- Swimming and sunbathing on the beach
- Fishing and boating in Lake Ontario
- Hiking and biking nearby trails
- Exploring Salmon River and local state parks

Unique Experiences: With direct access to a private beach on Lake Ontario, Brennan Beach RV Resort provides a relaxing yet activity-filled camping experience. Whether enjoying the sunset over the lake or fishing, this resort offers a perfect family vacation setting.

Feedback: Guests love the beach access and variety of activities, making it a favorite for family getaways.

Branches of Niagara Campground & Resort

📍 2659 Whitehaven Rd, Grand Island, NY 14072

📞 (716) 773-7600 — $$

Campground Description:

This family-friendly campground near Niagara Falls offers spacious RV sites, cabins, and tent camping. With on-site activities like zip-lining, fishing, and kayaking, Branches of Niagara Campground ensures a memorable experience for all ages. Its prime location makes it a great base for exploring Niagara Falls and surrounding attractions.

Types of Sites Available:

- RV sites with full hookups
- Tent camping sites
- Cabin rentals

Amenities:

- Free Wi-Fi and cable TV
- Heated pool and splash pad
- Zip-line course

Activities:

- Zip-lining, fishing, and kayaking on the lake
- Exploring Niagara Falls
- Hiking and biking nearby

Unique Experiences: With a range of outdoor activities and close proximity to Niagara Falls, this campground offers adventure and relaxation in one destination.

Feedback: Guests praise the clean facilities and variety of activities, making it ideal for families.

Moose Hillock Camping Resort

📍 10366 NY-149, Fort Ann, NY 12827

📞 (518) 792-4500 — $$

Campground Description:

Located near Lake George, Moose Hillock offers a family-friendly camping experience with a massive tropical-themed swimming pool, spacious sites, and access to outdoor activities like hiking and fishing. The Adirondacks provide a stunning backdrop for this resort, which is known for its organized events and fun atmosphere.

Types of Sites Available:

- RV sites with full hookups
- Tent camping sites
- Cabin rentals

Amenities:

- Free Wi-Fi
- Tropical-themed pool with slides
- Picnic areas
- Dog park

Activities:

- Swimming in the tropical pool
- Hiking nearby trails
- Fishing and boating at Lake George

Unique Experiences: The resort's tropical-themed pool and spacious sites make it a hit with families, offering both relaxation and adventure.

Feedback: Guests appreciate the well-maintained facilities and variety of activities for children.

Lake George RV Park

📍 74 State Route 149, Lake George, NY 12845

📞 (518) 792-3775 — $$

Campground Description:

Park offers a premium camping experience with extensive amenities such as multiple pools, tennis courts, bike trails, and more. Located near Lake George Village, this award-winning park is ideal for families and groups looking to explore the Adirondacks.

Types of Sites Available:

- RV sites with full hookups
- Tent camping sites

Activities:

- Swimming in the pools
- Hiking and biking
- Visiting Lake George Village

Amenities:

- Indoor and outdoor pools
- Fitness center
- Playground
- Dog park
- Shuttle service

Unique Experiences: This luxury RV park provides an extensive range of amenities in a prime Adirondack location, offering both relaxation and outdoor adventure.

Feedback: Highly praised for cleanliness and wide variety of activities, this park is a favorite for family vacations.

HIDDEN GEMS

Draper's Acres

Address: 1264 NY-73, Lake Placid, NY 12946

Campground Description:
A peaceful, family-run campground near Lake Placid, offering scenic mountain views and close proximity to hiking and outdoor activities.

Unique Experience: Enjoy a quiet retreat with easy access to Lake Placid's outdoor adventures.

Amenities:
• Full hookups
• Restrooms and showers

Activities:
• Hiking
• Fishing

Brookwood RV Resort

Address: 133 NY-9N, Ticonderoga, NY 12883

Campground Description:
A quiet RV resort in the Adirondacks, offering large, shaded sites and easy access to historical attractions like Fort Ticonderoga.

Unique Experience: Relax in the Adirondacks and explore nearby Lake George and historic landmarks.

Amenities:
• Full hookups
• Restrooms

Activities:
• Boating
• Historical tours

NATIONAL PARKS

Watkins Glen State Park

Address: 1009 N Franklin St, Watkins Glen, NY 14891

Campground Description:
Famous for its breathtaking gorge, Watkins Glen State Park offers scenic camping with access to stunning waterfalls and hiking trails.

Unique Experience: Walk along the gorge trails and witness 19 cascading waterfalls.

Amenities:
• Restrooms
• Picnic areas

Activities:
• Hiking
• Waterfall viewing

Letchworth State Park

Address: 1 Letchworth State Park, Castile, NY 14427

Campground Description:
Known as the "Grand Canyon of the East," Letchworth State Park offers beautiful camping with dramatic gorge views and waterfalls.

Unique Experience: Explore the deep gorge and waterfalls for stunning photography opportunities.

Amenities:
• Restrooms
• Picnic areas

Activities:
• Hiking
• Scenic drives

Finger Lakes National Forest

Address: Hector Ranger Station, 5218 NY-414, Hector, NY 14841

Campground Description:
Finger Lakes National Forest provides ample dispersed camping in a serene setting with access to lakes, trails, and wildlife.

Unique Experience: Camp in the heart of the Finger Lakes region with access to hiking and wine trails.

Amenities:
- Primitive campsites
- Access to trails

Activities:
- Hiking
- Wildlife watching

Adirondack State Park

Address: 1133 NY-86, Ray Brook, NY 12977

Campground Description:
Adirondack State Park offers vast boondocking opportunities in the largest protected natural area in the Lower 48 states, with mountains, lakes, and forests.

Unique Experience: Immerse yourself in the wilderness of the Adirondacks, perfect for hiking and paddling.

Amenities:
- Primitive campsites
- Access to lakes

Activities:
- Canoeing
- Hiking

Others Campgrounds

- Adirondack Gateway RV Resort & Campground (Gansevoort, NY)
- Lake George Battleground Campground (Lake George, NY)
- Deer Run Campground (Schenectady, NY)
- Whispering Pines Campsites & RV Park (Greenfield, NY)
- Lake George Escape Family Camping Resort (Diamond Point, NY)
- Frosty Acres Campground (Schenectady, NY)
- Twin Ells Campsites (West Chazy, NY)
- Arrowhead Marina & RV Park (Glenville, NY)
- Cooperstown KOA Journey (Richfield Springs, NY)
- Nick's Lake Campground (Old Forge, NY)

Others Boondocking

- North-South Lake Campground (Catskills area)
- Chapel Pond Area (Adirondacks, dispersed camping)
- Moose River Plains (Adirondacks, dispersed camping)
- West Canada Lake Wilderness Area
- Burnt-Rossman Hills State Forest

Others National Park

- Fire Island National Seashore (Watch Hill Campground)

New Jersey: The Garden State's Hidden Gems

New Jersey, often known for its bustling cities and shorelines, is also home to lush forests, scenic mountains, and quiet, natural beauty that makes it an unexpected gem for RVers. From the sandy beaches of the **Jersey Shore** to the peaceful trails of the **Pine Barrens**, New Jersey offers a variety of landscapes that are perfect for exploration by RV. It's a state where nature and history meet, offering everything from seaside retreats to colonial landmarks.

The best season to RV in New Jersey is **spring through fall**, from **April to October**. **Spring** brings blooming gardens and mild weather, making it a great time to explore New Jersey's state parks and coastal areas. **Summer** is the prime season for enjoying the **Jersey Shore**, where the beaches come alive with sunseekers and families. **Fall** is another beautiful time to visit, with the forests and mountains transforming into a vibrant palette of reds and golds, perfect for scenic drives and hikes. **Winter** can be cold and snowy, particularly in the northern part of the state, making RVing more challenging unless you're prepared for cold-weather conditions.

For RVers, the **Jersey Shore** is a must-visit destination. With miles of sandy beaches, bustling boardwalks, and charming coastal towns, it's a perfect place to park your RV and soak up the sun. Towns like **Cape May** offer a mix of Victorian charm and seaside beauty, while places like **Island Beach State Park** provide a more tranquil, natural setting right by the ocean.

New Jersey is also rich in history, and RVers can explore the state's colonial past by visiting sites like **Princeton** and **Morristown,** or take a trip to **Liberty State Park** for stunning views of the **Statue of Liberty** and **Ellis Island**. Inland, the **Pine Barrens** offer a quiet, forested escape, with camping spots nestled among the trees and opportunities for hiking, canoeing, and birdwatching.

New Jersey's campgrounds offer a variety of options, from full-service RV resorts near the coast to more rustic, peaceful spots in the mountains or forests. The state parks, like **Wharton State Forest** and **High Point State Park**, provide excellent campgrounds for RVers looking to experience the state's natural beauty while enjoying outdoor activities like fishing, hiking, and kayaking.

New Jersey's mix of coastal charm, rich history, and scenic outdoor escapes makes it an ideal destination for RVers. Whether you're looking to explore the beaches, hike through serene forests, or discover the state's historical landmarks, New Jersey offers something for everyone, with the added benefit of being just a short drive from major cities like New York and Philadelphia.

Liberty Harbor RV Park

📍 11 Marin Blvd, Jersey City, NJ 07302

📞 (201) 516-7500 — $$$

Campground Description:

Liberty Harbor RV Park is a unique urban RV park located just minutes from Manhattan, offering visitors a rare opportunity to camp near New York City. With stunning views of the Statue of Liberty, Ellis Island, and the NYC skyline, this RV park is ideal for those wanting to explore the city while staying in the comfort of their RV. Although the park offers basic amenities, its unbeatable location makes it a favorite for city explorers.

Types of Sites Available:

• RV sites with water and electricity hookups (no sewer)
• Tent camping is not available

Amenities:

• Free Wi-Fi
• Restrooms and showers
• Laundry facilities
• On-site marina
• 24-hour security
• Picnic tables
• Access to public transportation (ferry, subway)

Activities:

• Exploring Manhattan via ferry or subway
• Visiting Liberty State Park
• Enjoying waterfront views of the Statue of Liberty
• Walking along the Jersey City waterfront

Unique Experiences: Liberty Harbor RV Park offers the best of both worlds—urban camping with direct access to NYC's attractions while enjoying spectacular views of the harbor.

Feedback: Guests appreciate the convenient location, friendly staff, and incredible views, making this park a popular choice for urban adventurers.

Ocean View Resort

📍 2555 Route 9, Ocean View, NJ 08230

📞 (609) 624-0385 — $$

Campground Description:

Ocean View Resort, situated near the Jersey Shore, offers a family-friendly camping experience with access to a peaceful freshwater lake and the Atlantic beaches. The resort features spacious RV sites, tent camping, and cabins, providing a wide range of accommodations. Guests can enjoy swimming, fishing, and organized activities, ensuring a fun vacation for all ages.

Types of Sites Available:

• RV sites with full hookups
• Tent camping sites
• Cabin rentals

Amenities:

• Free Wi-Fi
• Swimming pool
• Canoe and kayak rentals
• Playground, mini-golf, dog park
• Freshwater lake with water activities

Activities:

• Swimming, fishing, and boating in the lake
• Shuttle service to nearby beaches
• Mini-golf, hiking, and biking on trails

Unique Experiences: Ocean View Resort offers a perfect balance of lakeside relaxation and beachside adventure, with plenty of family-friendly activities.

Feedback: Guests love the variety of activities and proximity to both the Jersey Shore and the peaceful lake, making it a favorite for summer getaways.

Seashore Campsites & RV Resort

720 Seashore Rd, Cape May, NJ 08204

(609) 884-4010 — $$

Campground Description:

Located in the scenic town of Cape May, Seashore Campsites & RV Resort offers a family-friendly escape with easy access to nearby beaches. This resort features a private lake, modern amenities, and a range of accommodations, making it an ideal spot for families, groups, and outdoor enthusiasts.

Types of Sites Available:
- RV sites with full hookups
- Tent camping sites
- Cabin rentals

Amenities:
- Free Wi-Fi
- Swimming pool and private lake
- Canoe and kayak rentals
- Picnic areas, playground, dog park

Activities:
- Swimming, fishing, and boating in the private lake
- Exploring Cape May's beaches and local attractions
- Mini-golf, basketball, volleyball

Unique Experiences: Seashore Campsites provides guests with a mix of beachside fun and lakefront relaxation, making it a perfect base for exploring the Jersey Shore.

Feedback: Guests appreciate the clean facilities, friendly staff, and easy access to Cape May's attractions, making it a popular summer vacation spot.

Big Timber Lake RV Camping Resort

116 Swainton-Goshen Rd, Cape May Court House, NJ 08210

(609) 465-4456 — $$

Campground Description:

Big Timber Lake RV Camping Resort, nestled in the woodlands of Cape May Court House, offers a peaceful camping experience with access to both a private lake and the Jersey Shore beaches. With spacious RV sites, tent camping, and cabin rentals, the resort provides a variety of outdoor activities, including swimming, fishing, and kayaking.

Types of Sites Available:
- RV sites with full hookups
- Tent camping sites
- Cabin rentals

Amenities:
- Free Wi-Fi
- Swimming pool and private lake
- Canoe and kayak rentals
- Playground, dog park, mini-golf

Activities:
- Swimming and fishing in the private lake
- Participating in family-friendly games and events
- Exploring nearby Cape May beaches and attractions

Unique Experiences: Big Timber Lake offers a serene woodland setting with plenty of activities, from lakefront fun to easy access to Cape May's attractions.

Feedback: Guests enjoy the variety of activities and proximity to both the beach and lake, making it a perfect spot for family vacations.

Cedar Creek Campground

Address: 1052 Atlantic City Blvd, Bayville, NJ 08721

Campground Description:
Located near the Pine Barrens, Cedar Creek Campground offers a peaceful, wooded setting with access to Cedar Creek for kayaking and canoeing.
Unique Experience: Paddle down Cedar Creek for a serene, nature-filled adventure.

Amenities:
• Kayak and canoe rentals
• Swimming pool

Activities:
• Paddling
• Fishing

High Point State Park

Address: 1480 NJ-23, Sussex, NJ 07461

Campground Description:
High Point State Park offers scenic camping with access to hiking trails, a lake for swimming, and panoramic views from the highest point in New Jersey.
Unique Experience: Enjoy breathtaking views from High Point Monument and hike through rugged terrain.

Amenities:
• Picnic areas
• Lake access

Activities:
• Hiking
• Swimming

Triplebrook Campground

Address: 58 Honey Run Rd, Blairstown, NJ 07825

Campground Description:
A family-friendly campground nestled in the mountains of northwestern New Jersey, offering beautiful views and plenty of outdoor activities.
Unique Experience: Enjoy mountain views and serene countryside in this quiet retreat.

Amenities:
• Pool
• Camp store

Activities:
• Hiking
• Fishing

Stokes State Forest

Address: 1 Coursen Rd, Branchville, NJ 07826

Campground Description:
Stokes State Forest features diverse terrain and miles of hiking trails, including the Appalachian Trail, along with peaceful camping areas.
Unique Experience: Camp in a tranquil forest setting and explore miles of scenic trails.

Amenities:
• Restrooms
• Fire pits

Activities:
• Hiking
• Wildlife viewing

Boondocking

Wharton State Forest

Address: 31 Batsto Rd, Hammonton, NJ 08037

Campground Description:
Wharton State Forest offers dispersed camping in the heart of the Pine Barrens, perfect for those seeking adventure in a unique ecosystem.

Unique Experience: Explore the historic Batsto Village and the vast, pine-covered wilderness.

Amenities:
• Primitive campsites
• Canoe access

Activities:
• Canoeing
• Hiking

Bass River State Forest

Address: 762 Stage Rd, Tuckerton, NJ 08087

Campground Description:
With remote camping options, Bass River State Forest is ideal for those who want to experience the Pine Barrens while enjoying hiking trails and lake activities.

Unique Experience: Enjoy peaceful camping by the lake in the quiet of the Pine Barrens.

Amenities:
• Primitive campsites
• Lake access

Activities:
• Fishing
• Hiking

Others Campgrounds

• Baker's Acres Campground (Little Egg Harbor Township, NJ)
• Indian Rock RV Park & Campground (Jackson, NJ)
• Timberland Lake Campground (Jackson, NJ)
• Harmony Ridge Campground (Branchville, NJ)
• Beachcomber Camping Resort (Cape May, NJ)
• Pine Haven Campground (Ocean View, NJ)
• Long Beach RV Resort (Barnegat, NJ)
• Pleasant Acres Farm Campground (Sussex, NJ)
• Mountain View Campground (Wantage, NJ)
• Turkey Swamp Park (Freehold, NJ)

Others Boondocking

• Belleplain State Forest (designated areas)
• Brendan T. Byrne State Forest
• Bass River State Forest (additional dispersed spots)
• Whittingham Wildlife Management Area
• Great Bay Boulevard Wildlife Management Area

Pennsylvania: A Blend of History and Nature

Pennsylvania is a state where history and natural beauty come together, offering RVers a wide range of experiences, from exploring the rolling hills and forests of the **Appalachian Mountains** to visiting historic landmarks like **Gettysburg** and **Philadelphia**. Known as the **Keystone State**, Pennsylvania is rich in both outdoor adventures and cultural heritage, making it a destination that appeals to all types of travelers.

The best season to RV in Pennsylvania is **spring through fall**, from **April to October**. **Spring** is perfect for enjoying the blooming flowers and mild temperatures, especially in the state's many parks and forests. **Summer** is ideal for camping, hiking, and enjoying the state's lakes and rivers, with plenty of festivals and outdoor activities to keep you entertained. **Fall** is a magical time in Pennsylvania, with the state's forests transforming into a stunning display of red, orange, and gold. **Winter**, while beautiful in some areas, can bring cold temperatures and snow, particularly in the northern and mountainous regions, making RV travel more challenging unless you're prepared for winter conditions.

One of the highlights of RVing in Pennsylvania is exploring its rich history. **Gettysburg National Military Park**, the site of the famous Civil War battle, offers a deep connection to the past, with RV-friendly campgrounds nearby that allow you to explore the historic battlefield and its museums. For those interested in early American history, **Philadelphia** offers a wealth of landmarks, including the **Liberty Bell** and **Independence Hall**, where you can step into the birthplace of American democracy.

For nature lovers, Pennsylvania's **Appalachian Mountains** and expansive forests provide endless opportunities for hiking, fishing, and camping. **Ricketts Glen State Park**, known for its stunning waterfalls and scenic hiking trails, is a favorite among RVers looking to experience the beauty of Pennsylvania's wilderness. The **Allegheny National Forest**, located in the northern part of the state, offers quiet, wooded campgrounds where you can immerse yourself in the tranquility of nature.

Pennsylvania's **Dutch Country** is another must-see for RVers. The rolling farmlands, covered bridges, and charming Amish communities in **Lancaster County** offer a peaceful, rural retreat. You can park your RV near picturesque farms and enjoy the simplicity and beauty of the countryside, with opportunities to explore local markets, traditional Amish crafts, and the unique culture of the region.

Whether you're drawn to Pennsylvania's rich history, its peaceful forests, or its charming small towns, the state offers a variety of campgrounds to suit every style. From full-service RV parks to more rustic sites in state parks, you'll find plenty of options for enjoying the state's natural beauty and cultural heritage.

For RVers seeking a mix of adventure, history, and relaxation, Pennsylvania is a state that offers it all. Whether you're exploring the historic sites, hiking in the mountains, or enjoying the fall foliage, Pennsylvania provides a wealth of experiences for every kind of traveler.

Pine Cradle Lake Family Campground

📍 220 Shoemaker Rd, Rome, PA 18837

📞 (570) 247-2424 — $$

Campground Description:

Located in the scenic Endless Mountains of Pennsylvania, this family-friendly campground offers a peaceful lakeside retreat with a variety of activities, making it ideal for outdoor enthusiasts and families.

Types of Sites Available:
- RV sites with full hookups
- Tent camping sites
- Cabin rentals

Amenities:
- Heated pool
- Fishing lake
- Walking and biking trails

Activities:
- Fishing and kayaking on Pine Cradle Lake
- Swimming in the heated pool
- Attending family-friendly events

Unique Experiences: A serene setting by the lake with modern amenities provides a peaceful escape, perfect for families looking for a nature-filled getaway.

Feedback: Guests appreciate the beautiful lake, clean facilities, and welcoming atmosphere, making it a top choice for families.

Gettysburg/Battlefield KOA

📍 20 Knox Rd, Gettysburg, PA 17325

📞 (717) 642-5713 — $$

Campground Description:

This peaceful, wooded campground near Gettysburg offers a perfect base for exploring Civil War history, with a range of amenities and activities for families and history buffs alike.

Types of Sites Available:
- RV sites with full hookups
- Tent camping sites
- Cabin rentals

Amenities:
- Swimming pool
- Mini-golf course
- Shuttle service to Gettysburg Battlefield

Activities:
- Exploring Gettysburg Battlefield
- Mini-golf and swimming
- Attending campground events and educational programs

Unique Experiences: Camping near the historic Gettysburg Battlefield offers a mix of education and outdoor fun in a relaxing, wooded setting.

Feedback: Praised for its proximity to historical sites and family-friendly atmosphere, it's a popular choice for both short visits and extended stays.

Sara's Campground

📍 50 Peninsula Dr, Erie, PA 16505

📞 (814) 833-4560   — $$

Campground Description:

This beachfront campground along Lake Erie offers direct access to the beach and is close to Presque Isle State Park, making it a perfect spot for outdoor activities and lakeside relaxation.

Types of Sites Available:

- Beachfront RV and tent camping
- Shaded RV and tent camping

Amenities:

- Direct beach access
- Volleyball courts
- Water sports rentals

Activities:

- Swimming and beachcombing
- Kayaking and paddleboarding
- Exploring Presque Isle State Park

Unique Experiences: Beachfront camping with stunning views of Lake Erie makes Sara's Campground a unique and relaxing lakeside getaway.

Feedback: Guests love the beachfront sites and variety of activities, making it a favorite for summer fun and lakeside relaxation.

Sun Retreats Lancaster County

 576 Yellow Hill Rd, Narvon, PA 17555

 (717) 445-5525   — $$

Campground Description:

Located in the heart of Amish Country, this family-friendly campground offers a peaceful retreat with modern amenities and easy access to cultural attractions and scenic farmlands.

Types of Sites Available:

- RV sites with full hookups
- Tent camping sites
- Cabin rentals

Amenities:

- Swimming pool and splash pad
- Mini-golf course
- Dog park

Activities:

- Swimming and playing mini-golf
- Exploring Amish farms and markets
- Attending campground events

Unique Experiences: A relaxing retreat in Amish Country with easy access to local attractions and plenty of on-site family-friendly activities.

Feedback: Guests praise the clean facilities and friendly atmosphere, making it a top choice for families looking to explore Lancaster County.

HIDDEN GEMS

Miller's Campground

Address: 2944 PA-981, New Alexandria, PA 15670

Campground Description:
A family-owned campground offering a quiet and rustic camping experience with easy access to local lakes and hiking trails.
Unique Experience: Enjoy a laid-back, natural setting perfect for fishing and relaxing by the campfire.

Amenities:
• Restrooms
• Picnic areas

Activities:
• Fishing
• Hiking

Mountain Top Campground

Address: 873 Sun Mine Rd, Tarentum, PA 15084

Campground Description:
A scenic, hilltop campground with panoramic views of the surrounding countryside, perfect for RV and tent campers alike.
Unique Experience: Take in breathtaking sunset views from the hilltop and enjoy peaceful, spacious campsites.

Amenities:
• Full hookups
• Laundry facilities

Activities:
• Hiking
• Stargazing

NATIONAL PARKS

Hickory Run State Park

Address: 3613 PA-534, White Haven, PA 18661

Campground Description:
This state park offers wooded and open campsites near waterfalls, boulder fields, and forested trails.
Unique Experience: Explore the iconic Boulder Field and hike through dense forests.

Amenities:
• Restrooms
• Picnic areas

Activities:
• Hiking
• Fishing

Ricketts Glen State Park

Address: 695 State Route 487, Benton, PA 17814

Campground Description:
Known for its stunning waterfalls and diverse hiking trails, this state park is a hiker's paradise.
Unique Experience: Discover 22 named waterfalls as you hike the Falls Trail, surrounded by scenic woodland.

Amenities:
• Restrooms
• Boat rentals

Activities:
• Waterfall hikes
• Boating

Boondocking

Allegheny National Forest

Address: Allegheny National Forest, PA

Campground Description:
This expansive national forest offers remote, dispersed camping opportunities among rolling hills and streams.

Unique Experience: Enjoy the solitude of boondocking while hiking or fishing in the serene forest.

Amenities:
• Primitive campsites
• Stream access

Activities:
• Hiking
• Wildlife watching

Tioga State Forest

Address: Tioga State Forest, PA

Campground Description:
Boondocking sites scattered throughout this state forest allow for remote camping near lakes and hardwood forests.

Unique Experience: Camp in peaceful isolation with access to hiking trails and scenic overlooks.

Amenities:
• Primitive campsites
• Lake access

Activities:
• Fishing
• Hiking

Others Campgrounds

• French Creek State Park (Elverson, PA)
• Bald Eagle State Park (Howard, PA)
• Raystown Lake Recreation Area (Hesston, PA)
• Otter Lake Camp Resort (East Stroudsburg, PA)
• Blue Rocks Family Campground (Lenhartsville, PA)
• Knoebels Campground (Elysburg, PA)
• Locust Lake State Park (Barnesville, PA)
• Promised Land State Park (Greentown, PA)
• Ohiopyle State Park (Ohiopyle, PA)
• Caledonia State Park (Fayetteville, PA)

Others Boondocking

• Sproul State Forest (dispersed camping areas)
• Susquehannock State Forest (dispersed camping areas)
• Loyalsock State Forest (dispersed camping areas)
• Michaux State Forest (dispersed camping areas)
• Weiser State Forest (dispersed camping areas)

Others National Park

• Delaware Water Gap National Recreation Area (Dingmans Campground)

Ohio: The Heart of the Midwest

Ohio, located in the heart of the Midwest, offers a diverse mix of landscapes, from rolling farmlands and lush forests to scenic rivers and lakes. For RVers, Ohio is a hidden gem, filled with beautiful state parks, historic small towns, and vibrant cities. Whether you're exploring the serene shores of **Lake Erie**, hiking through the **Hocking Hills**, or enjoying the cultural offerings of **Cincinnati** or **Cleveland**, Ohio is a state that has something for everyone.

The best season to RV in Ohio is **spring through fall**, from **April to October**. **Spring** brings mild temperatures and blooming flowers, making it a perfect time to explore Ohio's parks and trails. **Summer** is ideal for lake activities and outdoor festivals, with warm days and cool nights. **Fall** is arguably the best time to visit, as the state's forests burst into vibrant colors, offering stunning views and ideal hiking weather. **Winter** can be cold and snowy, particularly in northern Ohio, making RV travel more challenging unless you are prepared for cold-weather camping or plan to explore the winter attractions like skiing in **Mad River Mountain**.

One of the most popular destinations for RVers in Ohio is **Hocking Hills State Park**, a stunning region of waterfalls, gorges, and lush forests. With its dramatic rock formations and miles of hiking trails, Hocking Hills is a must-visit for those seeking natural beauty and adventure. The park offers RV-friendly campgrounds with plenty of access to outdoor activities like zip-lining, canoeing, and rock climbing.

For RVers who love water, **Lake Erie** is the place to be. Ohio's northern coastline offers beautiful beaches, quaint lakeside towns, and opportunities for boating, fishing, and swimming. The **Lake Erie Islands**, such as **Put-in-Bay** and **Kelleys Island**, provide a unique RV experience, where you can take a ferry to explore the islands and enjoy the relaxing lake atmosphere.

Ohio is also rich in history, with attractions like the **National Museum of the United States Air Force** in **Dayton** and **Cuyahoga Valley National Park**, which offers a mix of history and nature along the scenic **Cuyahoga River**. The park's towpath trail, which follows the historic **Ohio & Erie Canal**, is perfect for biking and hiking, and RVers will find campgrounds nearby that make it easy to explore this green oasis near the bustling cities of Cleveland and Akron.

Ohio's campgrounds are spread throughout the state, offering a mix of fully equipped RV resorts and more rustic, nature-focused spots in state parks and forests. Whether you're camping along a lake, in the middle of the woods, or close to a vibrant city, Ohio provides plenty of options for RVers seeking a variety of experiences.

With its mix of outdoor adventure, history, and Midwestern charm, Ohio is an excellent destination for RVers looking for a little bit of everything. Whether you're enjoying the peace of a lakeside campground or exploring the state's vibrant cities, Ohio invites you to experience the heart of the Midwest in all its forms.

Cross Creek Camping Resort

3190 S Old State Rd, Delaware, OH 43015

(740) 549-2267 — $$

Campground Description:

This family-friendly resort near Alum Creek State Park offers a variety of activities and well-maintained facilities, making it a great destination for families and groups.

Types of Sites Available:

- RV sites with full hookups
- Tent camping sites
- Cabin rentals

Amenities:

- Heated pool
- Playground
- Dog park
- Free Wi-Fi

Activities:

- Swimming
- Mini-golf
- Family-friendly events

Unique Experiences:
Organized activities and close proximity to Alum Creek State Park create a perfect outdoor adventure.

Feedback:
Guests love the clean facilities, family atmosphere, and variety of activities.

Berlin RV Park & Campground

5898 State Route 39, Millersburg, OH 44654

(330) 674-4774 — $$

Campground Description:

Located in Ohio's Amish Country, this quiet and peaceful park offers a relaxing escape surrounded by scenic landscapes, ideal for exploring local Amish markets.

Types of Sites Available:

- RV sites with full hookups
- Tent camping sites

Amenities:

- Free Wi-Fi
- Picnic areas with BBQs
- Dog park

Activities:

- Exploring Amish markets
- Walking trails
- Picnicking

Unique Experiences:
Guests can immerse themselves in Amish Country culture, with nearby craft shops and traditional dining experiences.

Feedback:
Praised for its peaceful setting, friendly staff, and clean facilities, it's a favorite for a countryside retreat.

Alton RV Park

6550 Alton Rd, Galloway, OH 43119

(614) 878-9127   — $$

Campground Description:

Just outside Columbus, Alton RV Park offers a peaceful retreat with easy access to the city's top attractions, ideal for exploring Columbus.

Types of Sites Available:

- RV sites with full hookups

Amenities:

- Free Wi-Fi
- Pet-friendly areas
- Picnic tables

Activities:

- Exploring Columbus Zoo
- Visiting Ohio State University
- Relaxing at the park

Unique Experiences: Conveniently located near Columbus, making it an excellent base for city exploration while enjoying a peaceful retreat.

Feedback: Guests appreciate the convenient location, friendly staff, and well-kept grounds.

Sauder Village Campground

22611 OH-2, Archbold, OH 43502

(800) 590-9755   — $$

Campground Description:

Sauder Village Campground offers a blend of modern amenities and historical charm, perfect for families and history buffs. Adjacent to the living history site of Sauder Village, guests can experience Ohio's rural heritage.

Types of Sites Available:

- RV sites with full hookups
- Tent camping sites
- Cabin rentals

Amenities:

- Free Wi-Fi
- Laundry facilities
- Fishing pond

Activities:

- Exploring Sauder Village
- Fishing
- Walking and biking on scenic trails

Unique Experiences: Guests can step back in time at Sauder Village, experiencing a recreated 19th-century community while enjoying modern camping conveniences.

Feedback: Known for its clean facilities, friendly staff, and unique historical experience, it's popular among families and history lovers alike.

HIDDEN GEMS

Tucker's Landing RV Park
Address: 46205 OH-7, Marietta, OH 45750

Campground Description:
A peaceful RV park along the Ohio River, perfect for quiet getaways with scenic riverfront views.
Unique Experience: Relax by the river while watching boats pass and enjoy the tranquility of nature.

Amenities:
• Full hookups
• River access

Activities:
• Fishing
• Boating

Walnut Creek Campground and Resort
Address: 2342 Walnut Creek Rd, Chillicothe, OH 45601

Campground Description:
A family-friendly resort-style campground offering a variety of outdoor activities and comfortable camping options.
Unique Experience: Stay in a beautiful rural setting with access to a variety of recreational amenities.

Amenities:
• Full hookups
• Swimming pool

Activities:
• Swimming
• Hiking

NATIONAL PARKS

Indian Lake State Park
Address: 13156 OH-235 N, Lakeview, OH 43331

Campground Description:
A popular destination known for its lakefront camping and access to water activities like boating and fishing.
Unique Experience: Camp along the shores of Indian Lake and enjoy its crystal-clear waters.

Amenities:
• Restrooms
• Boat ramps

Activities:
• Boating
• Fishing

John Bryan State Park
Address: 3790 OH-370, Yellow Springs, OH 45387

Campground Description:
A scenic park featuring dramatic limestone gorges and lush forests, ideal for nature lovers.
Unique Experience: Hike the breathtaking Clifton Gorge trail while staying in this serene park.

Amenities:
• Picnic areas
• Hiking trails

Activities:
• Hiking
• Rock climbing

Boondocking

Wayne National Forest

Address: 13700 US-33, Nelsonville, OH 45764

Campground Description:
Dispersed camping in Ohio's only national forest, offering expansive woodlands and peaceful solitude.
Unique Experience: Camp off the beaten path in a lush, tranquil forest setting.

Amenities:
• Primitive campsites
• Access to trails

Activities:
• Hiking
• Wildlife watching

Burr Oak State Park

Address: 10220 Burr Oak Lodge Rd, Glouster, OH 45732

Campground Description:
Boondocking is available in this peaceful park known for its scenic lake and extensive trails.
Unique Experience: Enjoy serene lake views and explore the park's abundant wildlife.

Amenities:
• Primitive campsites
• Lake access

Activities:
• Fishing
• Hiking

Others Campgrounds

• Buckeye Lake/Columbus East KOA Holiday (Buckeye Lake, OH)
• Lazy River At Granville (Granville, OH)
• Woodside Lake Park (Streetsboro, OH)
• Wapakoneta KOA (Wapakoneta, OH)
• Tall Timbers Campground (Port Clinton, OH)
• Evergreen Park RV Resort (Dundee, OH)
• Streetsboro / Cleveland SE KOA Holiday (Streetsboro, OH)
• Sandusky / Bayshore KOA Holiday (Sandusky, OH)
• Wolfie's Campground (Zanesville, OH)
• River Trail Crossing RV Park (Butler, OH)

Others Boondocking

• Zaleski State Forest
• Shawnee State Forest
• Caesar Creek Lake (designated boondocking areas)
• AEP ReCreation Land (dispersed camping)
• Mosquito Creek Wildlife Area

Others National Park

• Cuyahoga Valley National Park (The Stanford Backcountry Campsites)

Indiana: The Crossroads of America

Indiana may be known as the "Crossroads of America," but for RVers, it's far more than just a place to pass through. With its wide open spaces, charming small towns, and surprisingly beautiful landscapes, Indiana offers a peaceful and relaxing experience for those traveling by RV. Whether you're exploring the rolling hills of southern Indiana or the quiet shores of Lake Michigan in the north, this state offers a little something for everyone.

The best season to visit Indiana in an RV is **spring through fall**, from **April to October**. **Spring** is a wonderful time to explore the state's forests and farmlands, as everything comes into bloom. **Summer** is ideal for enjoying Indiana's many lakes and rivers, and the warmer months bring plenty of outdoor festivals and activities to the small towns and cities throughout the state. **Fall** is perhaps the most scenic time to visit, especially in the southern part of the state, where places like Brown County come alive with autumn colors. **The season to avoid** is **winter**, as it can be quite cold and snowy, making travel and camping challenging, particularly in northern Indiana.

What I've always loved about RVing in Indiana is the simplicity and charm of it all. This is a state where you can truly slow down, breathe in the fresh air, and enjoy the rolling landscapes dotted with picturesque farms and quiet woodlands. You can take a peaceful drive along scenic byways like the Indiana National Road or explore the historic towns and quaint shops that line the streets of places like Nashville, Indiana.

Indiana's campgrounds are some of the most peaceful you'll find in the Midwest. From the shores of Patoka Lake in the south to the Indiana Dunes National Park in the north, there's a variety of places to park your RV and enjoy the natural beauty that surrounds you. And for those who enjoy history, Indiana's connection to the early days of American pioneers and the historic stops along the famous Lincoln Highway make it a rewarding destination for those interested in learning about the country's past.

For RVers seeking a mix of relaxation, scenic beauty, and a touch of Americana, Indiana is a hidden gem. It's a place where you can take the road less traveled and discover the quiet beauty of the Midwest, all while enjoying the warmth and friendliness of the people who call this state home.

Lake Rudolph Campground & RV Resort

📍 78 N Holiday Blvd, Santa Claus, IN 47579

📞 (812) 937-4458   — $$

Campground Description:

A family-friendly resort in Santa Claus, Indiana, adjacent to Holiday World & Splashin' Safari, offering a variety of accommodations with on-site activities like swimming, fishing, and mini-golf.

Types of Sites Available:
- RV sites with full hookups
- Tent camping, cabins, rental RVs

Amenities:
- Swimming pool, splash pad, fishing, paddleboat rentals
- Mini-golf, playground, sports courts
- Shuttle to Holiday World

Activities:
- Swimming, fishing, boating, mini-golf
- Themed events and activities
- Easy access to Holiday World & Splashin' Safari

Unique Experiences:
A festive, family-friendly camping experience with plenty of activities and convenient access to the theme park.

Feedback:
Praised for its family-friendly atmosphere and clean facilities, a favorite for families visiting Holiday World.

Heartland Resort

📍 1613 W 300 N, Greenfield, IN 46140

📞 (317) 326-3181   — $$

Campground Description:

A scenic, family-friendly resort near Indianapolis offering fishing, mini-golf, and a peaceful retreat, with RV sites, cabins, and tent camping.

Types of Sites Available:
- RV sites with full hookups
- Tent camping, cabins

Activities:
- Fishing, swimming, mini-golf
- Social events, playground fun

Amenities:
- Swimming pool, fishing lakes, mini-golf
- Playground, picnic areas, event pavilion

Unique Experiences:
Offers a peaceful atmosphere with plenty of outdoor activities and proximity to Indianapolis for easy day trips.

Feedback: Highly rated for its clean facilities, variety of activities, and friendly staff.

Cornerstone Campground

75 W County Rd 500 S, New Castle, IN 47362

(765) 987-8700 — $$

Campground Description:

A peaceful, family-friendly campground offering RV sites, tent camping, and cabins, with amenities like a swimming pool, fishing pond, and sports courts.

Types of Sites Available:

- RV sites with full hookups
- Tent camping, cabins

Amenities:

- Swimming pool, fishing pond, sports courts
- Playground, picnic areas, pavilion

Activities:

- Swimming, fishing, sports courts
- Social events and family-friendly games

Unique Experiences: A tranquil and friendly campground with plenty of activities for all ages.

Feedback: Praised for its spacious sites, friendly staff, and clean facilities, making it a favorite for families.

Indianapolis KOA

5896 W 200 N, Greenfield, IN 46140

(317) 894-1397 — $$

Campground Description:

A family-friendly KOA near Indianapolis offering RV sites, cabins, and tent camping, with modern amenities like a pool and dog park. Ideal for those exploring Indianapolis while enjoying a peaceful stay.

Types of Sites Available:

- RV sites with full hookups
- Tent camping, cabins

Amenities:

- Swimming pool, dog park, playground
- Restrooms, showers, picnic areas

Activities:

- Swimming, playground, pet-friendly activities
- Exploring nearby Indianapolis attractions

Unique Experiences: A perfect balance of city exploration and relaxing outdoor activities, with easy access to Indianapolis.

Feedback: Highly rated for its clean facilities and proximity to Indianapolis, a favorite for families.

HIDDEN GEMS

Hidden Paradise Campground

Address: 802 E Jefferson St, St. Paul, IN 47272

Campground Description:
A peaceful campground nestled around a quarry lake, offering family-friendly camping with plenty of water-based activities.

Unique Experience: Enjoy swimming and snorkeling in the crystal-clear waters of a spring-fed quarry.

Amenities:
• Full RV hookups
• Quarry swimming area

Activities:
• Swimming and kayaking
• Fishing in the quarry

Lehman's Lakeside RV Resort

Address: 19609 Harmony Rd, Union, IL 60180

Campground Description:
This lakeside RV resort offers a relaxing escape with scenic views and water activities, ideal for families looking for a quiet getaway.

Unique Experience: Camp by the water with easy access to boating and fishing.

Amenities:
• Full RV hookups
• Restrooms and showers

Activities:
• Fishing and boating
• Relaxing by the campfire

NATIONAL PARKS

Indiana Dunes National Park

Address: 1215 N State Road 49, Porter, IN 46304

Campground Description:
Situated along the southern shore of Lake Michigan, this national park features unique dune formations, sandy beaches, and diverse ecosystems.

Unique Experience: Hike along the dunes and enjoy stunning views of Lake Michigan.

Amenities:
• Restrooms and showers
• Picnic areas

Activities:
• Hiking on dune trails
• Swimming at the beach

Brown County State Park

Address: 1810 State Road 46 E, Nashville, IN 47448

Campground Description:
Known for its rolling hills and beautiful fall foliage, Brown County State Park is a popular destination for hiking, horseback riding, and camping.

Unique Experience: Explore scenic vistas and wooded trails in Indiana's largest state park.

Amenities:
• Restrooms and showers
• Horseback riding facilities

Activities:
• Hiking through forested trails
• Horseback riding

Boondocking

Hoosier National Forest

Address: 811 Constitution Ave, Bedford, IN 47421

Campground Description:
This expansive forest offers a variety of dispersed camping opportunities, allowing visitors to camp amid dense forests, hills, and lakes.
Unique Experience: Experience the solitude of camping deep within Indiana's national forest.

Amenities:
• Primitive campsites
• Vault toilets

Activities:
• Hiking and exploring nature
• Wildlife viewing

Morgan-Monroe State Forest

Address: 6220 Forest Rd, Martinsville, IN 46151

Campground Description:
A vast state forest with dispersed camping opportunities, offering quiet, secluded sites surrounded by nature.
Unique Experience: Enjoy primitive camping in a serene woodland setting with access to miles of hiking trails.

Amenities:
• Primitive campsites
• Picnic tables

Activities:
• Hiking and birdwatching
• Camping in solitude

Others Campgrounds

• Tall Sycamore Campground
• White River Campground
• Hardin Ridge Recreation Area
• Twin Mills Camping Resort
• Ouabache State Park Campground
• Versailles State Park Campground
• Salamonie Lake Campground
• Prophetstown State Park Campground
• Summit Lake State Park Campground
• Turkey Run State Park Campground

Others Boondocking

• Salamonie River State Forest (dispersed camping)
• Greene-Sullivan State Forest (dispersed areas)
• Harrison-Crawford State Forest (dispersed camping available)
• Ferdinand State Forest (dispersed camping spots)
• Jackson-Washington State Forest

Illinois: A Midwest Gem

Illinois often surprises RVers with its diverse landscapes, from the bustling city of Chicago to the peaceful, rolling farmlands and tranquil state parks. While it may not have the towering mountains or expansive coastlines of other states, Illinois offers a unique blend of urban excitement and natural beauty, making it a perfect stop for those seeking both adventure and relaxation.

The best season to RV in Illinois is **spring through fall**, from **April to October**. **Spring** brings mild temperatures and the renewal of life in the state's many forests, parks, and gardens. **Fall** is another ideal time to visit, especially if you're traveling through southern Illinois, where the Shawnee National Forest comes alive with brilliant autumn colors. **Summer** is great for exploring Illinois' lakes, rivers, and outdoor festivals, though the heat and humidity can make some days challenging, particularly in the southern regions. **Winter** is the season to avoid for most RVers, as the cold and snow can make traveling and camping difficult, especially in northern Illinois where snowstorms are common.

One of the best things about RVing in Illinois is the variety of experiences you can have in one trip. You can spend your morning hiking along the scenic cliffs of Starved Rock State Park, and by the afternoon, you're exploring the cultural and historical richness of Chicago. The city offers unique RV parks and campsites just outside the urban area, giving you easy access to world-class museums, theaters, and dining. Then, just a few hours away, you can immerse yourself in the quiet beauty of the countryside or take in the peaceful shores of Lake Michigan.

For RVers, Illinois offers plenty of excellent campgrounds, from the well-equipped state parks to more rustic spots perfect for getting away from it all. The state is also home to some of the most scenic drives in the Midwest, with the Great River Road following the Mississippi River, offering stunning views and charming small towns along the way. And don't forget about the historic Route 66, where you can relive the golden age of road travel with quirky roadside attractions and iconic stops along the way.

Illinois is a state that offers something for everyone. Whether you're looking for the vibrancy of a big city or the calm of a quiet forest, you'll find it here. RVing through Illinois lets you experience the best of both worlds—urban adventure and rural peace, all within a day's drive.

Sycamore RV Resort

📍 375 E North Ave, Sycamore, IL 60178

📞 (815) 895-5590 — $$

Campground Description:

A tranquil lakeside resort in Sycamore, Illinois, with private lakes, offering fishing, swimming, and boating for a peaceful outdoor escape.

Types of Sites Available:
- RV sites with full hookups
- Tent camping sites

Activities:
- Fishing, swimming, boating
- Hiking, nature walks

Amenities:
- Private lakes for swimming, fishing, boating
- Free Wi-Fi, restrooms, showers
- Picnic areas, fire pits, playground

Unique Experiences: Enjoy peaceful lakeside camping with plenty of outdoor fun for the whole family.

Feedback: Praised for its clean facilities and serene environment, popular with families and couples.

Holiday Acres RV Resort

📍 12008 US-20, Garden Prairie, IL 61038

📞 (815) 547-7846 — $$

Campground Description:

Family-friendly resort with outdoor activities, including swimming, fishing, and mini-golf, offering a fun, community-driven experience.

Types of Sites Available:
- RV sites with full hookups
- Tent camping

Activities:
- Fishing, swimming, mini-golf
- Seasonal and themed events

Amenities:
- Swimming pool, fishing pond
- Restrooms, showers, laundry
- Mini-golf, playground, sports courts

Unique Experiences: Fun-filled, family-oriented resort with plenty of activities and nearby hiking trails.

Feedback: Highly rated for its variety of activities and family-friendly environment.

Rustic Acres RV Park

7408 E State Route 4, New Douglas, IL 62074

(217) 456-1122 — $$

Campground Description:

Part of the Yogi Bear's Jellystone Park™, this family-friendly campground offers themed events and activities centered around Yogi Bear for kids and families.

Types of Sites Available:
- RV sites with full hookups
- Tent camping, cabins

Activities:
- Yogi Bear-themed events
- Mini-golf, playground fun

Amenities:
- Swimming pool, playground
- Mini-golf, sports courts
- Planned activities and themed weekends

Unique Experiences: Yogi Bear-themed events and activities create a lively and engaging atmosphere for families.

Feedback: Loved for its family-friendly environment, clean facilities, and fun activities for kids.

Archway RV Park

4810 Broadway St, Mt. Vernon, IL 62864

(618) 244-0399 — $$

Campground Description:

A quiet, convenient RV park with easy highway access, ideal for travelers or extended stays, offering a peaceful environment near local attractions.

Types of Sites Available:
- RV sites with full hookups
- Tent camping

Activities:
- Relaxing, exploring Mt. Vernon
- Visiting local attractions

Amenities:
- Free Wi-Fi, restrooms, showers
- Playground, picnic tables
- Fire pits at select sites

Unique Experiences: A comfortable stopover with modern amenities and access to local dining and parks.

Feedback: Highly praised for its clean facilities, friendly staff, and convenient location near highways.

HIDDEN GEMS

NATIONAL PARKS

Lehmans Lakeside RV Resort

Address: 19609 Harmony Rd, Union, IL 60180

Campground Description:
A family-friendly lakeside campground offering scenic views and a relaxing atmosphere. Perfect for RV travelers seeking a peaceful retreat.
Unique Experience: Enjoy lakeside camping with easy access to fishing and water sports.

Amenities:
• Full RV hookups
• Restrooms and showers

Activities:
• Fishing and boating on the lake
• Relaxing by the campfire

Starved Rock State Park

Address: 2668 E 875th Rd, Oglesby, IL 61348

Campground Description:
A popular state park known for its dramatic sandstone cliffs, waterfalls, and scenic hiking trails along the Illinois River.
Unique Experience: Hike through lush canyons and discover hidden waterfalls.

Amenities:
• Restrooms and showers
• Picnic areas

Activities:
• Hiking through canyons
• Wildlife watching

D&W Lake Camping and RV Park

Address: 411 W Hensley Rd, Champaign, IL 61822

Campground Description:
A peaceful RV park set beside a small lake, offering a serene atmosphere just minutes from downtown Champaign.
Unique Experience: Camp by the water while enjoying the proximity to city conveniences.

Amenities:
• Full RV hookups
• Laundry facilities

Activities:
• Fishing in the lake
• Exploring nearby Champaign

Shabbona Lake State Park

Address: 100 Preserve Rd, Shabbona, IL 60550

Campground Description:
A peaceful state park offering excellent fishing, camping, and hiking opportunities around the serene Shabbona Lake.
Unique Experience: Fish on one of the best fishing lakes in Illinois.

Amenities:
• Restrooms and showers
• Fishing piers

Activities:
• Fishing for bass and crappie
• Hiking around the lake

Boondocking

Shawnee National Forest

Address: 50 Highway 145 S, Harrisburg, IL 62946

Campground Description:
Located in southern Illinois, Shawnee National Forest offers dispersed camping in a diverse landscape of forests, rivers, and rugged terrain.

Unique Experience: Camp in the heart of a dense forest with access to breathtaking natural features like rock formations and waterfalls.

Amenities:
• Primitive campsites
• Vault toilets

Activities:
• Hiking and exploring rock formations
• Wildlife watching

Garden of the Gods Recreation Area

Address: 50 Highway 145 S, Harrisburg, IL 62946

Campground Description:
A stunning boondocking location within Shawnee National Forest, known for its towering rock formations and panoramic views.

Unique Experience: Camp among awe-inspiring rock formations and enjoy spectacular sunsets.

Amenities:
• Primitive campsites
• Vault toilets

Activities:
• Hiking to the scenic viewpoints
• Photography of rock formations

Others Campgrounds

• Timber Trails RV Park
• Whispering Pines Campground
• Lincoln's New Salem State Park Campground
• Crazy Horse Campground
• Camp Lakewood Campground
• Sangchris Lake State Park Campground
• North Sandusky Campground
• Thomson Causeway Campground
• Jubilee College State Park
• Pere Marquette State Park Campground

Others Boondocking

• Apple River Canyon State Park (dispersed camping)
• Shawnee National Forest (various dispersed camping spots)
• Mississippi Palisades State Park (some dispersed camping areas)
• Trail of Tears State Forest (dispersed camping zones)
• Sam Parr State Fish and Wildlife Area

Michigan: The Great Lakes State, A Waterfront Haven

Michigan is a paradise for RVers who love water, nature, and adventure. Known as the "Great Lakes State," Michigan offers miles upon miles of shoreline, crystal-clear lakes, and forests that stretch as far as the eye can see. Whether you're exploring the sandy beaches of Lake Michigan or heading deep into the Upper Peninsula for a rugged, off-the-grid experience, Michigan's natural beauty is sure to leave you breathless.

The best season to RV in Michigan is **late spring through early fall**, from **May to October**. **Summer** is prime time to enjoy the state's incredible waterfronts, with warm weather perfect for swimming, boating, and fishing. **Fall** is another ideal season to visit, with cooler temperatures and Michigan's famous fall foliage turning the forests into a sea of red, orange, and gold. **Winter**, while beautiful, can be harsh, with heavy snowfalls and freezing temperatures, especially in the Upper Peninsula, making RVing challenging unless you're equipped for cold-weather camping.

One of the best parts of RVing in Michigan is the access to the **Great Lakes**, the largest freshwater system in the world. You can camp right on the shores of **Lake Michigan**, **Lake Huron**, or **Lake Superior**, where the sunsets are some of the most stunning you'll ever see. Popular destinations like **Sleeping Bear Dunes National Lakeshore** offer sweeping views of the dunes and crystal-clear waters, perfect for a relaxing yet adventure-filled getaway.

For RVers who love a mix of adventure and solitude, Michigan's **Upper Peninsula** (the U.P.) is a must. The rugged, unspoiled landscapes here are perfect for hiking, exploring waterfalls, and camping in remote areas. Places like **Pictured Rocks National Lakeshore** and **Tahquamenon Falls State Park** provide breathtaking views and a sense of tranquility that's hard to find elsewhere. The U.P. is also known for its lighthouses, rustic campgrounds, and a slower pace of life that makes it ideal for escaping the rush of everyday life.

Michigan's campgrounds are as varied as its landscapes, with well-equipped state parks, national forests, and more rustic, off-the-beaten-path options available. Whether you prefer a campground with full amenities or a quiet, lakeside retreat, Michigan has something for every type of RVer.

For those who love outdoor activities, Michigan offers endless opportunities for fishing, kayaking, hiking, and biking. And with its friendly small towns, fresh local produce, and a laid-back atmosphere, Michigan is a place that invites you to stay a little longer and savor every moment.

Mackinaw Mill Creek Camping

9730 US Highway 23, Mackinaw City, MI 49701

(231) 436-5584 — $$

Campground Description:

Mackinaw Mill Creek Camping, located on Lake Huron, provides scenic views of the Mackinac Bridge and Island. This large, family-friendly campground offers a variety of accommodations, including RV sites, tent camping, and cabins, making it an ideal base for exploring Northern Michigan's natural beauty and nearby attractions.

Types of Sites Available:

- RV sites with full and partial hookups
- Tent camping sites
- Cabin rentals

Amenities:

- Free Wi-Fi in select areas
- Swimming beach on Lake Huron
- Mini-golf, nature trails

Activities:

- Swimming and fishing along the lake
- Exploring Mackinaw City and ferry to Mackinac Island
- Mini-golf and family-friendly games

Unique Experiences:

Lakeside camping with breathtaking views of the Mackinac Bridge, ideal for outdoor enthusiasts and families.

Feedback: Praised for its scenic location, family-friendly atmosphere, and proximity to Mackinac Island.

Poncho's Pond RV Park

5335 W Wallace Ln, Ludington, MI 49431

(231) 845-6655 — $$

Campground Description:

Poncho's Pond RV Park offers a relaxing retreat around a scenic pond in Ludington, Michigan. Perfect for families and travelers, this park features spacious RV sites with full hookups, a variety of on-site amenities like pools and a hot tub, and easy access to Ludington State Park and Lake Michigan.

Types of Sites Available:

- RV sites with full hookups

Amenities:

- Indoor and outdoor pools, hot tub
- Playground, fishing pond
- Free Wi-Fi and cable TV

Activities:

- Swimming in the pools
- Fishing in the pond
- Exploring Ludington State Park and nearby beaches

Unique Experiences: A peaceful, family-friendly RV park with beautiful views and easy access to Michigan's natural attractions.

Feedback: Guests love the relaxing environment, clean facilities, and range of family-friendly amenities.

Indigo Bluffs RV Park & Resort

📍 6760 W Empire Hwy, Empire, MI 49630

📞 (231) 326-5050 — $$$

Campground Description:

Located near Sleeping Bear Dunes National Lakeshore, Indigo Bluffs offers an upscale camping experience with premium RV sites, a heated pool, and nature trails. The resort is a perfect mix of luxury and outdoor adventure, providing guests with a peaceful, scenic setting in Northern Michigan.

Types of Sites Available:

- RV sites with full hookups
- Premium RV sites with patios

Amenities:

- Heated pool, nature trails
- Clubhouse, fire pits
- Free Wi-Fi

Activities:

- Swimming and lounging by the heated pool
- Hiking and exploring the nearby Sleeping Bear Dunes National Lakeshore
- Visiting the nearby beaches of Lake Michigan
- Hiking in Sleeping Bear Dunes
- Swimming, biking
- Exploring local towns like Empire and Glen Arbor

Unique Experiences: Luxurious camping with access to the natural beauty of Sleeping Bear Dunes, ideal for outdoor lovers and families.

Feedback: Highly praised for its beautiful setting, premium amenities, and friendly atmosphere.

Petoskey RV Resort

📍 5505 Charlevoix Ave, Petoskey, MI 49770

📞 (231) 347-0905 — $$$

Campground Description:

Petoskey RV Resort offers a luxurious camping experience near Lake Michigan's Little Traverse Bay. With beautifully landscaped grounds and top-tier amenities, including a heated pool and fitness center, this upscale resort is ideal for those seeking comfort and relaxation while exploring the Petoskey area.

Types of Sites Available:

- RV sites with full hookups
- Luxury cottages

Amenities:

- Heated pool, fitness center
- Tennis and pickleball courts
- Fire pits, nature trails

Activities:

- Swimming and tennis
- Hiking and biking
- Exploring downtown Petoskey and nearby attractions

Unique Experiences: A premier RV resort with upscale amenities, offering a perfect balance of relaxation and outdoor adventure.

Feedback: Guests appreciate the resort's peaceful setting, beautiful grounds, and proximity to Petoskey's attractions.

Honcho Rest Campground

Address: 9544 US-31, Kewadin, MI 49648

Campground Description:
A peaceful campground on the shores of Torch Lake, offering a laid-back atmosphere perfect for nature lovers.

Unique Experience: Enjoy stunning lakeside views and access to Torch Lake's crystal-clear waters, ideal for relaxing or water activities.

Amenities:
• Lake access
• Picnic areas

Activities:
• Boating
• Fishing

Tiki RV Park & Campground

Address: 547 State St, St. Ignace, MI 49781

Campground Description:
A family-friendly RV park located near the Mackinac Bridge, offering convenient access to Upper Peninsula attractions.

Unique Experience: Enjoy the proximity to Mackinac Island ferries and explore the scenic Upper Peninsula.

Amenities:
• RV hookups
• Camp store

Activities:
• Exploring Mackinac Island
• Biking

Tahquamenon Falls State Park

Address: 41382 W M-123, Paradise, MI 49768

Campground Description:
This park is home to the stunning Tahquamenon Falls, one of the largest waterfalls east of the Mississippi River.

Unique Experience: Camp near the breathtaking Upper Falls and hike along scenic forest trails.

Amenities:
• Restrooms
• Picnic areas

Activities:
• Hiking
• Wildlife viewing

Sleeping Bear Dunes National Lakeshore

Address: 9922 Front St, Empire, MI 49630

Campground Description:
Famous for its towering dunes and scenic lakeshore, this park offers camping near some of the most beautiful landscapes in Michigan.

Unique Experience: Hike the iconic dunes and take in panoramic views of Lake Michigan.

Amenities:
• Hiking trails
• Restrooms

Activities:
• Dune climbing
• Swimming

Boondocking

Hiawatha National Forest

Address: 820 Rains Dr, Gladstone, MI 49837

Campground Description:
This vast forest offers dispersed camping among its scenic woodlands, perfect for a secluded camping experience.

Unique Experience: Camp deep in the forest with access to the Great Lakes and serene inland lakes.

Amenities:
• Dispersed campsites
• Hiking trails

Activities:
• Hiking
• Fishing

Ottawa National Forest

Address: 1400 US-2, Ironwood, MI 49938

Campground Description:
A pristine wilderness area with miles of trails and dispersed camping options for those seeking a true backcountry experience.

Unique Experience: Explore the quiet beauty of the Upper Peninsula with opportunities for fishing and hiking.

Amenities:
• Primitive campsites
• Fishing access

Activities:
• Hiking
• Wildlife watching

Others Campgrounds

• Traverse Bay RV Resort (Traverse City, MI)
• Duck Creek RV Resort (Muskegon, MI)
• South Haven Sunny Brook RV Resort (South Haven, MI)
• Silver Lake Resort & Campground (Mears, MI)
• Oak Grove Campground & Resort (Holland, MI)
• Cedarville RV Park (Cedarville, MI)
• Bay City State Park Campground (Bay City, MI)
• Lake Leelanau RV Park (Lake Leelanau, MI)
• Algonac State Park Campground (Marine City, MI)
• Rifle River Campground (Sterling, MI)

Others Boondocking

• Nordhouse Dunes Wilderness
• Manistee National Forest (dispersed camping areas)
• Yankee Springs Recreation Area
• Sturgeon River Gorge Wilderness
• Pinckney Recreation Area (dispersed options)

Others National Park

• Pictured Rocks National Lakeshore
• Isle Royale National Park

Wisconsin: Lakeside Bliss and Forest Adventures

Wisconsin, known as the "Badger State," offers RVers a rich blend of natural beauty, outdoor activities, and Midwestern charm. With its thousands of lakes, dense forests, and rolling farmlands, Wisconsin is a paradise for those seeking peaceful campgrounds, water adventures, and scenic drives. Whether you're exploring the picturesque shores of **Lake Michigan**, hiking in the **Northwoods**, or discovering charming small towns, Wisconsin provides a perfect backdrop for your RV adventure.

The best season to RV in Wisconsin is **spring through fall**, from **May to October**. **Summer** is ideal for water lovers, with warm weather perfect for swimming, boating, and fishing on the state's many lakes. **Fall** brings cooler temperatures and spectacular foliage, especially in the forests of northern Wisconsin, making it a prime time for scenic drives and hiking. **Winter**, while cold and snowy, can be a fun time for RVers who are prepared for winter camping and want to enjoy snowmobiling, skiing, or ice fishing in the state's snowy wonderland.

For RVers, the **Great Lakes** are a major attraction. **Lake Michigan's** eastern shoreline, with its sandy beaches and stunning coastal vistas, offers plenty of RV-friendly campgrounds and opportunities for beachcombing, boating, and exploring quaint towns like **Sheboygan** and **Door County**. **Door County**, often called the "Cape Cod of the Midwest," is a must-visit for its charming lighthouses, wineries, and orchards, as well as its peaceful campgrounds with lake views.

Inland, the **Wisconsin Dells** is a popular destination for families and outdoor enthusiasts alike. Known for its scenic river gorges, water parks, and hiking trails, the Dells offer a mix of natural beauty and fun attractions. RVers can camp near the river and explore the area's unique sandstone formations, take boat tours, or enjoy the many adventure parks.

For those seeking solitude and pristine nature, **Northern Wisconsin's Northwoods** region is a vast expanse of forests, lakes, and rivers. The **Chequamegon-Nicolet National Forest** is perfect for RVers looking for remote campgrounds where they can fish, kayak, and hike in the serene wilderness. **Apostle Islands National Lakeshore**, located on the northern coast of Lake Superior, is another hidden gem, offering stunning sea caves, historic lighthouses, and opportunities for boating and island-hopping.

Wisconsin's small towns, such as **Bayfield**, **Mineral Point**, and **Spring Green**, offer a taste of Midwestern charm with local festivals, artisan markets, and farm-to-table dining. RVers can enjoy the laid-back vibe of these communities, exploring historic sites, local farms, and breweries that highlight Wisconsin's famous cheese and beer culture.

Wisconsin's campgrounds range from well-equipped RV resorts to more rustic, nature-focused sites in state parks and forests. Whether you're camping by a lake, in the Northwoods, or near a charming town, Wisconsin offers a variety of options for every type of RVer.

For RVers seeking outdoor adventure, peaceful lakeside retreats, and the friendly warmth of the Midwest, Wisconsin is a state that has it all. Whether you're relaxing by the Great Lakes, exploring the forests of the Northwoods, or enjoying the small-town charm, Wisconsin promises an unforgettable RV experience filled with nature and serenity.

Devil's Lake State Park Campground

📍 S5975 Park Rd, Baraboo, WI 53913

📞 (608) 356-8301 — $$

Campground Description:

Wisconsin's largest state park, known for stunning 500-foot quartzite bluffs and crystal-clear Devil's Lake, offering excellent hiking, rock climbing, and water activities.

Types of Sites Available:

- RV sites with electric hookups
- Tent sites
- Group sites

Amenities:

- Restrooms and showers
- Fire pits and picnic areas
- Swimming beach on Devil's Lake

Activities:

- Hiking, rock climbing, and water sports
- Fishing and wildlife watching

Unique Experiences: Explore unique geological formations like Balanced Rock, while enjoying year-round outdoor recreation in a beautiful natural setting.

Feedback: Guests praise the stunning views, well-maintained trails, and family-friendly atmosphere.

Wisconsin Dells KOA

📍 S235A Stand Rock Rd, Wisconsin Dells, WI 53965

📞 (608) 254-4177 — $$

Campground Description:

A family-friendly KOA located near Wisconsin Dells' waterparks and scenic tours, offering a mix of relaxation and fun.

Types of Sites Available:

- RV sites with full hookups
- Tent sites
- Cabin rentals

Amenities:

- Swimming pool
- Playground
- Shuttle to local attractions

Activities:

- Swimming, biking, and campfire relaxation
- Nearby waterparks, shopping, and scenic tours

Unique Experiences: Convenient shuttle service to explore nearby attractions, while enjoying on-site amenities for all ages.

Feedback: Guests enjoy the clean facilities, family-friendly vibe, and proximity to popular attractions.

Mirror Lake State Park Campground

 E10320 Fern Dell Rd, Baraboo, WI 53913

(608) 254-2333   ___ $$

Campground Description:

A peaceful, wooded campground near Wisconsin Dells with access to the calm, scenic waters of Mirror Lake, perfect for paddling and fishing.

Types of Sites Available:
- RV sites (no hookups)
- Tent sites
- Group camping sites

Amenities:
- Restrooms and showers
- Fire pits and picnic areas
- Canoe, kayak, and paddleboard rentals

Activities:
- Paddling, hiking, and fishing
- Wildlife watching and exploring nearby trails

Unique Experiences: Enjoy calm waters and scenic hiking trails while staying close to Wisconsin Dells for added adventure.

Feedback: Guests love the quiet setting, clean trails, and proximity to water activities.

Lake Kegonsa State Park Campground

 2405 Door Creek Rd, Stoughton, WI 53589

(608) 873-9695   ___ $$

Campground Description:

A serene lakeside retreat in south-central Wisconsin offering access to Lake Kegonsa for boating, fishing, and hiking.

Types of Sites Available:
- RV sites (no hookups)
- Tent sites
- Group camping sites

Amenities:
- Restrooms and showers
- Swimming beach on Lake Kegonsa
- Boat launch and fishing piers

Activities:
- Boating, fishing, and swimming
- Hiking on scenic forest trails

Unique Experiences: Experience tranquil lakeside camping with water sports and nature exploration, close to the town of Stoughton for cultural activities.

Feedback: Guests appreciate the clean facilities, spacious sites, and peaceful surroundings.

HIDDEN GEMS

Governor Dodge State Park Campground

Address: 4175 State Hwy 23, Dodgeville, WI 53533

Campground Description:
A scenic campground located in one of Wisconsin's largest state parks, known for its beautiful lakes and sandstone bluffs.

Unique Experience: Enjoy camping with access to hiking trails, lakes for swimming, and kayaking amidst stunning geological features.

Amenities:
• Restrooms
• Picnic areas

Activities:
• Hiking
• Swimming

Chippewa County Campground

Address: 14100 128th St, Chippewa Falls, WI 54729

Campground Description:
A peaceful, less-known campground offering lakefront camping and outdoor recreation.

Unique Experience: Relax by Chippewa Lake, with great opportunities for fishing, boating, and quiet nature walks.

Amenities:
• Boat launch
• Picnic areas

Activities:
• Fishing
• Boating

NATIONAL PARKS

Apostle Islands National Lakeshore

Address: 415 Washington Ave, Bayfield, WI 54814

Campground Description:
A pristine lakeshore with camping opportunities on the mainland and several islands, offering scenic views of Lake Superior.

Unique Experience: Explore sea caves, kayak through crystal-clear waters, and camp on islands surrounded by nature.

Amenities:
• Primitive sites
• Water access

Activities:
• Kayaking
• Hiking

Glacier National Park (Pine County, WI)

Address: Pine County, WI (exact location varies)

Campground Description:
A hidden gem near Pine County, this campground provides serene surroundings and access to glacial landscapes.

Unique Experience: Discover quiet hiking trails and scenic views of the area's natural beauty.

Amenities:
• Restrooms
• Picnic areas

Activities:
• Hiking
• Nature walks

Boondocking

Chequamegon National Forest

Address: Northern Wisconsin (various dispersed camping locations)

Campground Description:
A vast forest offering boondocking opportunities in remote areas, with access to hiking, fishing, and wildlife viewing.

Unique Experience: Camp in the heart of Wisconsin's northern wilderness with miles of trails and beautiful forested areas.

Amenities:
• Primitive sites
• Scenic views

Activities:
• Hiking
• Wildlife viewing

Ottawa National Forest

Address: Northern Wisconsin (various dispersed camping locations)

Campground Description:
A peaceful boondocking location providing access to lakes, rivers, and dense forest in a remote setting.

Unique Experience: Enjoy solitude and off-grid camping with access to fishing, kayaking, and stunning forested landscapes.

Amenities:
• Primitive sites
• Water access

Activities:
• Fishing
• Kayaking

Others Campgrounds

• Peninsula State Park Campground (Fish Creek, WI)
• Harrington Beach State Park Campground (Belgium, WI)
• Point Beach State Forest Campground (Two Rivers, WI)
• Hartman Creek State Park Campground (Waupaca, WI)
• Buckhorn State Park Campground (Necedah, WI)
• High Cliff State Park Campground (Sherwood, WI)
• Brunet Island State Park Campground (Cornell, WI)
• Nelson Dewey State Park Campground (Cassville, WI)
• Perrot State Park Campground (Trempealeau, WI)
• Wildcat Mountain State Park Campground (Ontario, WI)

Others Boondocking

• Nicolet National Forest (dispersed camping)
• Kettle Moraine State Forest (Northern Unit, dispersed camping)
• Black River State Forest (dispersed camping)
• Northern Highland-American Legion State Forest (dispersed camping)
• Kickapoo Valley Reserve (dispersed camping)

Others National Park

• Apostle Islands National Lakeshore (Stockton Island Campground)
• Ice Age National Scenic Trail (dispersed camping at certain trail sections)

Minnesota: Land of 10,000 Lakes, A Nature Lover's Paradise

Minnesota, known as the "Land of 10,000 Lakes," is a haven for RVers who are drawn to water, forests, and the great outdoors. Whether you're exploring the pristine shores of its countless lakes, wandering through the dense forests, or taking in the beauty of its scenic byways, Minnesota offers endless opportunities for adventure and relaxation. The state's combination of natural beauty and outdoor activities makes it an ideal destination for those looking to immerse themselves in the wilderness.

The best season to RV in Minnesota is **late spring through early fall**, from **May to October**. **Summer** is prime time for water lovers, with warm days perfect for swimming, boating, and fishing in Minnesota's many lakes. **Fall** is also a fantastic time to visit, as the cooler temperatures and stunning autumn foliage transform the state's forests into a tapestry of red, orange, and gold. **Winter** in Minnesota can be harsh, with freezing temperatures and heavy snowfall, so RVing during this time is best suited for those who are prepared for cold-weather camping or are seeking out winter sports like snowmobiling and ice fishing.

For RVers, Minnesota's greatest appeal lies in its vast network of lakes and waterways. Whether you're camping along the shores of **Lake Superior**, the largest of the Great Lakes, or relaxing by one of the state's many inland lakes, the water is always nearby. **Boundary Waters Canoe Area Wilderness**, located in the northern part of the state, offers a truly unique experience for those looking to get away from it all. While RV camping is limited within the wilderness itself, nearby campgrounds offer easy access to this pristine area, where you can paddle through crystal-clear waters surrounded by dense forests and untouched wildlife.

Minnesota's state parks are some of the best in the country, with well-maintained campgrounds that offer a range of amenities. Parks like **Itasca State Park**, home to the headwaters of the Mississippi River, and **Voyageurs National Park**, which spans over 200,000 acres of water and wilderness, provide RVers with access to breathtaking scenery and endless outdoor activities, from hiking and fishing to stargazing on clear, crisp nights.

One of the best things about RVing in Minnesota is the variety of landscapes you can explore in a single trip. From the rugged cliffs and forests of the **North Shore** to the gentle rolling prairies in the southern part of the state, Minnesota offers a little something for everyone. Whether you're seeking solitude in nature or looking for a family-friendly destination with plenty of activities, Minnesota delivers in every season.

Dakota Meadows RV Park

 2341 Park Pl NW, Prior Lake, MN 55372

📞 (952) 445-8800 — $$

Campground Description:

Dakota Meadows RV Park in Prior Lake, Minnesota, offers modern camping near Mystic Lake Casino. With spacious RV sites and amenities like a fitness center and free shuttle service to the casino, it's a great option for relaxation and entertainment.

Types of Sites Available:

- RV sites with full hookups

Amenities:

- Free Wi-Fi, fitness center
- Shuttle to Mystic Lake Casino
- Dog park

Activities:

- Exploring Prior Lake
- Casino entertainment
- Walking and biking trails

Unique Experiences: A perfect blend of outdoor relaxation and casino entertainment, with easy access to nature and nightlife.

Feedback: Praised for its clean facilities, friendly staff, and convenient location near both recreation and entertainment.

St. Cloud Clearwater RV Park

 454 Co Rd 143, Clearwater, MN 55320

📞 (320) 558-2876 $$

Campground Description:

St. Cloud Clearwater RV Park offers a peaceful, family-friendly camping experience in central Minnesota, with spacious RV sites and plenty of amenities like a pool and sports courts.

Types of Sites Available:

- RV sites with full hookups
- Tent camping sites
- Cabin rentals

Amenities:

- Free Wi-Fi, swimming pool
- Sports courts, playground

Activities:

- Fishing, kayaking, hiking
- Family-friendly games
- Exploring nearby St. Cloudgames and activities at the playground

Unique Experiences: A scenic and peaceful campground with easy access to outdoor activities and local attractions.

Feedback: Praised for its family-friendly atmosphere, clean facilities, and variety of activities for all ages.

Autumn Woods RV Park

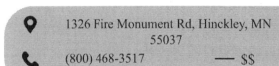

📍 1067 Autumn Woods Cir SW, Rochester, MN 55902

📞 (507) 990-2983 —— $$

Campground Description:

Located in Rochester, Minnesota, Autumn Woods RV Park offers a quiet, comfortable camping experience with easy access to the Mayo Clinic and city amenities.

Types of Sites Available:

- RV sites with full hookups

Amenities:

- Free Wi-Fi, dog park
- Access to biking and walking trails

Activities:

- Exploring Rochester
- Biking and walking on nature trails

Unique Experiences: A peaceful RV park with proximity to Mayo Clinic and Rochester's city life, perfect for long-term stays.

Feedback: Highly praised for its clean facilities, quiet atmosphere, and convenience to local amenities.

Grand Casino Hinckley RV Resort

📍 1326 Fire Monument Rd, Hinckley, MN 55037

📞 (800) 468-3517 —— $$

Campground Description:

Grand Casino Hinckley RV Resort offers a mix of outdoor fun and casino entertainment, with spacious RV sites, a pool, mini-golf, and a shuttle to the casino.

Types of Sites Available:

- RV sites with full hookups

Amenities:

- Free Wi-Fi, pool, hot tub
- Shuttle to Grand Casino

Activities:

- Casino entertainment
- Mini-golf, swimming
- Exploring local parks

Unique Experiences: Combines camping with casino excitement, offering entertainment and relaxation in one location.

Feedback: Guests love the clean facilities, fun activities, and convenient access to the casino.

Trails RV Park

Address: 9425 State 371 NW, Walker, MN 56484

Campground Description:
A peaceful RV park nestled in the woods of northern Minnesota, providing a quiet getaway for outdoor enthusiasts.

Unique Experience: Enjoy the serene forest setting with easy access to nearby lakes and trails.

Amenities:
• Full RV hookups
• Picnic areas

Activities:
• Hiking
• Fishing

Big Pines RV Park

Address: 501 Central Ave S, Park Rapids, MN 56470

Campground Description:
Located near the scenic Heartland Trail, this campground offers a great base for outdoor activities and exploration.

Unique Experience: Relax in a wooded setting while enjoying close proximity to Park Rapids' attractions.

Amenities:
• Full hookups
• Restrooms

Activities:
• Biking
• Wildlife viewing

Itasca State Park

Address: 36750 Main Park Dr, Park Rapids, MN 56470

Campground Description:
Home to the headwaters of the Mississippi River, Itasca State Park offers camping in a historic and beautiful setting.

Unique Experience: Walk across the headwaters of the Mississippi and explore miles of hiking trails.

Amenities:
• Restrooms
• Boat rentals

Activities:
• Hiking
• Canoeing

Gooseberry Falls State Park

Address: 3206 MN-61, Two Harbors, MN 55616

Campground Description:
This park is known for its stunning waterfalls and beautiful lakeshore along Lake Superior.

Unique Experience: Camp near breathtaking waterfalls and explore scenic hiking trails along the shore.

Amenities:
• Restrooms
• Picnic areas

Activities:
• Hiking
• Waterfall viewing

Boondocking

Superior National Forest

Address: 8901 Grand Ave Pl, Duluth, MN 55808

Campground Description:
A vast wilderness with dispersed camping opportunities in scenic spots near lakes and forests.

Unique Experience: Enjoy the tranquility of the wilderness with access to lakes and hiking trails.

Amenities:
• Dispersed campsites
• Hiking trails

Activities:
• Hiking
• Canoeing

Chippewa National Forest

Address: 200 Ash Ave NW, Cass Lake, MN 56633

Campground Description:
This national forest offers remote boondocking sites surrounded by lakes, rivers, and lush forests.

Unique Experience: Camp in secluded areas and enjoy the rich wildlife of northern Minnesota.

Amenities:
• Primitive campsites
• Fishing access

Activities:
• Fishing
• Wildlife watching

Others Campgrounds

• Lebanon Hills Campground (Eagan, MN)
• Fenske Lake Campground (Ely, MN)
• Wildwood RV Park & Campground (Taylors Falls, MN)
• Lake Bemidji State Park (Bemidji, MN)
• Grand Marais RV Park & Campground (Grand Marais, MN)
• Split Rock Lighthouse State Park Campground (Two Harbors, MN)
• Baker Park Reserve Campground (Maple Plain, MN)
• Mille Lacs Kathio State Park Campground (Onamia, MN)
• Scenic State Park (Bigfork, MN)
• Wild River State Park (Center City, MN)

Others Boondocking

• Cloquet Valley State Forest
• Beltrami Island State Forest
• Kabetogama State Forest
• Finland State Forest
• George Washington State Forest

Others National Park

• Voyageurs National Park

Iowa: Rolling Hills and Heartland Hospitality

Iowa is often considered the heart of the Midwest, with its endless fields of corn, gentle rolling hills, and a sense of peace that RVers crave when looking for a relaxing escape. But Iowa offers much more than just open farmland—it's a state full of hidden gems, scenic drives, and outdoor adventures that are perfect for anyone exploring by RV. Whether you're visiting the bluffs along the Mississippi River or the peaceful prairies in the west, Iowa is a welcoming place where you can slow down and enjoy the beauty of the land.

The best season to RV in Iowa is **late spring through fall**, from **May to October**. In **spring**, the state blooms with wildflowers and the landscape turns lush and green, making it an ideal time to explore the countryside and state parks. **Summer** is perfect for enjoying Iowa's many rivers, lakes, and outdoor festivals, although the heat and humidity can pick up in July and August. **Fall** is one of the most beautiful times to visit, with cool, crisp air and vibrant autumn colors painting the landscape. **The season to avoid** is **winter**, as temperatures can drop significantly, and snowstorms can make traveling and camping more difficult.

Iowa is a state where simplicity meets beauty. The winding roads take you through some of the most peaceful landscapes in the Midwest, where you'll pass through small towns that seem frozen in time, each with their own unique charm. RVers can enjoy camping near the river bluffs in the east, exploring the scenic Great River Road along the Mississippi, or finding a quiet spot in one of the state's many well-kept parks.

Iowa's campgrounds are as varied as its landscapes, from the picturesque lakeside spots in the northern part of the state to the more rustic, back-to-nature campsites scattered throughout the rolling hills. One of my favorite places to RV is near the Loess Hills, a unique and stunning area that offers hiking, wildlife viewing, and some of the most scenic vistas in the Midwest. And if you're a fan of small-town charm, Iowa's many quaint towns and friendly people will make you feel right at home.

For RVers looking to escape the hustle and bustle, Iowa offers a slower, more relaxed pace of life. It's a state where you can park your RV under a canopy of stars, enjoy a peaceful night by the campfire, and wake up to the sound of nature all around you. Whether you're exploring the state's hidden gems or just passing through, Iowa's heartland hospitality will leave a lasting impression.

Clear Lake State Park

2730 S Lakeview Dr, Clear Lake, IA 50428

(641) 357-4212 — $$

Campground Description:

Lakeside camping experience with sandy beaches, boating, and fishing. Ideal for families and outdoor enthusiasts, located along the southeast shore of Clear Lake.

Types of Sites Available:
- RV sites with electric hookups
- Tent camping sites

Amenities:
- Sandy beach, boat ramp, fishing pier
- Picnic areas, playground
- Restrooms, showers, free Wi-Fi

Activities:
- Swimming, boating, fishing
- Hiking, birdwatching
- Exploring nearby attractions like the Surf Ballroom

Unique Experiences: A lakeside retreat with clear waters, perfect for water sports and outdoor adventure in Northern Iowa.

Feedback: Highly rated for its beautiful setting, well-maintained facilities, and lakeside activities.

Lake Anita State Park

55111 750th St, Anita, IA 50020

(712) 762-3564 — $$

Campground Description:

A peaceful park surrounding scenic Lake Anita, offering hiking, fishing, and a relaxing atmosphere for nature lovers.

Types of Sites Available:
- RV sites with electric hookups
- Tent camping sites

Amenities:
- Sandy beach, boat ramp, fishing pier
- Hiking and biking trails
- Picnic areas, restrooms, showers

Activities:
- Swimming, boating, fishing
- Hiking and birdwatching
- Picnicking and relaxing by the lake

Unique Experiences: A tranquil lakeside escape with outdoor activities like hiking and boating, offering scenic views of Lake Anita.

Feedback: Praised for its peaceful atmosphere and clean facilities, ideal for family getaways and outdoor enthusiasts.

On-Ur-Wa RV Park

1111 28th St, Onawa, IA 51040

(712) 423-1387 — $$

Campground Description:

Conveniently located near I-29, offering spacious RV sites with full hookups and a peaceful setting near Lewis and Clark State Park.

Types of Sites Available:

- RV sites with full hookups

Amenities:

- Free Wi-Fi, restrooms, laundry
- Picnic areas, dog park
- RV dump station

Activities:

- Fishing, boating at nearby lakes
- Exploring Lewis and Clark State Park
- Birdwatching and local events

Unique Experiences: A peaceful stopover with easy highway access and proximity to outdoor activities, perfect for RV travelers.

Feedback: Praised for its clean facilities and convenient location, a great stopover for road-trippers.

Morwood Campground and Resort

180th St, Moravia, IA 52571

(641) 724-3450 — $$

Campground Description:

A family-friendly resort near Lake Rathbun, offering fishing, boating, and outdoor recreation, with spacious RV sites, cabins, and tent camping.

Types of Sites Available:
- RV sites with full hookups
- Tent camping, cabins

Amenities:
- Swimming pool, fishing pond
- Boat rentals nearby, playground
- Picnic areas, restrooms, showers

Activities:

- Fishing, boating, hiking
- Swimming, nature walks
- Exploring nearby Honey Creek Resort

Unique Experiences: Offers a relaxing lakeside retreat with access to Lake Rathbun's water sports and scenic views.

Feedback: Highly rated for its family-friendly atmosphere and range of activities, especially popular with outdoor lovers.

HIDDEN GEMS

Squaw Creek Park

Address: 4305 Squaw Ln, Marion, IA 52302

Campground Description:
A beautiful park offering scenic RV and tent camping with easy access to hiking and biking trails, perfect for nature lovers.

Unique Experience: Enjoy camping near the creek, surrounded by wooded landscapes.

Amenities:
• Full RV hookups
• Hiking trails

Activities:
• Biking and hiking
• Wildlife watching

BEYONDER Getaway at Lazy Acres RV Park

Address: 4776 32nd Ave Dr, Vinton, IA 52349

Campground Description:
A quiet RV park with spacious sites, offering a peaceful retreat with plenty of family-friendly activities.

Unique Experience: Relax at the tranquil pond with catch-and-release fishing.

Amenities:
• Full RV hookups
• Fishing pond

Activities:
• Fishing
• Biking

NATIONAL PARKS

Pilot Knob State Park

Address: 2148 Pilot Knob Rd, Forest City, IA 50436

Campground Description:
Pilot Knob is one of Iowa's oldest state parks, known for its forested trails and beautiful, scenic views from the "Pilot Knob" hilltop.

Unique Experience: Hike to the top of the scenic Pilot Knob for stunning views of the surrounding landscape.

Amenities:
• Restrooms and showers
• Picnic areas

Activities:
• Hiking trails
• Wildlife observation

Prairie Rose State Park

Address: 680 Road M47, Harlan, IA 51537

Campground Description:
This state park offers lakeside camping with easy access to boating, fishing, and hiking, making it a popular spot for outdoor enthusiasts.

Unique Experience: Camp along the lake and enjoy the beautiful prairie and wetland landscapes.

Amenities:
• Restrooms and showers
• Boat launch

Activities:
• Fishing and boating
• Hiking

Boondocking

Shawnee National Forest

Address: 50 Hwy 145 S, Harrisburg, IL 62946

Campground Description:
Shawnee National Forest offers ample opportunities for dispersed camping in a scenic, remote environment, surrounded by rolling hills and forests.

Unique Experience: Enjoy primitive camping in the heart of the forest, with access to incredible hiking trails and rock formations.

Amenities:
- Primitive campsites
- Vault toilets

Activities:
- Hiking and exploring
- Wildlife viewing

Hoosier National Forest

Address: 811 Constitution Ave, Bedford, IN 47421

Campground Description:
This national forest offers diverse camping opportunities, including boondocking, surrounded by dense woods and peaceful landscapes.

Unique Experience: Experience complete solitude while camping off-the-grid deep in the forest.

Amenities:
- Primitive campsites
- Fire rings

Activities:
- Hiking
- Camping in remote areas

Others Campgrounds

- Deer Run Resort (Coon Rapids, IA)
- Timberline Campground (Waukee, IA)
- Lazy Acres RV Park (Center Point, IA)
- Sugar Bottom Campground (North Liberty, IA)
- Ledges State Park Campground (Madrid, IA)
- Rock Creek State Park Campground (Kellogg, IA)
- Pammel State Park Campground (Winterset, IA)
- Lake Macbride State Park Campground (Solon, IA)
- Geode State Park Campground (Danville, IA)
- Backbone State Park Campground (Dundee, IA)

Others Boondocking

- Yellow River State Forest (dispersed camping areas)
- Loess Hills State Forest (dispersed sites)
- Stephens State Forest (boondocking available)
- Lake Rathbun Wildlife Area
- Volga River State Recreation Area

Missouri: A Gateway to Adventure

Missouri, often referred to as the "Show Me State," is a fantastic destination for RVers seeking a blend of outdoor adventure, rich history, and scenic beauty. From the majestic **Ozark Mountains** in the south to the rolling plains and rivers in the north, Missouri offers a diverse landscape that's perfect for exploring by RV. Whether you're kayaking in crystal-clear rivers, hiking through lush forests, or visiting historic cities like St. Louis and Kansas City, Missouri promises a memorable journey.

The best season to RV in Missouri is **spring through fall**, from **April to October**. **Spring** brings blooming wildflowers and mild temperatures, making it an ideal time to explore Missouri's many state parks and natural areas. **Fall** is equally beautiful, especially in the **Ozarks**, where the forests come alive with vibrant autumn colors. **Summer** is great for outdoor activities like boating, fishing, and swimming in Missouri's many lakes and rivers, but it can also be hot and humid, especially in the southern part of the state. **Winter**, particularly in the northern regions, can bring cold temperatures and occasional snow, so it's best to avoid RVing during the colder months unless you're well-prepared for winter conditions.

For RVers, Missouri's standout feature is the **Ozark Mountains**, a stunning region of forested hills, clear rivers, and breathtaking scenery. Whether you're camping near **Table Rock Lake**, floating down the **Current River**, or exploring the **Mark Twain National Forest**, the Ozarks offer a wealth of outdoor activities. One of my favorite spots to camp is **Meramec State Park**, where you can enjoy hiking, fishing, and exploring caves, all within a short drive of St. Louis.

Missouri's rich history is also a big draw for RVers. You can follow the **Lewis and Clark Trail** along the Missouri River, visit **Hannibal**, the boyhood home of Mark Twain, or stop in St. Louis to see the iconic **Gateway Arch**. For music lovers, **Branson** is a must-visit, offering a mix of live entertainment, family attractions, and RV-friendly campgrounds nestled in the heart of the Ozarks.

Missouri's campgrounds are well-maintained and varied, ranging from lakeside retreats with full amenities to more rustic spots in the heart of nature. Whether you're looking for a quiet riverside campsite or a resort-style RV park with plenty of activities, Missouri has something to offer for every type of traveler.

For those seeking a mix of adventure, relaxation, and a deep connection with nature, Missouri is a state that delivers in every season. It's a place where you can enjoy the simple pleasures of the outdoors while also diving into the state's fascinating history and culture.

America's Best Campground

📍 499 Buena Vista Rd, Branson, MO 65616

📞 (417) 336-4399   — $$

Campground Description:

America's Best Campground in Branson, Missouri, is a family-friendly RV park near the entertainment hub of Branson. It features spacious RV sites, tent camping, and cabins, with modern amenities and organized events, providing an ideal base for travelers to explore Branson's shows, shopping, and outdoor activities.

Types of Sites Available:
- RV sites with full hookups
- Tent camping sites
- Cabin rentals

Amenities:
- Free Wi-Fi, swimming pool, clubhouse
- Shuttle service to Branson attractions

Activities:
- Swimming, exploring Branson's shows, shopping
- Hiking, picnicking in the Ozarks

Unique Experiences: Convenient access to Branson's entertainment and the peaceful surroundings of the Ozarks.

Feedback: Highly praised for cleanliness, friendly staff, and a great location near Branson's attractions.

Basswood Resort

📍 15880 Interurban Rd, Platte City, MO 64079

📞 (816) 858-5556   — $$

Campground Description:

Basswood Resort in Platte City, Missouri, offers a peaceful camping experience with lush scenery, stocked fishing lakes, and a variety of accommodations. Family-friendly with modern amenities, it's an ideal spot for relaxation and outdoor activities, while also providing easy access to Kansas City's attractions.

Types of Sites Available:
- RV sites with full hookups
- Tent camping sites
- Cabin rentals

Amenities:
- Free Wi-Fi, swimming pool, fishing lakes
- Mini-golf, playground

Activities:
- Fishing, swimming, mini-golf
- Exploring nearby Kansas City

Unique Experiences: Scenic, peaceful surroundings combined with modern amenities and proximity to Kansas City.

Feedback: Praised for scenic beauty, family-friendly activities, and well-stocked fishing lakes.

Cottonwoods RV Park

5170 N Oakland Gravel Rd, Columbia, MO 65202

(573) 474-2747 — $$

Campground Description:

Cottonwoods RV Park in Columbia, Missouri, offers a tranquil camping experience close to the University of Missouri and Columbia's vibrant downtown. It features spacious RV sites, a swimming pool, and a dog park, making it ideal for families, long-term travelers, and visitors exploring the area.

Types of Sites Available:

- RV sites with full hookups
- Tent camping sites

Amenities:

- Free Wi-Fi, swimming pool, playground
- Dog park, fitness room

Activities:

- Swimming, hiking at Rock Bridge Memorial State Park
- Exploring Columbia's shops and restaurants

Unique Experiences: A peaceful campground with urban convenience, ideal for exploring Columbia and its natural beauty.

Feedback: Guests appreciate the quiet atmosphere, friendly staff, and proximity to local attractions.

Pin Oak Creek RV Park

1302 Highway AT, Villa Ridge, MO 63089

(636) 451-5656 — $$

Campground Description:

Pin Oak Creek RV Park in Villa Ridge, Missouri, offers family-friendly camping with a range of activities including paintball, mini-golf, and fishing. Located near Six Flags St. Louis, it's perfect for outdoor fun and easy access to regional attractions.

Types of Sites Available:

- RV sites with full hookups
- Tent camping sites
- Cabin rentals

Amenities:

- Free Wi-Fi, swimming pool, fishing pond
- Paintball, mini-golf

Activities:

- Paintball, mini-golf, fishing
- Visiting Six Flags St. Louis

Unique Experiences: A mix of outdoor recreation with proximity to Six Flags and other attractions.

Feedback: Praised for family-friendly activities, clean facilities, and convenient location near St. Louis attractions.

HIDDEN GEMS

Cozy C RV Campground
Address: 16733 US-54, Bowling Green, MO 63334

Campground Description:
A quiet and family-friendly campground located in the countryside, offering spacious sites and peaceful surroundings.

Unique Experience: Enjoy tranquil evenings under the stars and easy access to local attractions.

Amenities:
• Full hookups
• Laundry facilities

Activities:
• Fishing nearby
• Relaxing outdoors

Circle B Campground
Address: 473 E HWY 106, Eminence, MO 65466

Campground Description:
Nestled near the Current River, this campground is perfect for nature lovers and outdoor adventurers.

Unique Experience: Relax by the river or explore the nearby Ozark National Scenic Riverways.

Amenities:
• Full hookups
• Picnic tables

Activities:
• Canoeing
• Hiking

NATIONAL PARKS

Roaring River State Park
Address: 12716 Farm Rd 2239, Cassville, MO 65625

Campground Description:
A popular park located in the Ozark Mountains, famous for its trout fishing and scenic hiking trails.

Unique Experience: Fish for trout in the crystal-clear waters of Roaring River.

Amenities:
• Restrooms
• Fishing access

Activities:
• Trout fishing
• Hiking

Lake of the Ozarks State Park
Address: 403 MO-134, Kaiser, MO 65047

Campground Description:
Located on the shores of the Lake of the Ozarks, this park offers plenty of water-based activities and outdoor fun.

Unique Experience: Explore the lake by boat or relax on the beach.

Amenities:
• Restrooms
• Boat ramps

Activities:
• Boating
• Swimming

Boondocking

Mark Twain National Forest

Address: 401 Fairgrounds Rd, Rolla, MO 65401

Campground Description:
This vast forest offers dispersed camping opportunities in serene, wooded areas.
Unique Experience: Enjoy hiking and camping in solitude among the forest's lush landscape.

Amenities:
• Dispersed campsites
• Hiking trails

Activities:
• Hiking
• Wildlife viewing

Berryman Recreation Area

Address: Forest Rd 2266, Potosi, MO 63664

Campground Description:
Located within Mark Twain National Forest, this area is known for its challenging trails and natural beauty.
Unique Experience: Camp near the Berryman Trail, perfect for hiking and biking.

Amenities:
• Primitive campsites
• Trail access

Activities:
• Mountain biking
• Hiking

Others Campgrounds

• Bennett Spring State Park Campground (Lebanon, MO)
• Meramec State Park Campground (Sullivan, MO)
• Table Rock State Park Campground (Branson, MO)
• Harry S Truman State Park Campground (Warsaw, MO)
• Montauk State Park Campground (Salem, MO)
• Pomme de Terre State Park Campground (Pittsburg, MO)
• Wakonda State Park Campground (La Grange, MO)
• Long Branch State Park Campground (Macon, MO)
• Sam A. Baker State Park Campground (Patterson, MO)
• Big Lake State Park Campground (Craig, MO)

Others Boondocking

• Hawn State Park (dispersed camping in nearby areas)
• Corps of Engineers Land (specific areas near lakes)
• Truman Lake (some dispersed camping spots)
• Pomme de Terre Lake (dispersed camping in designated areas)
• Mark Twain Lake (specific areas for boondocking)

North Dakota: The Quiet Beauty of the Northern Plains

North Dakota, often overlooked by travelers, is a hidden gem for RVers seeking wide-open spaces, serene landscapes, and a deep connection to nature. From the sweeping prairies to the rugged beauty of the **Badlands**, North Dakota offers a quiet, peaceful experience for those who want to escape the crowds and explore the untouched wilderness of the Northern Plains. Whether you're hiking through national parks, tracing the footsteps of explorers, or simply relaxing by a peaceful river, North Dakota invites RVers to slow down and take in the beauty around them.

The best season to RV in North Dakota is **late spring through early fall**, from **May to September**. **Summer** is the ideal time to visit, with long, sunny days perfect for outdoor adventures. **Spring** brings blooming wildflowers and a sense of renewal, while **fall** offers crisp air and golden prairie landscapes. **Winter**, however, can be harsh, with frigid temperatures and heavy snow, making it challenging for RV travel unless you are equipped for cold weather and looking for a winter adventure.

North Dakota's standout attraction for RVers is **Theodore Roosevelt National Park**, a breathtaking landscape of rugged badlands, rolling hills, and roaming wildlife. Named after the president who found solace and inspiration here, this park offers plenty of opportunities for hiking, wildlife viewing, and camping under the vast North Dakota sky. Watching bison, wild horses, and prairie dogs roam freely in the park is an unforgettable experience, and RVers can find campgrounds nestled in the heart of this stunning natural wonder.

For history buffs, North Dakota offers a chance to follow the paths of **Lewis and Clark** along the **Missouri River**, with several historic sites and interpretive centers dedicated to the famous explorers. **Fort Union Trading Post National Historic Site**, located along the river, offers a glimpse into the fur trading history that shaped the region. RVers can camp along the riverbanks, where the tranquil setting offers a perfect place to unwind and enjoy the peaceful surroundings.

The state's vast prairies and rolling farmland also provide a scenic backdrop for RVers looking to explore off the beaten path. **Lake Sakakawea**, one of the largest man-made reservoirs in the U.S., offers excellent fishing, boating, and camping opportunities. You can park your RV by the water, cast a line, and watch the sunset over the wide-open plains.

North Dakota's campgrounds range from quiet state parks to more rugged, wilderness settings, perfect for those seeking solitude and a connection to nature. Whether you're exploring the badlands, relaxing by a lake, or driving along scenic byways, the state's campgrounds offer a mix of amenities and peaceful settings that make it an ideal stop for RVers.

For RVers who appreciate wide-open spaces, stunning landscapes, and the quiet beauty of the Northern Plains, North Dakota offers a unique and rewarding experience. It's a state where you can feel truly immersed in nature, with the opportunity to explore untouched wilderness and discover the simple pleasures of the great outdoors.

Roughrider RV Resort

📍 4501 16th St SW, Minot, ND 58701

📞 (701) 839-7878 — $$

Campground Description:

Roughrider RV Resort in Minot, ND, offers a convenient and relaxing RV camping experience with modern amenities and easy access to the area's attractions. Ideal for families and travelers, the resort is close to popular destinations like Roosevelt Park Zoo and the North Dakota State Fairgrounds, making it a perfect stop for exploring the area.

Types of Sites Available:

- RV sites with full hookups
- Pull-through and back-in sites

Amenities:
- Free Wi-Fi and cable TV
- Playground for children
- Laundry facilities
- Pet-friendly areas and dog park

Activities:

- Exploring nearby Roosevelt Park Zoo and Scandinavian Heritage Park

- Relaxing by the campfire and attending local events

Unique Experiences:
A peaceful retreat with access to Minot's attractions and events, making it great for families and adventurers.

Feedback:
Guests love the clean facilities and the relaxing atmosphere, with praise for the friendly staff and spacious sites.

Jan's RV Park and Lodge

📍 100 1st St SE, Leeds, ND 58346

📞 (701) 466-2244 — $$

Campground Description:

Jan's RV Park and Lodge in Leeds, ND, offers a quiet and welcoming camping experience, ideal for nature lovers and those exploring Devils Lake. This small, family-owned park provides personal service and comfortable accommodations, making it a great stop for fishing trips, bird watching, and exploring the surrounding area.

Types of Sites Available:

- RV sites with full hookups
- Lodge accommodations

Amenities:
- Free Wi-Fi
- Fire pits at select sites
- Lodge with rooms for rent

Activities:

- Kayaking, fishing, hiking
- Beachcombing, birdwatching

Unique Experiences: Perfect for travelers seeking a peaceful retreat with personal attention and access to natural beauty.

Feedback: Guests appreciate the friendly staff, clean facilities, and the peaceful, small-town atmosphere, especially for bird watching and fishing.

Red Trail Campground

📍 250 E River Rd S, Medora, ND 58645

📞 (701) 623-4317   — $$

Campground Description:

Red Trail Campground in Medora, ND, offers a scenic and historic camping experience near Theodore Roosevelt National Park. With breathtaking views of the Badlands, the campground provides modern amenities in a natural setting, perfect for exploring the region's attractions like the Medora Musical and Maah Daah Hey Trail.

Types of Sites Available:

- RV sites with full hookups
- Tent camping sites

Amenities:

- Free Wi-Fi
- Playground for children• Fire pits at select sites

Activities:

- Kayaking, fishing, hiking
- Beachcombing, birdwatching

Unique Experiences: A beautiful base for outdoor enthusiasts and history buffs, with direct access to Medora's Western charm and stunning Badlands scenery.

Feedback: Praised for its scenic location and easy access to local attractions, Red Trail Campground is popular among families and nature lovers.

Buffalo Gap Campground

📍 Buffalo Gap Campground, Medora, ND 58645

📞 (701) 227-7800   — $

Campground Description:

Buffalo Gap Campground, near Medora, ND, offers a rustic, peaceful camping experience with access to the Maah Daah Hey Trail and Theodore Roosevelt National Park. This no-frills campground provides basic amenities and is perfect for campers seeking solitude and natural beauty in the Badlands.

Types of Sites Available:

- Tent camping sites
- RV sites (no hookups)

Amenities:

- Restrooms (vault toilets)
- Fire rings at each site

Activities:

- Kayaking, fishing, hiking
- Beachcombing, birdwatching

Unique Experiences: A back-to-nature campground ideal for hikers and nature lovers looking for tranquility and access to the region's trails and parks.

Feedback: Guests love the peaceful setting and easy access to the trail, making it a popular choice for hikers and those seeking a quiet escape.

Mellow Moose Campground

Address: 1201 34th Ave NW, Minot, ND 58703

Campground Description:
A quiet, family-friendly campground located just outside of Minot, offering spacious sites and a peaceful atmosphere.

Unique Experience: Enjoy a relaxing stay surrounded by North Dakota's open skies and peaceful countryside.

Amenities:
• Full hookups
• Restrooms and showers

Activities:
• Hiking nearby
• Fishing

Fort Stevenson State Park Campground

Address: 1252A 41st Ave NW, Garrison, ND 58540

Campground Description:
Located on the shores of Lake Sakakawea, this state park offers excellent camping with scenic lake views and access to recreational activities.

Unique Experience: Camp with stunning views of the lake and explore the historical fort site.

Amenities:
• Full hookups
• Boat ramp

Activities:
• Boating
• Fishing

Theodore Roosevelt National Park (Cottonwood Campground)

Address: 315 2nd Ave, Medora, ND 58645

Campground Description:
Nestled along the Little Missouri River, Cottonwood Campground offers a peaceful camping experience amidst the rugged beauty of Theodore Roosevelt National Park.

Unique Experience: Explore the park's badlands and observe bison, elk, and prairie dogs in their natural habitat.

Amenities:
• Restrooms
• Picnic areas

Activities:
• Wildlife viewing
• Hiking

Lake Metigoshe State Park

Address: 261 State Park Rd, Bottineau, ND 58318

Campground Description:
A beautiful state park set around Lake Metigoshe, offering forested campsites and year-round outdoor recreation opportunities.

Unique Experience: Enjoy water-based activities and explore the Turtle Mountains.

Amenities:
• Restrooms
• Boat ramp

Activities:
• Canoeing
• Hiking

Boondocking

Little Missouri National Grassland

Address: 99 23rd Ave W, Dickinson, ND 58601

Campground Description:
Dispersed camping in North Dakota's largest national grassland, offering stunning open landscapes and solitude.

Unique Experience: Camp under the stars in the vast, undisturbed grasslands.

Amenities:
- Primitive campsites
- Access to trails

Activities:
- Wildlife watching
- Hiking

Sweet Briar Lake

Address: Morton County, ND 58535

Campground Description:
Boondocking available at Sweet Briar Lake, providing a peaceful lakeside experience with fishing and relaxation opportunities.

Unique Experience: Camp by the lake and enjoy excellent fishing spots in this secluded area.

Amenities:
- Primitive campsites
- Lake access

Activities:
- Fishing
- Boating

Others Campgrounds

- Lewis and Clark State Park Campground (Epping, ND)
- Beaver Lake State Park Campground (Napoleon, ND)
- Grahams Island State Park Campground (Devils Lake, ND)
- Lake Sakakawea State Park Campground (Pick City, ND)
- Icelandic State Park Campground (Cavalier, ND)
- Turtle River State Park Campground (Arvilla, ND)
- Cross Ranch State Park Campground (Center, ND)
- Lake Tschida Recreation Area (Elgin, ND)
- North Park Campground (Dickinson, ND)
- Spiritwood Lake Resort Campground (Jamestown, ND)

Others Boondocking

- Sheyenne National Grassland
- Little Missouri River (dispersed camping)
- Maah Daah Hey Trail (dispersed camping areas)
- Beaver Creek Recreation Area
- Lake Ilo National Wildlife Refuge

Others National Park

- Theodore Roosevelt National Park (Juniper Campground)

South Dakota: A Land of Monuments and Wilderness

South Dakota is a state that captivates RVers with its blend of natural beauty, iconic landmarks, and vast open spaces. Known for its rugged landscapes and historic monuments, South Dakota is a destination where the spirit of the American West comes alive. Whether you're gazing up at the majestic faces of **Mount Rushmore**, exploring the surreal beauty of the **Badlands**, or camping near the serene **Black Hills**, South Dakota offers RVers an adventure filled with history, nature, and awe-inspiring views.

The best season to RV in South Dakota is **spring through fall**, from **May to October**. **Summer** is the peak season, offering warm temperatures and clear skies, making it ideal for exploring the state's many outdoor attractions. **Fall** brings cooler weather and fewer crowds, making it a great time to visit the national parks and take scenic drives through the changing landscape. **Winter**, especially in the northern and western parts of the state, can be cold and snowy, making RV travel more challenging unless you're well-prepared for winter conditions.

One of South Dakota's crown jewels for RVers is the **Black Hills National Forest**, a stunning region of granite peaks, pine forests, and crystal-clear lakes. This area is home to some of the state's most famous landmarks, including **Mount Rushmore National Memorial** and **Crazy Horse Memorial**. There are plenty of campgrounds in and around the Black Hills, offering easy access to hiking, fishing, and sightseeing, while giving you a peaceful place to rest surrounded by nature.

The **Badlands National Park** is another must-see for RVers. Its unique, otherworldly landscape of sharp peaks, deep canyons, and colorful rock formations is like nothing else in the country. The park offers RV-friendly campgrounds where you can watch the sun set over the striking badlands terrain and marvel at the star-filled skies.

For those interested in history and the Wild West, a stop at **Deadwood** is essential. This historic town, once a gold rush settlement, offers a glimpse into the past with its well-preserved buildings, museums, and reenactments of famous shootouts. You can park your RV nearby and explore the town's rich heritage, then head out to nearby trails for hiking or horseback riding.

South Dakota's campgrounds range from full-service RV parks to more rustic, remote spots where you can truly connect with nature. Whether you're camping in the heart of the Black Hills, along the Missouri River, or near the quiet beauty of **Custer State Park**, South Dakota's campgrounds provide a perfect base for exploring the state's natural wonders.

For RVers seeking a mix of breathtaking landscapes, iconic American landmarks, and outdoor adventure, South Dakota is a state that delivers on all fronts. From the towering monuments to the vast, open prairies, South Dakota offers an RV experience that's both unforgettable and deeply rooted in the history and beauty of the American West.

Custer Mountain Campground

1111 Mt Rushmore Rd, Custer, SD 57730

(605) 673-5548 $$

Campground Description:

Located in the Black Hills, this scenic campground provides a peaceful retreat near top attractions like Custer State Park, Mount Rushmore, and Crazy Horse Memorial.

Types of Sites Available:
- RV sites with full hookups
- Tent camping sites
- Cabin rentals

Amenities:
- Free Wi-Fi
- Picnic areas and fire pits
- Hiking trails

Activities:
- Hiking and exploring the Black Hills
- Visiting Custer State Park, Mount Rushmore, and Crazy Horse Memorial
- Fishing and wildlife viewing

Unique Experiences: Guests enjoy the serene setting and proximity to South Dakota's most iconic landmarks, making it an ideal base for exploring the Black Hills.

Feedback: Praised for its quiet atmosphere, clean facilities, and friendly staff, it's a popular choice for outdoor adventure and relaxation.

Sioux Falls KOA

1401 East Robur Dr, Sioux Falls, SD 57104

(605) 332-9987 $$

Campground Description:

This family-friendly KOA offers modern amenities and easy access to Sioux Falls attractions like Falls Park and the Great Plains Zoo, making it a convenient stop for Midwest travelers.

Types of Sites Available:
- RV sites with full hookups
- Tent camping sites
- Cabin rentals

Amenities:
- Swimming pool and mini-golf
- Dog park
- Free Wi-Fi

Activities:
- Swimming and mini-golf
- Exploring Sioux Falls' attractions
- Attending organized campground events

Unique Experiences: The combination of convenience and comfort, along with family-friendly activities, makes this KOA a great base for exploring Sioux Falls.

Feedback: Guests appreciate the clean facilities and helpful staff, making it a top choice for short visits and extended stays.

Rapid City RV Park

📍 4110 S Hwy 16, Rapid City, SD 57701

📞 (605) 342-2751 — $$

Campground Description:

Located near downtown Rapid City and major attractions like Mount Rushmore, this RV park offers a peaceful stay with beautiful views of the Black Hills.

Types of Sites Available:

- RV sites with full hookups
- Tent camping sites

Amenities:

- Swimming pool
- Dog park
- Free Wi-Fi

Activities:

- Visiting Mount Rushmore and Crazy Horse Memorial
- Hiking and wildlife viewing in the Black Hills
- Exploring downtown Rapid City

Unique Experiences: This campground's proximity to major attractions and scenic views make it a great choice for exploring the Black Hills.

Feedback: Praised for its convenient location and clean facilities, it's a popular spot for travelers visiting South Dakota's top landmarks.

Cherry Creek State Park

📍 26267 219th St, Fort Pierre, SD 57532

📞 (605) 223-7722 — $$

Campground Description:

Located near Fort Pierre, this state park offers a peaceful camping experience with access to fishing, hiking, and wildlife viewing in a serene natural setting.

Types of Sites Available:

- Tent camping sites
- Primitive RV sites

Amenities:

- Fishing access
- Picnic areas with BBQ grills
- Hiking trails

Activities:

- Fishing in nearby lakes
- Hiking and wildlife watching
- Exploring Fort Pierre's historical sites

Unique Experiences: Guests can enjoy a rustic, nature-focused camping experience with excellent opportunities for fishing and hiking in South Dakota's beautiful landscape.

Feedback: Praised for its peaceful environment and natural beauty, it's an ideal destination for nature lovers seeking a quiet retreat.

HIDDEN GEMS

Buffalo Ridge Camp Resort

Address: 245 Centennial Dr, Keystone, SD 57751

Campground Description:
A well-maintained, family-friendly resort near Mount Rushmore, offering a variety of camping options with beautiful views of the Black Hills.

Unique Experience: Camp near iconic Mount Rushmore while enjoying the natural beauty of South Dakota's Black Hills.

Amenities:
• Full hookups
• Pool

Activities:
• Hiking
• Mount Rushmore tours

Lake Oahe Campground

Address: 20439 Marina Rd, Pierre, SD 57501

Campground Description:
A lakeside campground offering fishing, boating, and peaceful camping along the expansive Lake Oahe.

Unique Experience: Enjoy stunning sunsets and excellent fishing opportunities on one of the largest reservoirs in the U.S.

Amenities:
• Boat ramp
• Picnic areas

Activities:
• Boating
• Fishing

NATIONAL PARKS

Badlands National Park (Cedar Pass Campground)

Address: 20681 SD-240, Interior, SD 57750

Campground Description:
Located in the heart of the Badlands, this campground offers breathtaking views of the rugged rock formations and easy access to hiking trails.

Unique Experience: Witness the stunning landscapes and wildlife of the Badlands up close, with incredible sunrises and sunsets.

Amenities:
• Restrooms
• Picnic tables

Activities:
• Hiking
• Wildlife viewing

Wind Cave National Park (Elk Mountain Campground)

Address: Wind Cave National Park, Hot Springs, SD 57747

Campground Description:
A quiet, wooded campground offering a peaceful retreat with access to one of the world's longest caves.

Unique Experience: Explore the fascinating underground formations of Wind Cave and enjoy the peaceful surroundings above ground.

Amenities:
• Restrooms
• Fire rings

Activities:
• Cave tours
• Hiking

Boondocking

Black Hills National Forest

Address: 1019 N 5th St, Custer, SD 57730

Campground Description:

Offering a variety of dispersed camping sites throughout the forest, this is a perfect location for those seeking solitude in the wilderness.

Unique Experience: Camp in the heart of the Black Hills with easy access to hiking, wildlife, and scenic drives.

Amenities:
• Primitive sites
• Scenic trails

Activities:
• Hiking
• Wildlife watching

Buffalo Gap National Grassland

Address: Buffalo Gap National Grassland, SD

Campground Description:

A vast expanse of grassland offering dispersed camping with scenic views and opportunities to experience South Dakota's prairie ecosystems.

Unique Experience: Boondock under the stars on the open prairie, surrounded by the rugged beauty of the Badlands.

Amenities:
• Primitive sites
• Scenic overlooks

Activities:
• Wildlife viewing
• Photography

Others Campgrounds

• Broken Arrow Horse Campground (Custer, SD)
• Rafter J Bar Ranch Campground (Hill City, SD)
• Big Pine Campground (Custer, SD)
• Whispering Pines Campground (Rapid City, SD)
• Beaver Lake Campground (Custer, SD)
• Outlaw Ranch (Custer, SD)
• Mountain View RV Park & Campground (Hill City, SD)
• Riverview RV Park & Campground (Pierre, SD)
• Heartland RV Park & Cabins (Hermosa, SD)
• KOA Palmer Gulch Resort (Hill City, SD)

Others Boondocking

• Badlands Overlook (near Badlands National Park)
• Buffalo Gap National Grassland (other sections)
• Pactola Reservoir (near Rapid City, SD)
• Bismarck Lake (Custer, SD)
• Bear Butte State Park (Sturgis, SD)

Nebraska: The Heart of the Great Plains

Nebraska, with its vast prairies, rolling sandhills, and historic trails, is a hidden gem for RVers seeking a peaceful and scenic journey through the heart of the Great Plains. Often overlooked by travelers, Nebraska offers a quiet charm that invites you to slow down and take in the wide-open landscapes, dramatic sunsets, and a rich history tied to the early pioneers who traveled westward.

The best season to RV in Nebraska is **late spring through early fall**, from **May to October**. **Summer** is ideal for exploring Nebraska's many parks and natural attractions, with warm days perfect for hiking, fishing, and enjoying the outdoors. **Fall** is a beautiful time to visit, as the rolling hills and prairies are touched by the golden hues of autumn. **Winter**, however, can be cold and windy, particularly on the plains, making RV travel more challenging unless you're prepared for colder conditions.

For RVers, Nebraska's wide-open spaces offer a sense of freedom and solitude that is hard to find elsewhere. The **Sandhills** region, a vast expanse of grass-covered dunes, is a highlight for those seeking an off-the-beaten-path adventure. You can explore the area's quiet beauty, camp by tranquil lakes, and take in the incredible wildlife that calls the Sandhills home. One of the best ways to experience Nebraska's history is by following the **Oregon Trail**, where you can visit landmarks like **Chimney Rock** and **Scotts Bluff National Monument**, both offering stunning views and a deep connection to the past.

Nebraska's campgrounds range from state parks and forested areas to more rustic, peaceful spots nestled along rivers and lakes. **Lake McConaughy**, one of the state's largest lakes, offers excellent RV camping with opportunities for boating, fishing, and relaxing by the water. For those interested in history, camping near the **Platte River** allows you to retrace the steps of early pioneers while enjoying the serene beauty of the river valley.

Nebraska's quiet landscapes and open roads make it a perfect destination for RVers who want to escape the hustle and bustle of more crowded places. Whether you're exploring the prairies, following historic trails, or simply enjoying a peaceful night under the stars, Nebraska offers a unique and rewarding experience for those willing to take the road less traveled.

Robidoux RV Park

585 Five Rocks Rd, Gering, NE 69341

(308) 436-2046 — $$

Campground Description:

Robidoux RV Park is nestled in the scenic landscape of Gering, Nebraska, near Scotts Bluff National Monument. Offering spacious RV sites and modern amenities, the park is ideal for travelers seeking to explore Nebraska's natural beauty and history. Its quiet surroundings, close to hiking, biking, and historical sites, make it perfect for both short and long-term stays.

Types of Sites Available:
- RV sites with full hookups
- Pull-through and back-in sites

Amenities:
- Free Wi-Fi, restrooms, laundry
- Playground, picnic areas, dog park

Activities:
- Exploring Scotts Bluff National Monument
- Walking and biking paths, fishing nearby

Unique Experiences: Stunning views of Scotts Bluff with modern comforts, offering a peaceful base for outdoor adventures.

Feedback: Praised for clean facilities, friendly staff, and beautiful views of the bluffs.

Grand Island KOA

904 S B Rd, Doniphan, NE 68832

(308) 382-6728 — $$

Campground Description:

Grand Island KOA, located near Doniphan, Nebraska, offers a family-friendly camping experience with easy access to local attractions like the Platte River and the Stuhr Museum. The campground provides spacious RV sites, cabins, and tent camping, as well as on-site activities, including mini-golf and a pool.

Types of Sites Available:
- RV sites with full hookups
- Tent camping sites
- Cabin rentals

Amenities:
- Free Wi-Fi, swimming pool, mini-golf
- Playground, picnic areas, dog park

Activities:
- Swimming, mini-golf, exploring Grand Island
- Fishing and boating nearby

Unique Experiences: A fun, family-friendly environment with a range of amenities and close proximity to local attractions.

Feedback: Highly rated for its clean facilities, family-friendly activities, and relaxing atmosphere.

Victorian Acres RV Park

6591 NE-2, Nebraska City, NE 68410

(402) 873-6866 — $$

Campground Description:

Victorian Acres RV Park offers a peaceful, well-maintained camping experience in Nebraska City, known for its rich history and beautiful apple orchards. With spacious RV sites and modern amenities, the park is a tranquil retreat with easy access to local attractions.

Types of Sites Available:

- RV sites with full hookups
- Tent camping sites

Amenities:

- Free Wi-Fi, restrooms, laundry
- Picnic areas, walking trails, dog park

Activities:

- Exploring Nebraska City and Arbor Lodge
- Picnicking, walking trails, local festivals

Unique Experiences: A quiet, scenic campground with beautiful landscapes and access to Nebraska City's rich history and attractions.

Feedback: Praised for its clean facilities, peaceful setting, and friendly staff.

Prairie Oasis RV Park

913 Road B, Henderson, NE 68371

(402) 723-5227 — $$

Campground Description:

Prairie Oasis RV Park, located in Henderson, Nebraska, provides a peaceful retreat surrounded by beautiful prairie landscapes. Offering fishing, paddle boating, and walking trails, the park is a perfect stop for travelers seeking relaxation in nature.

Types of Sites Available:

- RV sites with full hookups
- Tent camping sites
- Cabin rentals

Amenities:

- Free Wi-Fi, restrooms, laundry
- Playground, picnic areas, scenic pond

Activities:

- Fishing and paddle boating on the pond
- Walking and biking trails

Unique Experiences: A tranquil prairie escape with a charming pond and family-friendly amenities, perfect for relaxing and outdoor fun.

Feedback: Guests appreciate the serene setting, clean facilities, and friendly staff, making it a great stop for travelers and families.

HIDDEN GEMS

NATIONAL PARKS

Eugene T. Mahoney State Park

Address: 28500 W Park Hwy, Ashland, NE 68003

Campground Description:
A popular park offering a family-friendly camping experience with modern amenities and beautiful views of the Platte River.
Unique Experience: Enjoy a blend of outdoor activities and family fun in one of Nebraska's most developed parks.

Amenities:
• Full hookups
• Pool and water park

Activities:
• Hiking
• Fishing

Chadron State Park

Address: 15951 Gold Rush Byway, Chadron, NE 69337

Campground Description:
Nebraska's oldest state park, offering stunning views of the Pine Ridge area and a variety of outdoor recreation activities.
Unique Experience: Explore Nebraska's unique Pine Ridge with hiking trails and scenic overlooks.

Amenities:
• Cabins and campsites
• Picnic areas

Activities:
• Hiking
• Fishing

Blue Heron Campground

Address: 78596 Jeffres Ln, Gothenburg, NE 69138

Campground Description:
A quiet riverside campground in central Nebraska, ideal for those looking for a peaceful nature getaway.
Unique Experience: Relax by the Platte River and enjoy the serenity of this lesser-known camping spot.

Amenities:
• Electric hookups
• Restrooms

Activities:
• Birdwatching
• Canoeing

Indian Cave State Park

Address: 65296 720 Rd, Shubert, NE 68437

Campground Description:
A scenic park along the Missouri River, famous for its historic cave and lush wooded trails.
Unique Experience: Discover the prehistoric cave carvings and hike through dense, beautiful forests.

Amenities:
• Electric hookups
• Restrooms

Activities:
• Hiking
• Exploring historical sites

Boondocking

Merritt Reservoir

Address: Hwy 97, Valentine, NE 69201

Campground Description:
A remote camping area by the reservoir offering excellent fishing and stargazing opportunities.
Unique Experience: Camp under some of the darkest skies in Nebraska, perfect for stargazing and fishing.

Amenities:
- Primitive campsites
- Boat ramp

Activities:
- Fishing
- Stargazing

Buffalo Bill Ranch State Recreation Area

Address: 2921 Scouts Rest Ranch Rd, North Platte, NE 69101

Campground Description:
Dispersed camping near the historic ranch of Buffalo Bill Cody, offering a glimpse into Nebraska's frontier history.
Unique Experience: Immerse yourself in the Wild West atmosphere while camping in a scenic and quiet area.

Amenities:
- Primitive campsites
- Restrooms

Activities:
- Exploring historic sites
- Wildlife viewing

Others Campgrounds

- Fort Kearny State Recreation Area (Kearney, NE)
- Mormon Island State Recreation Area (Doniphan, NE)
- Two Rivers State Recreation Area (Waterloo, NE)
- Rock Creek Station State Historical Park (Fairbury, NE)
- Lake Minatare State Recreation Area (Minatare, NE)
- Louisville State Recreation Area (Louisville, NE)
- Ponca State Park (Ponca, NE)
- Box Butte Reservoir State Recreation Area (Hemingford, NE)
- Niobrara State Park (Niobrara, NE)
- Lake McConaughy State Recreation Area (Ogallala, NE)

Others Boondocking

- Oglala National Grassland
- Halsey National Forest (dispersed sites)
- Samuel R. McKelvie National Forest
- Nebraska Sandhills (various areas for dispersed camping)
- Platte River areas (dispersed camping spots)

Kansas: Endless Skies and Prairie Beauty

Kansas, often referred to as the "Sunflower State," is a place where the wide-open skies stretch endlessly above, and the golden prairies roll gently below. While it may not have the dramatic landscapes of other states, Kansas offers a peaceful, laid-back atmosphere that is perfect for RVers seeking a calm and scenic escape. Driving through Kansas feels like traveling through the heart of America, where the beauty is subtle but constant, and the sunsets are some of the most breathtaking you'll ever see.

The best season to RV in Kansas is **spring through fall**, from **April to October**. In **spring**, the prairies are vibrant with wildflowers, and the weather is mild—ideal for exploring the many outdoor spaces the state has to offer. **Fall** is equally beautiful, with cooler temperatures and the golden hues of the harvest season. **Summer** can be hot, particularly in the southern parts of the state, but if you enjoy sunshine and warm weather, it's a great time to explore Kansas' lakes and rivers. **Winter** is the season to avoid, as cold winds and occasional snowstorms can make RV travel less enjoyable, especially on the open plains.

What I love most about Kansas is its simplicity. The long stretches of road allow you to take in the quiet beauty of the prairie, where small towns appear like oases, each with its own charm and story to tell. RVers can enjoy scenic byways like the Flint Hills National Scenic Byway, where the tallgrass prairie stretches as far as the eye can see, or visit the many state parks that offer peaceful, well-maintained campgrounds.

Kansas is also home to some truly unique attractions. One of my favorites is the Monument Rocks, a series of towering chalk formations that rise dramatically from the flat plains. And for history buffs, a visit to the Santa Fe Trail or the historic sites related to the state's frontier past offers a glimpse into the rich history of the American West.

The campgrounds in Kansas are as inviting as the state itself, offering both well-equipped RV parks and more rustic, quiet spots perfect for a night under the stars. Whether you're camping along one of the state's scenic rivers or tucked away in a quiet corner of the prairies, you'll find that Kansas has a way of making you feel at home.

For RVers who crave wide-open spaces, simple pleasures, and the beauty of the prairie, Kansas is the perfect destination. It's a place where you can slow down, enjoy the moment, and reconnect with the natural world.

Goodland KOA Journey

📍 1114 E US Hwy 24, Goodland, KS 67735

📞 (785) 890-5701 — $$

Campground Description:

Located off I-70, this campground offers a peaceful stop for road-trippers and RV enthusiasts. Proximity to attractions like the Van Gogh painting makes it great for exploring.

Types of Sites Available:

- RV sites, tent camping, cabins

Amenities:
- Free Wi-Fi • Seasonal swimming pool
- Restrooms and showers
- Laundry facilities
- Playground for children
- Dog park and pet-friendly areas

Activities:

- Swimming in the seasonal pool
- Exploring nearby attractions like the giant Van Gogh painting and High Plains Museum
- Birdwatching and wildlife viewing in the surrounding area

Unique Experiences: A relaxing stop with modern amenities and close proximity to Goodland's attractions.

Feedback: Praised for cleanliness, friendly staff, and convenient highway access.

Salina KOA

📍 1109 W Diamond Dr, Salina, KS 67401

📞 (785) 827-3182 — $$

Campground Description:

Conveniently located near I-70, this KOA offers family-friendly activities, including mini-golf and a seasonal pool. Ideal for travelers exploring the Salina area.

Types of Sites Available:
- RV sites with full hookups
- Tent camping sites
- Deluxe cabins and camping cabins

Amenities:
- Free Wi-Fi
- Seasonal swimming pool
- Mini-golf course
- Playground for children

Activities:

- Swimming and relaxing by the seasonal pool
- Playing mini-golf
- Playground fun for kids
- Walking pets in the dog park
- Exploring local attractions like Rolling Hills Zoo and the Smoky Hill Museum

Unique Experiences: A family-friendly campground with easy access to nearby attractions and plenty of on-site fun.

Feedback: Highly rated for its activities, clean facilities, and friendly atmosphere.

Ellis Lakeside Campground

100 Kansas 247, Ellis, KS 67637

(785) 726-4812 — $

Campground Description:

Quiet lakeside camping along Big Creek Lake with fishing, hiking, and peaceful surroundings. Perfect for nature lovers.

Types of Sites Available:
- RV sites with full hookups
- Tent camping sites

Amenities:
- Free Wi-Fi • Dump station
- Restrooms and showers
- Fishing dock and boat ramp
- Fire pits at select sites
- Walking and biking trails nearby

Activities:
- Fishing and boating on Big Creek Lake
- Birdwatching and wildlife viewing
- Hiking and biking along local trails
- Playing at the playground
- Picnicking by the lake
- Exploring the historic town of Ellis, including the Walter P. Chrysler Boyhood Home

Unique Experiences: Tranquil lakeside camping with easy access to nature and local historical sites.

Feedback: Loved for its serene location, lakeside views, and relaxed atmosphere.

Crawford State Park

1 W Lake Rd, Farlington, KS 66734

(620) 362-3671 — $$

Campground Description:

Lakeside park with boating, fishing, and hiking. A scenic destination with beautiful woodlands and plenty of outdoor activities.

Types of Sites Available:
- RV sites with electric and water hookups
- Tent camping sites
- Primitive and modern cabins for rent

Amenities:
- Boat ramp and dock access
- Fishing piers • Fire pits at select sites
- Hiking trails
- Camp store for essentials

Activities:
- Fishing for bass, crappie, and catfish in Crawford Lake
- Boating, canoeing, and kayaking on the lake
- Hiking and exploring the park's scenic trails
- Birdwatching and wildlife viewing
- Picnicking and BBQs at the picnic shelters

Unique Experiences: A picturesque lakeside retreat with excellent outdoor opportunities, ideal for families and nature lovers.

Feedback: Praised for its natural beauty, clean facilities, and variety of activities.

HIDDEN GEMS

Topeka Hilltop Campground
Address: 3341 SE 29th St, Topeka, KS 66605

Campground Description:
A quiet, hilltop campground offering beautiful views of the surrounding countryside, perfect for a peaceful getaway.
Unique Experience: Enjoy a serene camping experience with panoramic views of Topeka.

Amenities:
• Full RV hookups
• Restrooms and showers

Activities:
• Hiking nearby trails
• Wildlife watching

Washington City Campground
Address: 902 D St, Washington, KS 66968

Campground Description:
A small city-run campground with convenient access to local parks, ideal for travelers looking for a simple, no-frills stay.
Unique Experience: Stay in a quiet community campground with access to local shops and restaurants.

Amenities:
• Electric hookups
• Picnic tables

Activities:
• Exploring local parks
• Biking around town

NATIONAL PARKS

Clinton State Park
Address: 798 N 1415 Rd, Lawrence, KS 66049

Campground Description:
A large state park offering lakeside camping with access to boating, fishing, and scenic trails.
Unique Experience: Camp by the beautiful Clinton Lake with stunning sunset views.

Amenities:
• Restrooms and showers
• Full RV hookups

Activities:
• Boating and fishing
• Hiking

Pomona State Park
Address: 22900 S Pomona Dam Rd, Vassar, KS 66543

Campground Description:
A tranquil park located on the shores of Pomona Lake, known for its excellent fishing and peaceful campsites.
Unique Experience: Relax by the water's edge and enjoy the calm of Pomona Lake.

Amenities:
• Boat ramps
• Restrooms and showers

Activities:
• Fishing and boating
• Picnicking

Boondocking

Cedar Bluff State Park

Address: 32001 KS-147, Ellis, KS 67637

Campground Description:
A remote park with expansive views and plenty of boondocking opportunities, perfect for those who love wide-open spaces.

Unique Experience: Experience off-the-grid camping in a wide, open prairie setting.

Amenities:
• Primitive campsites
• Boat ramps

Activities:
• Fishing
• Hiking

El Dorado State Park

Address: 618 NE Bluestem Rd, El Dorado, KS 67042

Campground Description:
A popular state park with multiple boondocking spots near the reservoir, offering a blend of wilderness and water recreation.

Unique Experience: Boondock by El Dorado Lake, surrounded by nature and serenity.

Amenities:
• Primitive campsites
• Vault toilets

Activities:
• Boating
• Wildlife watching

Others Campgrounds

• Milford State Park Campground (Milford, KS)
• Tuttle Creek State Park Campground (Manhattan, KS)
• Kanopolis State Park Campground (Marquette, KS)
• Prairie Dog State Park Campground (Norton, KS)
• Perry State Park Campground (Ozawkie, KS)
• Wilson State Park Campground (Sylvan Grove, KS)
• Big Hill Lake Campground (Cherryvale, KS)
• Meade State Park Campground (Meade, KS)
• Glen Elder State Park Campground (Glen Elder, KS)
• Scott State Park Campground (Scott City, KS)

Others Boondocking

• Cimarron National Grassland
• Sandsage Bison Range & Wildlife Area
• Smoky Valley Ranch
• Maxwell Wildlife Refuge
• Cheney Wildlife Area

Delaware: The Hidden Gem of the East Coast

Delaware might be small in size, but for RVers, it offers a perfect blend of scenic coastline, charming towns, and outdoor adventures. Tucked between larger states, Delaware often flies under the radar, which means fewer crowds and a more relaxed pace, ideal for anyone looking to enjoy some peace and quiet on their RV travels. From the serene beaches along the Atlantic Coast to the tranquil forests inland, Delaware provides a surprising variety of landscapes for its size.

The best season to explore Delaware in an RV is **spring through fall**, from **April to October**. **Spring** brings mild weather and blooming wildflowers, making it a great time to visit the state's parks and nature reserves. **Fall**, on the other hand, offers cooler temperatures and vibrant foliage, perfect for outdoor activities like hiking and biking. **Summer** is prime time for beachgoers, with the coastal towns like Rehoboth Beach and Bethany Beach coming alive with activity. **The season to avoid** is **winter**, from **December to February**, when the cold, damp weather can make camping less enjoyable, and some campgrounds may close for the season.

One of Delaware's best-kept secrets is its beautiful coastline. The beaches are clean, the water is refreshing, and there's always a sense of calm that's hard to find in the more crowded coastal areas further north. RVers can easily set up camp near the water and enjoy the relaxed vibe of beach towns where you can spend your days sunbathing, fishing, or strolling along the boardwalks.

Inland, Delaware offers charming towns, historical sites, and plenty of outdoor spaces to explore. The state parks, like Cape Henlopen and Trap Pond, are excellent for camping and provide access to activities like kayaking, hiking, and birdwatching. For a small state, Delaware has a lot to offer, especially if you're looking for a more low-key RVing experience.

Delaware's compact size means you can see a lot in a short amount of time. Whether you're looking to relax by the beach or explore the rich history and natural beauty of the inland areas, this state offers something for every type of traveler. It's a hidden gem that offers all the charm of the East Coast without the hustle and bustle.

Treasure Beach RV Park & Campground

37291 Lighthouse Rd, Selbyville, DE 19975

📞 (302) 436-8001 — $$

Campground Description:

A family-friendly waterfront campground along Assawoman Bay, perfect for beach lovers and outdoor enthusiasts. Close to Ocean City, MD, offering boating, fishing, crabbing, and plenty of on-site activities.

Types of Sites Available:
- RV sites with full hookups
- Tent sites, cottages
- Waterfront sites

Amenities:
- Pool, private beach, boat ramp
- Fishing pier, sports courts
- Laundry, camp store

Activities:
- Boating, fishing, kayaking
- Swimming, exploring Ocean City
- Family-friendly games and events

Unique Experiences: Offers a blend of beachside relaxation and coastal adventure with direct access to Assawoman Bay and nearby Ocean City.

Feedback: Ideal for families and groups seeking beach fun and outdoor recreation with convenient access to local attractions.

Homestead Campground

25165 Prettyman Rd, Georgetown, DE 19947

📞 (302) 684-4278 — $$

Campground Description:

A peaceful, family-friendly campground in Georgetown, DE, offering easy access to Rehoboth Beach and Lewes. Perfect for a quiet getaway with plenty of on-site activities like mini-golf and a pool.

Types of Sites Available:
- RV sites with full hookups
- Tent camping, cabins

Amenities:
- Pool, mini-golf, playground
- Picnic areas, laundry, camp store
- Sports courts, planned events

Activities:
- Swimming, mini-golf, hiking
- Exploring nearby beaches
- Fishing, kayaking, and boating

Unique Experiences: Combines countryside relaxation with access to Delaware's popular beach towns and offers family-friendly activities on-site.

Feedback: Great for families and couples seeking a quiet camping experience with access to both inland and coastal activities.

Delaware Seashore State Park

📍 39415 Inlet Rd, Rehoboth Beach, DE 19971

📞 (302) 227-2800 ⎯ $$

Campground Description:

A scenic coastal campground near Rehoboth Beach, offering RV and tent sites close to the beach. Ideal for beach lovers and outdoor adventurers looking to enjoy sunbathing, fishing, and water sports.

Types of Sites Available:

- RV sites with water/electric hookups
- Tent sites, waterfront sites

Amenities:

- Bathhouses, fishing pier
- Laundry, camp store, playground
- Boat ramp, beach access

Activities:

- Swimming, fishing, crabbing
- Kayaking, paddleboarding, hiking
- Exploring Rehoboth Beach and Dewey Beach

Unique Experiences: A perfect coastal camping experience with direct beach access and proximity to local attractions like Rehoboth Beach's boardwalk.

Feedback: Ideal for beach lovers and families looking for a scenic and active camping experience close to the ocean.

Cape Henlopen State Park

📍 15099 Cape Henlopen Dr, Lewes, DE 19958

📞 (302) 645-8983 ⎯ $$

Campground Description:

Located in Lewes, DE, Cape Henlopen State Park offers beachside camping with rich historical significance. The park features stunning coastal views, hiking trails, and WWII bunkers for exploration.

Types of Sites Available:

- RV sites with water/electric hookups
- Tent sites, cabins

Amenities:

- Bathhouses, fishing pier
- Laundry, playground, camp store
- Picnic areas, boat ramp

Activities:

- Swimming, beachcombing, fishing
- Hiking, biking, kayaking
- Exploring WWII bunkers and trails

Unique Experiences: Blends coastal beauty with history, offering access to pristine beaches, wildlife, and WWII fortifications.

Feedback: A top choice for families, history enthusiasts, and nature lovers looking for a beachside escape with lots to explore.

HIDDEN GEMS

Gulls Way Campground

Address: 32369 Long Neck Rd, Dagsboro, DE 19939

Campground Description:
Gulls Way Campground offers a family-friendly camping experience near the Indian River, with scenic views and a peaceful atmosphere perfect for a relaxing getaway.

Unique Experience: Enjoy serene riverfront camping with access to boating and fishing in a quiet, laid-back setting.

Amenities:
• Fishing pier
• Boat ramp

Activities:
• Boating on the Indian River
• Fishing off the pier

Tuckahoe Acres Camping Resort

Address: 36031 Tuckahoe Trail, Dagsboro, DE 19939

Campground Description:
Tuckahoe Acres Camping Resort is a large, family-oriented campground with plenty of outdoor recreation, including a pool, sports courts, and organized activities for kids.

Unique Experience: Family fun in the heart of Delaware with organized events, swimming, and riverside views.

Amenities:
• Swimming pool
• Sports courts

Activities:
• Swimming and outdoor games
• Boating and kayaking

NATIONAL PARKS

Cape Henlopen State Park

Address: 15099 Cape Henlopen Dr, Lewes, DE 19958

Campground Description:
Cape Henlopen State Park offers beachfront camping with access to sandy shores, historic sites, and excellent trails for biking and hiking.

Unique Experience: Camp by the ocean and explore Delaware's rich coastal history while enjoying outdoor recreation along the Atlantic Coast.

Amenities:
• Beach access
• Biking trails

Activities:
• Swimming and beachcombing
• Biking along the scenic coastal trails

Delaware Seashore State Park

Address: 39415 Inlet Rd, Rehoboth Beach, DE 19971

Campground Description:
Delaware Seashore State Park offers oceanside camping with direct access to the Atlantic Ocean, making it a prime spot for beach lovers and water sports enthusiasts.

Unique Experience: Wake up to the sound of the ocean and enjoy easy access to water activities like swimming, fishing, and surfing.

Amenities:
• Oceanside campsites
• Boat ramps

Activities:
• Surfing and swimming in the ocean
• Boating and fishing in the inlet

Boondocking

Prime Hook National Wildlife Refuge

Address: 11978 Turkle Pond Rd, Milton, DE 19968

Campground Description:
Prime Hook National Wildlife Refuge allows dispersed camping in designated areas, offering a secluded camping experience surrounded by diverse wildlife and wetlands.

Unique Experience: Experience the tranquility of camping in a wildlife refuge, with opportunities for birdwatching and nature photography.

Amenities:
- Primitive campsites
- Wildlife observation areas

Activities:
- Birdwatching and wildlife viewing
- Nature photography

Assawoman Wildlife Area

Address: Assawoman Wildlife Area, Frankford, DE

Campground Description:
Assawoman Wildlife Area provides coastal boondocking with scenic marsh views, ideal for those looking to camp off-grid and enjoy peaceful surroundings.

Unique Experience: Escape to the Delaware coast for a quiet boondocking experience surrounded by coastal marshlands and abundant wildlife.

Amenities:
- Primitive campsites
- Coastal views

Activities:
- Kayaking and paddling in the marshes
- Wildlife and birdwatching

Others Campgrounds

- Killens Pond State Park Campground
- Tall Pines Campground
- Holly Lake Campsites
- Lums Pond State Park Campground
- G & R Campground
- Trap Pond State Park Campground
- Massey's Landing
- Leisure Point Resort
- Ponderosa Pines Campground
- Yogi Bear's Jellystone Park Campground

Others Boondocking

- Bombay Hook National Wildlife Refuge (designated areas)
- Redden State Forest (dispersed camping)
- Blackbird State Forest (dispersed camping)
- Woodland Beach Wildlife Area (designated areas)
- Little Creek Wildlife Area (designated areas)

Maryland: A Perfect Blend of Coast and Countryside

Maryland may be small, but it packs a punch when it comes to diversity and beauty for RVers. From the scenic Chesapeake Bay and its charming coastal towns to the rolling hills and farmlands of western Maryland, this state offers a rich blend of outdoor activities and historical landmarks. Whether you're drawn to the coastline for fresh seafood or exploring the forests and mountains for a more rugged experience, Maryland is a hidden gem for RV enthusiasts.

The best season to RV in Maryland is **spring through fall**, from **April to October**. **Spring** brings the beauty of blooming wildflowers and mild temperatures, making it a great time to explore the state's parks and coastal areas. **Summer** is ideal for beachgoers, with places like Ocean City and Assateague Island offering plenty of sun, sand, and surf. **Fall** is another perfect time to visit, especially for RVers who want to enjoy cooler weather and vibrant autumn foliage, particularly in the western part of the state. **Winter** can be cold and snowy, particularly in the mountainous regions, so it's generally the season to avoid unless you're prepared for chilly conditions.

What makes Maryland such a great destination for RVers is the state's balance of coastal charm and inland beauty. One of the highlights is Assateague Island National Seashore, where you can camp near the ocean and wake up to wild ponies grazing on the dunes. For history buffs, Maryland offers countless historic sites, from Civil War battlefields like Antietam to the rich maritime history of towns like Annapolis and St. Michaels.

Maryland's campgrounds are as varied as its landscapes. Whether you're looking to set up camp by the water or prefer a more rustic, wooded retreat, you'll find plenty of options. The state parks, like Cunningham Falls and Deep Creek Lake, provide excellent spots for hiking, fishing, and boating, while RVers who love the coast can enjoy the unique experience of camping right on the beach at Assateague Island.

One of the things that stands out most about RVing in Maryland is how easy it is to travel between its diverse regions. In a single day, you can go from the Eastern Shore's tranquil beaches to the rolling hills and forests of western Maryland, or explore the vibrant cultural scene of Baltimore. Whether you're looking for a quiet spot by the bay or a more adventurous mountain escape, Maryland offers something for every kind of RVer.

Cherry Hill Park

9800 Cherry Hill Rd, College Park, MD 20740

(301) 937-7116 $$$

Campground Description:

Located near Washington, D.C., Cherry Hill Park offers full-service amenities for those exploring the nation's capital. It features spacious RV sites, tent camping, and cabin rentals, making it ideal for families and solo travelers. Guests enjoy pools, mini-golf, and shuttle service to D.C.

Types of Sites Available:

- RV sites with full hookups
- Tent camping sites
- Cabin rentals

Amenities:

- Two swimming pools, hot tub
- Mini-golf, café, camp store
- Dog park, fitness room

Activities:

- Swimming, mini-golf
- Shuttle service to D.C. attractions

Unique Experiences: Perfect for sightseeing in D.C. while enjoying relaxing campground amenities.

Feedback: Highly rated for location and friendly staff, with easy access to Washington, D.C. attractions.

Ramblin' Pines Family Campground & RV Park

801 Hoods Mill Rd, Woodbine, MD 21797

(410) 795-5161 $$

Campground Description:

Set in the lush countryside, Ramblin' Pines offers a fun-filled camping experience with spacious sites and amenities like a swimming pool, mini-golf, and a dog park. A great destination for families, its proximity to Baltimore and Washington, D.C. makes it an excellent choice for combining nature with urban attractions.

Types of Sites Available:

- RV sites with full hookups
- Tent camping sites
- Cabin rentals

Amenities:

- Pool, mini-golf, splash pad
- Hiking trails, playground
- Dog park, fitness center

Activities:

- Mini-golf, hiking
- Swimming, nature walks

Unique Experiences: A peaceful, family-oriented retreat with fun activities for all ages, plus easy access to nearby cities.

Feedback: Loved for its clean facilities and friendly atmosphere, perfect for families seeking a relaxing getaway.

Sun Outdoors Frontier Town

8428 Stephen Decatur Hwy, Berlin, MD 21811

(800) 228-5590 — $$

Campground Description:

This Wild West-themed campground near Ocean City offers unique family-friendly experiences with an on-site water park, Wild West shows, and mini-golf. Located on the bay, it's perfect for water activities and fun cowboy-themed entertainment.

Types of Sites Available:

- RV sites with full hookups
- Tent camping sites
- Vacation rentals

Amenities:

- Water park, Wild West shows
- Mini-golf, playground
- Shuttle to Ocean City

Activities:

- Water park, Wild West shows
- Mini-golf, fishing, crabbing

Unique Experiences: Guests enjoy live cowboy shows, a water park, and proximity to Ocean City's beaches and boardwalk.

Feedback: Praised for its Wild West theme, family-friendly amenities, and range of activities. A favorite for adventure-filled vacations.

Bar Harbor RV Park & Marina

4228 Birch Ave, Abingdon, MD 21009

(410) 679-0880 — $$

Campground Description:

A peaceful waterfront RV park with stunning views of the Bush River. It offers modern amenities, a marina, and direct access to fishing and boating. Located near historic Havre de Grace, it's an ideal spot for nature lovers and boaters.

Types of Sites Available:

- RV sites with full hookups
- Pull-through and back-in sites
- Waterfront sites

Amenities:

- Marina, fishing pier
- Swimming pool
- Kayak rentals

Activities:

- Boating, fishing
- Swimming, kayaking

Unique Experiences: Scenic waterfront camping with marina access, perfect for boating and fishing enthusiasts.

Feedback: Praised for its waterfront views, clean facilities, and serene atmosphere, ideal for relaxation and boating.

HIDDEN GEMS

Double G RV Park

Address: 76 Double G Dr, McHenry, MD 21541

Campground Description:
A peaceful RV park near Deep Creek Lake, offering easy access to Maryland's largest freshwater lake and a relaxing environment.
Unique Experience: Enjoy boating, fishing, and the natural beauty of Deep Creek Lake.

Amenities:
• Full RV hookups
• Restrooms and showers

Activities:
• Boating
• Fishing

Ole Mink Farm Recreation Resort

Address: 12806 Mink Farm Rd, Thurmont, MD 21788

Campground Description:
Nestled in the Catoctin Mountains, this family-owned resort provides a peaceful getaway with scenic views and wooded campsites.
Unique Experience: Experience the serene mountain surroundings, perfect for outdoor lovers seeking a retreat.

Amenities:
• Cabins available
• Swimming pool

Activities:
• Hiking
• Wildlife watching

NATIONAL PARKS

Assateague Island National Seashore

Address: 7206 National Seashore Ln, Berlin, MD 21811

Campground Description:
A stunning coastal park known for its wild horses and pristine beaches, offering an unforgettable camping experience.
Unique Experience: Camp alongside wild horses and enjoy the unspoiled beauty of the Atlantic Ocean coastline.

Amenities:
• Beach access
• Fire pits

Activities:
• Beachcombing
• Wildlife watching

Patapsco Valley State Park

Address: 8020 Baltimore National Pike, Ellicott City, MD 21043

Campground Description:
This state park offers outdoor activities along the Patapsco River, with scenic trails, waterfalls, and historic sites.
Unique Experience: Explore miles of hiking and biking trails through picturesque woodlands and along the river.

Amenities:
• Picnic areas
• Restrooms

Activities:
• Hiking
• Biking

Boondocking

Assateague Island National Seashore
Address: 7206 National Seashore Ln, Berlin, MD 21811

Campground Description:
A premier boondocking destination with scenic beaches and wildlife, where you can camp under the stars by the ocean.
Unique Experience: Boondock right by the water, surrounded by wild horses and stunning sunsets over the Atlantic.

Amenities:
• Primitive campsites
• Fire rings

Activities:
• Swimming
• Birdwatching

Catoctin Mountain Park
Address: 6602 Foxville Rd, Thurmont, MD 21788

Campground Description:
A beautiful mountain park offering dispersed camping and an array of trails through dense forests and mountain streams.
Unique Experience: Enjoy peaceful boondocking spots surrounded by the tranquil beauty of the Catoctin Mountains.

Amenities:
• Primitive campsites
• Hiking trails

Activities:
• Hiking
• Fishing

Others Campgrounds

• Bar Harbor RV Park and Marina (Abingdon, MD)
• Buttonwood Beach RV Resort (Earleville, MD)
• Woodlands Camping Resort (Elkton, MD)
• Tuckahoe State Park Campground (Queen Anne, MD)
• Greenbrier State Park Campground (Boonsboro, MD)
• Point Lookout State Park Campground (Scotland, MD)
• Elk Neck State Park Campground (North East, MD)
• Cunningham Falls State Park (Thurmont, MD)
• Deep Creek Lake State Park (Swanton, MD)
• Rocky Gap State Park Campground (Flintstone, MD)

Others Boondocking

• Green Ridge State Forest
• Potomac State Forest
• Youghiogheny Wild River Natural Environment Area
• Savage River State Forest
• Maryland Appalachian Trail Shelters

Others National Park

• Catoctin Mountain Park

Virginia: History and Scenic Beauty

Virginia, often referred to as the "Mother of Presidents" and the gateway to the American South, offers RVers a captivating blend of rich history and diverse natural beauty. From the majestic peaks of the **Blue Ridge Mountains** to the serene shores of the **Chesapeake Bay**, Virginia provides an array of landscapes and experiences for those traveling by RV. Whether you're exploring historic landmarks like **Colonial Williamsburg**, hiking through **Shenandoah National Park**, or relaxing by the coast, Virginia invites RVers to experience its unique mix of past and present.

The best season to RV in Virginia is **spring through fall**, from **April to October**. **Spring** brings blooming flowers, particularly in Virginia's famous gardens and along scenic drives like the **Blue Ridge Parkway**. **Fall** is equally stunning, with the Appalachian Mountains coming alive with brilliant autumn colors. **Summer** is perfect for enjoying the state's beaches and waterways, though it can be humid, especially in the central and eastern regions. **Winter** can be cold in the mountains, but the milder weather in the lowlands and along the coast offers year-round camping opportunities.

One of the top destinations for RVers in Virginia is **Shenandoah National Park**, a stunning stretch of the **Blue Ridge Mountains** that offers scenic vistas, waterfalls, and over 200 miles of hiking trails, including sections of the famous **Appalachian Trail**. The **Skyline Drive**, which runs the length of the park, is one of the most beautiful drives in the U.S., offering sweeping views of the surrounding mountains and valleys. RV campgrounds within and near the park allow travelers to immerse themselves in the natural beauty of this iconic region.

For history lovers, Virginia's deep connection to the birth of America makes it a must-visit state. **Colonial Williamsburg** offers a fully immersive experience of life in the 18th century, while **Jamestown** and **Yorktown** provide fascinating insights into America's earliest settlements and the Revolutionary War. RVers can camp near these historic sites and enjoy easy access to walking tours, reenactments, and museums that bring Virginia's colonial and Civil War history to life.

Virginia's coastal regions, particularly the **Eastern Shore** and the **Chesapeake Bay**, offer a peaceful retreat with quiet beaches, charming fishing towns, and opportunities for boating, crabbing, and birdwatching. **Virginia Beach** is a popular coastal destination, with family-friendly campgrounds close to the ocean and plenty of activities to enjoy, from beachcombing to exploring the nearby wildlife refuges.

The **Blue Ridge Parkway** is another must-see for RVers traveling through Virginia. This scenic byway stretches for 469 miles along the Blue Ridge Mountains and offers numerous campgrounds, hiking trails, and picnic areas. It's a perfect route for those who want to take in the beauty of the Appalachian Mountains at a leisurely pace.

Virginia's campgrounds range from full-service RV resorts with modern amenities to rustic, nature-focused sites in state parks and forests. Whether you're camping in the heart of the mountains, near historic sites, or along the coast, Virginia's campgrounds provide the perfect base for exploring everything this diverse state has to offer.

For RVers seeking a mix of outdoor adventure, history, and scenic beauty, Virginia offers a rich and rewarding experience. Whether you're hiking in Shenandoah, walking through the streets of Colonial Williamsburg, or relaxing by the Chesapeake Bay, Virginia promises an RV journey full of discovery and unforgettable memories.

Cherry Hill Park

9800 Cherry Hill Rd, College Park, MD 20740

(301) 937-7116 — $$

Campground Description:

The closest RV park to Washington, D.C., Cherry Hill Park offers convenience for exploring the nation's capital while providing modern amenities like pools, a cafe, and shuttle services. Perfect for families and history enthusiasts.

Types of Sites Available:

- RV sites with full hookups
- Tent sites
- Cabin rentals (standard and deluxe)

Amenities:

- Free Wi-Fi,
- Swimming pools and cafe
- Playground,
- Shuttle service to D.C.

Activities:

- Swimming,
- Visiting D.C.'s historic sites,
- Picnicking
- Exploring local parks.

Unique Experiences: Easy access to Washington, D.C., with shuttle service and on-site amenities to relax after a day of sightseeing.

Feedback: Praised for its location, cleanliness, and friendly staff, with convenient access to the city.

Virginia Beach KOA

1240 General Booth Blvd, Virginia Beach, VA 23451

(757) 428-1444 — $$

Campground Description:

Located minutes from the beach, Virginia Beach KOA provides family-friendly amenities and activities, including pools, a splash pad, and shuttle service to the beach.

Types of Sites Available:

- RV sites with full hookups
- Tent camping
- Cabin rentals (standard and deluxe)

Amenities:

- Pools,
- Hot tub
- Bike rentals,

Activities:

- Beach trips,
- Biking
- Visiting local attractions like the Virginia Aquarium.

Unique Experiences: Perfect blend of beachside fun with a family-friendly camping experience, offering easy beach access and plenty of on-site activities.

Feedback: Guests love the location, clean facilities, and variety of family activities, making it ideal for a beach vacation.

Natural Bridge / Lexington KOA

📍 214 Killdeer Ln, Natural Bridge, VA 24578

📞 (540) 291-2770 —— $$

Campground Description:

Set in the Shenandoah Valley, this KOA offers a peaceful camping experience near iconic attractions like the Natural Bridge and Blue Ridge Parkway.

Types of Sites Available:
- RV sites with full hookups
- Tent camping
- Cabin rentals (standard and deluxe)

Amenities:
- Pool
- Dog park
- Fire pits
- Hiking trails nearby.

Activities:
- Kayaking, fishing, hiking
- Beachcombing, birdwatching

Unique Experiences: A relaxing retreat near Virginia's natural wonders, perfect for nature and history lovers.

Feedback: Guests appreciate the serene setting, friendly staff, and proximity to both outdoor adventures and historic attractions.

Lake Anna State Park Campground

📍 6800 Lawyers Rd, Spotsylvania Courthouse, VA 22551

📞 (540) 854-5503 —— $

Campground Description:

A lakeside retreat in central Virginia, offering water activities, hiking, and nature exploration on the shores of Lake Anna, one of the state's largest lakes.

Types of Sites Available:
- RV sites with water and electric
- Tent camping
- Cabin rentals
- Primitive campsites

Amenities:
- Boat launch
- Fishing piers
- Swimming beach
- Hiking trails

Activities:
- Boating
- Swimming
- Fishing,
- Hiking
- Wildlife watching
- Visiting nearby wineries and historical sites.

Unique Experiences: A peaceful lakeside setting perfect for water sports and nature lovers, with access to nearby Civil War battlefields and local wineries.

Feedback: Praised for its peaceful atmosphere, clean facilities, and diverse recreational options, offering both relaxation and adventure.

HIDDEN GEMS

Grayson Highlands State Park Campground

Address: 829 Grayson Highland Ln, Mouth of Wilson, VA 24363

Campground Description:
Nestled in the Blue Ridge Mountains, this campground offers access to scenic hiking and stunning views.
Unique Experience: Camp near wild ponies while exploring the high-altitude trails and breathtaking views of the Appalachian Mountains.

Amenities:
• Restrooms
• Fire pits

Activities:
• Hiking
• Wildlife viewing

Douthat State Park Campground

Address: 14239 Douthat State Park Rd, Millboro, VA 24460

Campground Description:
A peaceful lakeside campground in the Allegheny Mountains, perfect for nature lovers and families.
Unique Experience: Enjoy fishing and swimming in the clear waters of Douthat Lake, surrounded by miles of hiking trails.

Amenities:
• Restrooms
• Picnic areas

Activities:
• Fishing
• Hiking

NATIONAL PARKS

Shenandoah National Park (Big Meadows Campground)

Address: Mile 51.2 Skyline Dr, Shenandoah National Park, VA 22835

Campground Description:
A spacious campground in the heart of Shenandoah National Park, with stunning mountain vistas.
Unique Experience: Camp along Skyline Drive, with access to scenic overlooks, waterfalls, and trails.

Amenities:
• Restrooms
• Picnic areas

Activities:
• Hiking
• Wildlife viewing

Appomattox Court House National Historical Park Campground

Address: 111 National Park Dr, Appomattox, VA 24522

Campground Description:
Located near the site of General Lee's surrender, this campground offers a blend of history and outdoor adventure.
Unique Experience: Immerse yourself in American Civil War history while enjoying the park's peaceful, historic setting.

Amenities:
• Restrooms
• Picnic areas

Activities:
• Historic tours
• Hiking

Boondocking

George Washington National Forest

Address: Virginia (various dispersed camping locations)

Campground Description:
A vast forest offering dispersed camping opportunities for outdoor enthusiasts seeking seclusion.
Unique Experience: Camp in the heart of nature with access to hiking, fishing, and wildlife viewing in the Blue Ridge Mountains.

Amenities:
• Primitive sites
• Scenic views

Activities:
• Hiking
• Fishing

Jefferson National Forest

Address: Virginia (various dispersed camping locations)

Campground Description:
Remote dispersed camping in Virginia's Jefferson National Forest, ideal for those seeking solitude.
Unique Experience: Explore the forest's trails, streams, and abundant wildlife while camping in a quiet, natural setting.

Amenities:
• Primitive sites
• Scenic views

Activities:
• Wildlife watching
• Hiking

Others Campgrounds

• First Landing State Park Campground (Virginia Beach, VA)
• Smith Mountain Lake State Park Campground (Huddleston, VA)
• Pocahontas State Park Campground (Chesterfield, VA)
• Chippokes Plantation State Park Campground (Surry, VA)
• Belle Isle State Park Campground (Lancaster, VA)
• Hungry Mother State Park Campground (Marion, VA)
• Kiptopeke State Park Campground (Cape Charles, VA)
• Lake Fairfax Park Campground (Reston, VA)
• North Bend Park Campground (Boydton, VA)
• Occoneechee State Park Campground (Clarksville, VA)

Others Boondocking

• Croatan National Forest (various dispersed areas, VA)
• Laurel Fork Recreation Area (Blacksburg, VA)
• George Washington National Forest (dispersed camping near trailheads, VA)
• Jefferson National Forest (dispersed camping in remote sections, VA)
• Peters Mill Run (off-road and camping near Fort Valley, VA)

West Virginia: The Mountain State's Outdoor Paradise

West Virginia, often called the "Mountain State," offers RVers a breathtaking escape into the rugged beauty of the **Appalachian Mountains**. With its rolling hills, deep river gorges, and dense forests, West Virginia is a haven for outdoor enthusiasts. Whether you're hiking through the **Monongahela National Forest**, exploring the dramatic scenery of the **New River Gorge**, or relaxing by a tranquil mountain stream, West Virginia provides a perfect blend of adventure and serenity.

The best season to RV in West Virginia is **spring through fall**, from **April to October**. **Spring** brings blooming wildflowers, fresh green landscapes, and perfect hiking conditions. **Summer** offers warm temperatures ideal for camping, rafting, and enjoying the state's many lakes and rivers. **Fall** is especially magical, as the state's forests burst into vibrant reds, oranges, and yellows, creating some of the most stunning autumn scenery in the country. **Winter**, while beautiful in the mountains, can bring snow and cold, making RVing more challenging unless you're equipped for winter conditions and want to enjoy skiing or snowboarding in the higher elevations.

West Virginia is home to the **New River Gorge National Park and Preserve**, the state's crown jewel for RVers. Known for its deep gorge and the iconic **New River Gorge Bridge**, this park offers spectacular views, world-class whitewater rafting, and countless hiking trails that lead through lush forests and to scenic overlooks. RV campgrounds near the gorge provide the perfect base for exploring this dramatic landscape and experiencing the thrill of adventure sports like rock climbing, zip-lining, and mountain biking.

For those seeking a more peaceful experience, the **Monongahela National Forest** offers a vast expanse of wilderness, with pristine streams, high-elevation forests, and quiet campgrounds tucked away in the mountains. The **Seneca Rocks** area is popular for both hikers and climbers, offering stunning views of the towering rock formations. **Dolly Sods Wilderness**, with its unique ecosystem and alpine-like environment, provides RVers with a remote and tranquil escape.

West Virginia is also rich in history and culture, with small towns that offer a glimpse into the past. **Harpers Ferry**, located at the confluence of the Potomac and Shenandoah rivers, is both a historic site and a beautiful natural area. RVers can explore the town's role in the Civil War, visit the **Harpers Ferry National Historical Park**, and hike a section of the **Appalachian Trail**.

The **Greenbrier River** and **Summersville Lake** are popular destinations for RVers who enjoy water activities. Whether you're fishing, kayaking, or simply enjoying the peaceful waters, the campgrounds near these bodies of water provide a relaxing retreat surrounded by nature.

West Virginia's campgrounds range from well-equipped RV parks to rustic sites in state and national forests. Whether you're camping by a river, nestled in the mountains, or near one of the state's scenic byways, West Virginia's campgrounds provide an ideal starting point for exploring the beauty of the state.

For RVers seeking rugged landscapes, outdoor adventure, and a deep connection to nature, West Virginia offers a truly immersive experience. Whether you're rafting down the New River, hiking to a mountaintop vista, or simply enjoying the tranquility of a mountain stream, West Virginia is a state that invites you to explore and savor its untamed beauty.

Cacapon Resort State Park Campground

818 Cacapon Lodge Dr, Berkeley Springs, WV 25411

(304) 258-1022   — $

Campground Description:

A peaceful retreat in the Appalachian foothills, offering activities like hiking, golfing, fishing, and swimming, perfect for families and outdoor enthusiasts.

Types of Sites Available:
- Tent sites
- RV sites (no hookups)

Amenities:
- Restrooms and showers
- Swimming beach
- Hiking trails

Activities:
- Swimming and fishing at Cacapon Lake
- Hiking and wildlife watching

Unique Experiences: Enjoy the beautiful Appalachian surroundings with scenic trails and lake activities in a tranquil environment.

Feedback: Guests appreciate the peaceful setting, clean facilities, and the variety of activities available.

Blackwater Falls State Park Campground

1584 Blackwater Lodge Rd, Davis, WV 26260

(304) 259-5216   — $

Campground Description:

A scenic campground located near the famous Blackwater Falls, offering a peaceful mountain setting with year-round outdoor activities.

Types of Sites Available:
- RV sites with electric hookups
- Tent sites

Amenities:
- Restrooms and showers
- Hiking trails
- Picnic areas

Activities:
- Hiking to Blackwater Falls
- Cross-country skiing in winter

Unique Experiences: Camp near the iconic Blackwater Falls and enjoy hiking, fishing, and scenic views year-round.

Feedback: Guests love the proximity to the falls, clean facilities, and the park's natural beauty.

Holly River State Park Campground

680 State Park Rd, Hacker Valley, WV 26222

(304) 493-6353 — $

Campground Description:

A secluded campground in central West Virginia, offering access to waterfalls, hiking trails, and natural swimming holes.

Types of Sites Available:
- RV sites with electric hookups
- Tent sites

Amenities:
- Restrooms and showers
- Picnic areas
- Swimming pool

Activities:
- Hiking and swimming in natural pools
- Fishing in nearby streams

Unique Experiences: Explore scenic waterfalls and enjoy the tranquility of the forest in one of West Virginia's largest state parks.

Feedback: Guests enjoy the peaceful setting, well-maintained trails, and variety of outdoor activities.

Pipestem Resort State Park Campground

3405 Pipestem Dr, Pipestem, WV 25979

(304) 466-1800 — $$

Campground Description:

A large resort park offering luxury camping with access to outdoor activities such as hiking, golfing, and zip-lining in the scenic Appalachian Mountains.

Types of Sites Available:
- RV sites with full or partial hookups
- Tent sites

Amenities:
- Restrooms and showers
- Swimming pool
- Golf course

Activities:
- Zip-lining and hiking
- Swimming and fishing

Unique Experiences: Enjoy both relaxation and adventure with zip-lining, scenic overlooks, and access to the Bluestone River.

Feedback: Guests appreciate the wide range of activities and clean facilities, making it ideal for families and adventure seekers.

Bluestone State Park Campground

Address: 78 Summers County Rte 14, Hinton, WV 25951

Campground Description:
A serene campground located near Bluestone Lake, offering peaceful camping with stunning lake views.
Unique Experience: Enjoy camping by the lake with opportunities for fishing, boating, and wildlife watching.

Amenities:
• Restrooms
• Picnic areas

Activities:
• Fishing
• Boating

Greenbrier State Forest Campground

Address: 1541 Harts Run Rd, Caldwell, WV 24925

Campground Description:
A quiet forested campground nestled in Greenbrier State Forest, perfect for nature lovers seeking a peaceful escape.
Unique Experience: Camp surrounded by towering trees and explore the forest's scenic hiking and biking trails.

Amenities:
• Restrooms
• Fire pits

Activities:
• Hiking
• Biking

New River Gorge National Park (Summersville Lake Campground)

Address: 278 Summersville Lake Rd, Summersville, WV 26651

Campground Description:
A beautiful campground near Summersville Lake, offering easy access to New River Gorge National Park's famous cliffs and waterways.
Unique Experience: Experience world-class rock climbing, white-water rafting, and lake activities in a stunning natural setting.

Amenities:
• Restrooms
• Picnic areas

Activities:
• Rock climbing
• Boating

Harpers Ferry National Historical Park (Campgrounds near the park)

Address: 171 Shoreline Dr, Harpers Ferry, WV 25425

Campground Description:
Located near Harpers Ferry, this campground provides access to rich historical sites and scenic trails.
Unique Experience: Camp near historic Civil War landmarks and explore Harpers Ferry's hiking trails with stunning river views.

Amenities:
• Restrooms
• Fire pits

Activities:
• Historical tours
• Hiking

Boondocking

Monongahela National Forest

Address: West Virginia (various dispersed camping locations)

Campground Description:
A vast forest offering boondocking options, with access to rugged mountains, rivers, and diverse wildlife.

Unique Experience: Enjoy off-grid camping and explore the forest's extensive network of trails and scenic areas.

Amenities:
• Primitive sites
• Scenic views

Activities:
• Hiking
• Wildlife viewing

George Washington National Forest (West Virginia section)

Address: West Virginia (various dispersed camping locations)

Campground Description:
This national forest provides dispersed camping opportunities in remote areas with stunning mountain landscapes.

Unique Experience: Camp in solitude with access to hiking, fishing, and scenic drives through the Appalachian Mountains.

Amenities:
• Primitive sites
• Scenic views

Activities:
• Hiking
• Fishing

Others Campgrounds

• Stonewall Resort State Park Campground (Roanoke, WV)
• Seneca Shadows Campground (Seneca Rocks, WV)
• Tygart Lake State Park Campground (Grafton, WV)
• Mountwood Park Campground (Parkersburg, WV)
• North Bend State Park Campground (Cairo, WV)
• Watoga State Park Campground (Marlinton, WV)
• Kanawha State Forest Campground (Charleston, WV)
• Beech Fork State Park Campground (Barboursville, WV)
• Little Beaver State Park Campground (Beaver, WV)
• Chief Logan State Park Campground (Logan, WV)

Others Boondocking

• Spruce Knob (dispersed camping in Monongahela National Forest, WV)
• Dolly Sods Wilderness (dispersed camping sites, WV)
• Cranberry Wilderness (dispersed camping in the Monongahela National Forest, WV)
• Laurel Fork South Wilderness (dispersed camping in Monongahela National Forest, WV)
• Tea Creek Wildlife Management Area (dispersed camping, WV)

Others National Park

• New River Gorge National Park (Glade Creek Campground)
• Harpers Ferry National Historical Park (Camp Hill Campground)

Kentucky: Bluegrass Beauty and Adventure

Kentucky, with its rolling hills, lush forests, and world-famous bourbon, is a destination that offers a little bit of everything for RVers. Known as the "Bluegrass State," Kentucky combines southern hospitality with natural beauty, making it an ideal spot for those seeking outdoor adventure or simply a peaceful retreat. From the Appalachian Mountains in the east to the meandering rivers and horse country in the central region, Kentucky's diverse landscapes offer countless opportunities for exploration.

The best season to RV in Kentucky is **spring through fall**, from **April to October**. **Spring** is especially stunning, with the rolling hills turning a brilliant green and wildflowers blooming across the countryside. **Fall** is equally beautiful, with cooler temperatures and vibrant autumn colors painting the forests. **Summer** is perfect for outdoor activities, but it can get hot and humid, especially in the southern parts of the state. If you're comfortable with the warmth, it's a great time to explore the state's lakes, rivers, and forests. **The season to avoid** is **winter**, as it can be quite cold, particularly in the Appalachian region, and some campgrounds may close for the season due to weather conditions.

RVing in Kentucky means discovering a state full of natural wonders. One of the highlights is Mammoth Cave National Park, home to the world's longest cave system. Parking your RV nearby and taking a tour of the caves is an unforgettable experience. The state's horse country is another must-see, where the rolling bluegrass hills are dotted with some of the most beautiful horse farms in the world. And let's not forget about Kentucky's lakes and rivers—whether you're kayaking, fishing, or just enjoying a quiet day by the water, Kentucky's waterways provide endless relaxation and adventure.

The campgrounds in Kentucky are varied, from well-maintained state parks to more rustic sites in the heart of nature. Whether you're staying by one of the state's lakes, nestled in the foothills of the Appalachian Mountains, or relaxing in horse country, Kentucky's campgrounds offer a perfect mix of comfort and natural beauty. One of my favorite experiences is camping near Red River Gorge, where the stunning rock formations and hiking trails make for an incredible RV destination.

For those seeking a mix of history, adventure, and natural beauty, Kentucky is an ideal state to explore by RV. It's a place where you can enjoy a day at the races in Lexington, tour bourbon distilleries along the Bourbon Trail, or simply relax in one of the state's many beautiful parks. Wherever you go, Kentucky's charm and hospitality will make you feel right at home.

Kentucky Horse Park Campground

4089 Iron Works Pkwy, Lexington, KY 40511

(859) 259-4257 — $$

Campground Description:

Located in the heart of horse country, this campground is perfect for horse enthusiasts and families. It's close to the Kentucky Horse Park and offers modern amenities and scenic views.

Types of Sites Available:
- RV sites with electric and water hookups
- Tent camping sites
- Pull-through and back-in sites

Amenities:
- Seasonal swimming pool
- Hiking and biking trails
- Fishing ponds

Activities:
- Visiting the Kentucky Horse Park and its museums
- Exploring the Kentucky Horse Park and its museums
- Hiking and biking on scenic trails
- Fishing in the campground's ponds
- Relaxing by the swimming pool
- Visiting Lexington's famous horse farms

Unique Experiences: Guests can explore the world of horses while enjoying a peaceful campground near central Kentucky's attractions.

Feedback: Highly praised for its proximity to the Kentucky Horse Park, clean facilities, and family-friendly atmosphere.

4 Guys RV Park

472 L&E Railroad Pl, Stanton, KY 40380

(606) 663-4444 — $$

Campground Description:

This campground is located near Red River Gorge and Natural Bridge State Park, offering scenic surroundings and outdoor adventure for campers and families.

Types of Sites Available:
- RV sites with full hookups
- Tent camping sites

Amenities:
- Free Wi-Fi
- Playground and dog park
- Laundry facilities

Activities:
- Hiking and rock climbing in Red River Gorge
- Fishing and picnicking

Unique Experiences: Ideal for outdoor enthusiasts, this park provides easy access to hiking, climbing, and the stunning natural beauty of Kentucky.

Feedback: Guests love the clean facilities, friendly staff, and its convenient location near outdoor activities.

Ashland / Huntington West KOA Holiday

📍 80 KOA Lane, Argillite, KY 41121

📞 (606) 928-7600 $$

Campground Description:

A family-friendly campground in northeastern Kentucky, offering a peaceful setting with easy access to nearby attractions in Ashland and Huntington, WV. Guests can enjoy modern amenities and various outdoor activities, making it an ideal base for exploring the region or relaxing by the pool.

Types of Sites Available:
- RV sites with full hookups
- Tent camping sites
- Deluxe cabins and camping cabins

Amenities:
- Free Wi-Fi, restrooms, showers
- Seasonal swimming pool, mini-golf
- Fishing pond, playground

Activities:
- Swimming, mini-golf, and hiking
- Fishing in the pond
- Exploring nearby Ashland and Huntington

Unique Experiences: A peaceful and fun destination for families, with easy access to local attractions and plenty of on-site activities like mini-golf and fishing.

Feedback: Guests praise the friendly staff, clean facilities, and variety of activities, making it a favorite for families and travelers exploring Kentucky and West Virginia.

Callie's Lake and Campground

📍 5515 Campton Rd, Slade, KY 40376

📞 (606) 663-2291 $$

Campground Description:

Nestled in the heart of Red River Gorge, Callie's Lake and Campground offers a scenic escape for nature lovers, featuring a tranquil lake, spacious sites, and easy access to hiking, rock climbing, and fishing in the surrounding natural areas.

Types of Sites Available:
- RV sites with electric and water hookups
- Tent camping sites
- Cabin rentals

Amenities:
- Free Wi-Fi, restrooms, showers
- Lake for fishing, hiking trails nearby
- Picnic areas with BBQ grills

Activities:
- Fishing and relaxing by the lake
- Hiking and rock climbing in Red River Gorge
- Picnicking and stargazing

Unique Experiences: A serene lakeside retreat in a breathtaking natural setting, perfect for outdoor enthusiasts exploring Red River Gorge and Natural Bridge State Park.

Feedback: Visitors love the peaceful environment, friendly staff, and proximity to Red River Gorge, making it a favorite for nature lovers and families.

Elkhorn Creek RV Park

Address: 165 N Scruggs Ln, Frankfort, KY 40601

Campground Description:
A peaceful RV park located along Elkhorn Creek, offering a relaxing atmosphere with easy access to fishing and water activities.

Unique Experience: Enjoy fishing right from your campsite and the tranquility of Elkhorn Creek.

Amenities:
• Full RV hookups
• Fishing access

Activities:
• Fishing in Elkhorn Creek
• Kayaking

Duck Creek RV Park

Address: 2540 John Puryear Dr, Paducah, KY 42003

Campground Description:
A family-friendly RV park near downtown Paducah, providing modern amenities and a comfortable stay for all visitors.

Unique Experience: Stay close to Paducah's historic district while enjoying a peaceful camping experience.

Amenities:
• Full RV hookups
• Restrooms and showers

Activities:
• Visiting Paducah's downtown
• Walking trails nearby

Mammoth Cave National Park

Address: 1 Mammoth Cave Pkwy, Cave City, KY 42127

Campground Description:
Home to the world's longest cave system, Mammoth Cave National Park offers both tent and RV camping with access to incredible cave tours.

Unique Experience: Explore the depths of Mammoth Cave, one of the most extensive cave systems in the world.

Amenities:
• Restrooms and showers
• RV and tent sites

Activities:
• Cave tours
• Hiking

Natural Bridge State Resort Park

Address: 2135 Natural Bridge Rd, Slade, KY 40376

Campground Description:
A picturesque park known for its stunning natural sandstone arch, offering hiking and breathtaking views.

Unique Experience: Hike to the top of the Natural Bridge and take in panoramic views of the surrounding landscape.

Amenities:
• Restrooms and showers
• Picnic areas

Activities:
• Hiking to the Natural Bridge
• Wildlife watching

Daniel Boone National Forest

Address: 1700 Bypass Rd, Winchester, KY 40391

Campground Description:
A vast forest offering dispersed camping, perfect for those seeking a quiet, rustic experience surrounded by nature.
Unique Experience: Camp in the heart of the forest, surrounded by towering trees and untouched wilderness.

Amenities:
• Primitive campsites
• Vault toilets

Activities:
• Hiking
• Wildlife watching

Land Between the Lakes National Recreation Area

Address: 238 Visitor Center Dr, Golden Pond, KY 42211

Campground Description:
This expansive recreation area between Kentucky and Barkley lakes provides excellent opportunities for boondocking and exploring the outdoors.
Unique Experience: Enjoy boondocking in a stunning natural area with lakes on both sides.

Amenities:
• Primitive campsites
• Access to water activities

Activities:
• Fishing and boating
• Hiking

Others Campgrounds

• Taylorsville Lake State Park Campground (Taylorsville, KY)
• Levi Jackson Wilderness Road Park Campground (London, KY)
• Yatesville Lake State Park Campground (Louisa, KY)
• Paintsville Lake State Park Campground (Staffordsville, KY)
• Rough River Dam State Resort Park Campground (Falls of Rough, KY)
• General Butler State Resort Park Campground (Carrollton, KY)
• Kincaid Lake State Park Campground (Falmouth, KY)
• Blue Licks Battlefield State Resort Park Campground (Carlisle, KY)
• Nolin Lake State Park Campground (Mammoth Cave, KY)
• Pennyrile Forest State Resort Park Campground (Dawson Springs, KY)

Others Boondocking

• Peabody Wildlife Management Area
• Ballard Wildlife Management Area
• Lake Barkley Wildlife Management Area
• Sloughs Wildlife Management Area
• Big Rivers Wildlife Management Area & State Forest

Tennessee: A Land of Music and Mountains

Tennessee, with its rich musical heritage, stunning mountain landscapes, and vibrant cities, is a state that offers RVers a diverse range of experiences. Whether you're exploring the misty peaks of the **Great Smoky Mountains**, enjoying the rhythm of **Nashville's** live music scene, or discovering the peaceful beauty of the **Tennessee River Valley**, Tennessee is a state where history, culture, and nature come together to create unforgettable memories.

The best season to RV in Tennessee is **spring through fall**, from **April to October**. **Spring** brings blooming wildflowers and cool temperatures, making it a perfect time to explore the state's parks and scenic drives. **Fall** is a highlight for RVers, as the state's forests and mountains burst into brilliant colors, especially in the **Smokies**. **Summer** is ideal for water activities and outdoor adventures, though it can get humid, especially in the central and western regions. **Winter** in Tennessee is relatively mild, particularly in the lowlands, though the higher elevations of the **Smoky Mountains** can see snow, offering a different kind of adventure for winter RVers.

For nature lovers, **Great Smoky Mountains National Park** is the crown jewel of Tennessee. The park is home to mist-covered peaks, cascading waterfalls, and hundreds of miles of hiking trails, offering plenty of opportunities for adventure. There are several RV-friendly campgrounds in and around the park, allowing you to enjoy the natural beauty and peaceful serenity of the Smokies while having easy access to wildlife viewing, scenic drives, and outdoor activities.

Tennessee's vibrant cities are also a big draw for RVers. **Nashville**, known as the "Music City," is famous for its live music venues, including the legendary **Grand Ole Opry** and the honky-tonks along **Broadway**. RVers can camp near the city and immerse themselves in its rich musical culture, while also enjoying its Southern hospitality and great food. **Memphis**, home of the blues and **Graceland**, the legendary home of Elvis Presley, is another must-see for those interested in music history.

For a quieter experience, the **Tennessee River Valley** offers scenic byways, peaceful lakes, and charming small towns. RVers can camp along the riverbanks, enjoy fishing or boating, and take in the beauty of the rolling hills and tranquil waters. **Chickamauga Lake** and **Percy Priest Lake** are popular destinations for water sports, with campgrounds that offer lakefront views and easy access to outdoor activities.

Tennessee's campgrounds range from full-service RV parks to more rustic, nature-focused spots in state parks and national forests. Whether you're camping by a lake, in the mountains, or near one of the state's cultural hubs, Tennessee offers a variety of options for every type of traveler.

For RVers seeking a mix of outdoor adventure, rich musical history, and Southern charm, Tennessee is a state that truly has it all. Whether you're hiking in the Smokies, enjoying live music in Nashville, or relaxing by a peaceful river, Tennessee provides an RV experience that's as diverse as it is unforgettable.

Nashville KOA

📍 2626 Music Valley Dr, Nashville, TN 37214

📞 (615) 889-0282 — $$

Campground Description:

Located near downtown Nashville, this upscale KOA offers modern amenities and easy access to attractions like the Grand Ole Opry and Broadway, making it a great base for exploring Music City.

Types of Sites Available:
- RV sites with full hookups
- Tent camping sites
- Cabin rentals

Amenities:
- Swimming pool and hot tub
- Fitness center
- Shuttle to downtown Nashville

Activities:
- Swimming and relaxing by the pool
- Exploring Nashville's famous attractions
- Attending organized events at the campground

Unique Experiences: This KOA offers a convenient mix of luxury camping and proximity to Nashville's vibrant music and cultural scene.

Feedback: Praised for its clean facilities, friendly staff, and location near downtown, it's a favorite for those visiting Nashville.

Gatlinburg East / Smoky Mountain KOA

📍 4874 Hooper Hwy, Cosby, TN 37722

📞 (423) 487-5534 — $$

Campground Description:

Nestled near the Great Smoky Mountains National Park, this KOA offers a peaceful retreat with access to hiking trails, waterfalls, and Gatlinburg attractions, perfect for nature lovers and adventurers.

Types of Sites Available:
- RV sites with full hookups
- Tent camping sites
- Cabin rentals

Amenities:
- Swimming pool
- Playground
- Dog park

Activities:
- Hiking in the Great Smoky Mountains
- Swimming and relaxing by the pool
- Visiting Gatlinburg and Pigeon Forge

Unique Experiences: This KOA combines outdoor adventure with easy access to local attractions, making it ideal for both relaxation and exploration.

Feedback: Praised for its scenic setting, friendly staff, and proximity to the Smoky Mountains, it's a top choice for nature enthusiasts.

Pigeon Forge / Gatlinburg KOA

3122 Veterans Blvd, Pigeon Forge, TN 37863

(865) 453-7903 — $$

Campground Description:

Located near Dollywood and the Great Smoky Mountains, this KOA provides family-friendly amenities and a convenient base for exploring Pigeon Forge and Gatlinburg attractions.

Types of Sites Available:
- RV sites with full hookups
- Tent camping sites
- Cabin rentals

Amenities:
- Swimming pool and hot tub
- Mini-golf course
- Shuttle to local attractions

Activities:
- Swimming and playing mini-golf
- Visiting Dollywood and the Smoky Mountains
- Enjoying local shops and restaurants

Unique Experiences: With on-site activities and proximity to popular attractions, this KOA offers both fun and convenience for families.

Feedback: Guests love the clean facilities, helpful staff, and easy access to Dollywood and the Smoky Mountains.

Lake Livingston State Park

300 Park Road 65, Livingston, TX 77351

(936) 365-2201 — $

Campground Description:

Located on the shores of Lake Livingston, this state park offers a tranquil lakeside camping experience with opportunities for boating, fishing, and hiking.

Types of Sites Available:
- RV sites with full hookups
- Tent camping sites

Amenities:
- Fishing piers and boat ramps
- Swimming pool
- Hiking trails

Activities:
- Boating and fishing on Lake Livingston
- Hiking and birdwatching
- Swimming and picnicking

Unique Experiences: This state park provides a peaceful lakeside retreat, perfect for outdoor recreation and nature appreciation.

Feedback: Guests love the clean facilities, spacious campsites, and excellent access to water activities, making it a popular choice for family getaways.

The River's Edge Campground

Address: 1930 S Main St, Hendersonville, TN 37075

Campground Description:
A peaceful riverside campground offering shaded sites along the Cumberland River, perfect for nature lovers and anglers.

Unique Experience: Enjoy serene river views and excellent fishing opportunities in a quiet, wooded setting.

Amenities:
• Full hookups
• River access

Activities:
• Fishing
• Boating

Tims Ford State Park Campground

Address: 570 Tims Ford Dr, Winchester, TN 37398

Campground Description:
A scenic campground located along the shores of Tims Ford Lake, offering a great spot for water activities and hiking.

Unique Experience: Camp lakeside and explore miles of hiking trails with panoramic views of Tims Ford Lake.

Amenities:
• Electric and water hookups
• Bathhouse

Activities:
• Boating
• Hiking

Great Smoky Mountains National Park (Elkmont Campground)

Address: 434 Elkmont Rd, Gatlinburg, TN 37738

Campground Description:
Nestled in the heart of the Smokies, Elkmont Campground offers forested sites with easy access to hiking trails and historic areas.

Unique Experience: Camp under the canopy of the Smoky Mountains with close proximity to some of the park's most scenic trails and wildlife.

Amenities:
• Restrooms
• Picnic tables

Activities:
• Hiking
• Wildlife viewing

Norris Dam State Park Campground

Address: 125 Village Green Cir, Lake City, TN 37769

Campground Description:
A tranquil campground offering lakefront sites and access to Norris Lake for fishing and water sports.

Unique Experience: Enjoy peaceful lakefront camping with the backdrop of Norris Dam and the surrounding forest.

Amenities:
• Electric hookups
• Restrooms

Activities:
• Boating
• Fishing

Cherokee National Forest

Address: 2800 Ocoee St N, Cleveland, TN 37312

Campground Description:
A sprawling national forest offering dispersed camping with access to hiking, waterfalls, and stunning mountain views.

Unique Experience: Experience solitude in the Appalachian Mountains with abundant wildlife and scenic hiking trails.

Amenities:
• Primitive sites
• Hiking trails

Activities:
• Hiking
• Wildlife viewing

Land Between the Lakes National Recreation Area

Address: 238 Visitor Center Dr, Golden Pond, KY 42211

Campground Description:
A vast recreation area offering dispersed camping, water activities, and over 170,000 acres of forest to explore.

Unique Experience: Camp in a remote area surrounded by forests, lakes, and abundant wildlife in a peaceful, natural setting.

Amenities:
• Primitive sites
• Scenic overlooks

Activities:
• Boating
• Wildlife watching

Others Campgrounds

• Townsend / Great Smokies KOA Holiday (Townsend, TN)
• Pine Mountain RV Park (Pigeon Forge, TN)
• Anchor Down RV Resort (Dandridge, TN)
• Two Rivers Landing RV Resort (Sevierville, TN)
• Misty River Cabins & RV Resort (Walland, TN)
• Whispering River Resort (Walland, TN)
• Jellystone Park at Nashville (Nashville, TN)
• Sweetwater KOA Holiday (Sweetwater, TN)
• Clarksville RV Park & Campground (Clarksville, TN)
• Deer Run RV Resort (Crossville, TN)

Others Boondocking

• Prentice Cooper State Forest (Chattanooga, TN)
• North Cumberland Wildlife Management Area (Caryville, TN)
• Cherokee National Forest (various areas)
• Hatchie National Wildlife Refuge (Brownsville, TN)
• Big South Fork National River and Recreation Area (Jamestown, TN)

North Carolina: From Mountains to Coast, A Diverse Playground

North Carolina is a state of stunning contrasts, offering RVers the best of both mountains and coastlines. Whether you're winding through the misty peaks of the **Blue Ridge Mountains**, exploring the historic towns of the **Piedmont**, or basking in the sun on the beaches of the **Outer Banks**, North Carolina provides an incredible variety of landscapes and outdoor activities. For RVers who want to experience both rugged wilderness and serene seascapes, this state is an unbeatable destination.

The best season to RV in North Carolina is **spring through fall**, from **April to October**. **Spring** brings mild temperatures and blooming wildflowers, making it the perfect time to explore the state's parks and scenic byways. **Fall** is perhaps the most beautiful time to visit, especially in the **Blue Ridge Mountains**, where the autumn foliage creates a stunning tapestry of reds, oranges, and golds. **Summer** is ideal for beach lovers, with warm, sunny days along the coast, although it can get hot and humid in some inland areas. **Winter**, especially in the higher elevations of the mountains, can bring snow and cold, making RVing more challenging, but the milder temperatures along the coast provide a great escape from northern winters.

For mountain lovers, **Western North Carolina** is a dream come true. The **Blue Ridge Parkway**, one of the most scenic drives in the country, offers breathtaking views and access to numerous campgrounds nestled in the mountains. **Great Smoky Mountains National Park** is another highlight, offering stunning trails, wildlife viewing, and RV camping in the heart of the Appalachians. Whether you're hiking to waterfalls, exploring mountain towns like **Asheville**, or simply enjoying the peace of the forests, the western part of the state is a paradise for outdoor enthusiasts.

On the other side of the state, the **Outer Banks** offer a completely different kind of experience. This string of barrier islands, with their pristine beaches, historic lighthouses, and charming coastal villages, is a perfect spot for RVers seeking sun and sea. You can camp just steps from the Atlantic Ocean and explore historic sites like the **Wright Brothers National Memorial** in **Kitty Hawk**, or visit the **Cape Hatteras National Seashore**, known for its beautiful beaches and iconic lighthouse.

North Carolina's **Piedmont** region, located between the mountains and the coast, offers rolling hills, vibrant cities, and historic towns. **Raleigh**, **Durham**, and **Chapel Hill** make up the **Research Triangle**, a cultural hub with plenty of museums, parks, and restaurants to explore. For RVers, this region is a perfect blend of urban and rural, with plenty of campgrounds near lakes and rivers.

North Carolina's campgrounds are as varied as its landscapes. From the high-elevation sites in the mountains to the coastal spots near the Atlantic, RVers will find plenty of options to suit their style. The state's well-maintained parks, such as **Mount Mitchell State Park** and **Carolina Beach State Park**, offer excellent camping facilities with access to hiking, fishing, and scenic views.

Whether you're exploring the high peaks of the Smokies, relaxing on the beaches of the Outer Banks, or discovering the charm of small towns and rolling hills, North Carolina offers something for every kind of RVer. It's a state where you can experience the beauty of nature in all its forms, from the mountains to the sea.

Lakewood RV Resort

📍 59 Resort Lane, Flat Rock, NC 28731

📞 (828) 697-9523 — $$

Campground Description:

Lakewood RV Resort in Flat Rock, NC, offers an adult-oriented, peaceful retreat surrounded by the Blue Ridge Mountains. The resort features spacious RV sites and a range of modern amenities, perfect for travelers seeking relaxation and mountain serenity. Its proximity to Hendersonville and Asheville provides easy access to dining, shopping, and local attractions.

Types of Sites Available:
- RV sites with full hookups
- Pull-through and back-in sites

Amenities:
- Free Wi-Fi and cable TV
- Heated pool and hot tub
- Recreation hall and game room
- Dog park and pet-friendly areas

Activities:
- Relaxing by the heated pool and hot tub
- Exploring nearby Dupont State Forest and Chimney Rock State Park
- Attending organized social events

Unique Experiences: A peaceful adult-oriented RV resort, perfect for retirees and travelers looking for mountain serenity combined with modern conveniences.

Feedback: Guests appreciate the adult-focused, relaxing atmosphere and convenient location near outdoor attractions.

Asheville's Bear Creek RV Park & Campground

📍 81 S Bear Creek Rd, Asheville, NC 28806

📞 (828) 253-0798 — $$

Campground Description:

Located near Asheville, NC, Bear Creek RV Park offers a scenic camping experience with easy access to the Blue Ridge Mountains and Asheville's vibrant downtown. With modern amenities and a peaceful setting, the campground is ideal for those seeking a mix of outdoor adventure and city exploration.

Types of Sites Available:
- RV sites with full hookups
- Tent camping sites

Amenities:
- Free Wi-Fi and cable TV
- Heated pool
- Recreation room
- Dog park

Activities:
- Visiting Asheville's downtown shops and restaurants
- Hiking in Pisgah National Forest

Unique Experiences: A perfect base for exploring the Blue Ridge Parkway, Biltmore Estate, and Asheville's arts and music scene.

Feedback: Praised for its convenient location and well-maintained facilities, Bear Creek is a top choice for RVers exploring Asheville.

Carolina Pines RV Resort

5800 SC-90, Conway, SC 29526

(843) 896-0700 $$

Campground Description:

Carolina Pines RV Resort is a luxury camping destination near Myrtle Beach, offering top-tier amenities, including a water park, miniature golf, and organized activities. With spacious RV sites and on-site dining, this resort provides a fun and relaxing atmosphere for families, couples, and groups.

Types of Sites Available:
- RV sites with full hookups
- Cottage rentals

Amenities:
- Free Wi-Fi and cable TV
- Water park and lazy river
- Fitness center and on-site dining
- Shuttle service to Myrtle Beach

Activities:
- Swimming in the water park and lazy river
- Visiting Myrtle Beach's boardwalk

Unique Experiences: A luxurious RV resort combining relaxation and adventure, with easy access to Myrtle Beach's attractions.

Feedback: Guests love the upscale amenities and variety of activities, making it a favorite for family vacations.

Great Smoky Mountains KOA (Cherokee, NC)

92 KOA Campground Rd, Cherokee, NC 28719

(828) 497-9711 $$

Campground Description:

Located near the Great Smoky Mountains National Park, this KOA campground offers a family-friendly camping experience with access to outdoor adventures and cultural attractions in the Cherokee Indian Reservation. The campground features RV sites, cabins, and tent camping.

Types of Sites Available:
- RV sites with full hookups
- Tent camping sites
- Deluxe cabins

Amenities:
- Free Wi-Fi and cable TV
- Swimming pool and hot tub
- Playground and splash pad
- Fishing and tubing in the Oconaluftee River

Activities:
- Exploring Great Smoky Mountains National Park
- Tubing and fishing in the river

Unique Experiences:
A scenic base for outdoor enthusiasts and families, with opportunities to experience Cherokee culture and nature.
Feedback:
Praised for its friendly staff and access to outdoor recreation, this KOA is a popular choice for nature lovers.

Creekwood Farm RV Park

Address: 4696 Jonathan Creek Rd, Waynesville, NC 28785

Campground Description:
Nestled alongside a creek in the mountains, Creekwood Farm RV Park offers a peaceful, rural setting with spacious sites and friendly service.
Unique Experience: Relax by the creek while enjoying the scenic mountain views.

Amenities:
• Full hookups
• Restrooms and showers

Activities:
• Hiking nearby
• Fishing

Grandfather Campground

Address: 125 Riverside Dr, Banner Elk, NC 28604

Campground Description:
A serene, family-friendly campground located at the base of Grandfather Mountain, offering riverfront sites and easy access to outdoor adventures.
Unique Experience: Camp along the river and explore the famous Grandfather Mountain trails.

Amenities:
• Full hookups
• Restrooms

Activities:
• Hiking
• Fishing

Great Smoky Mountains National Park

Address: 107 Park Headquarters Rd, Gatlinburg, TN 37738 (Access from North Carolina side)

Campground Description:
The most visited national park in the U.S., the Great Smoky Mountains offers diverse wildlife, lush forests, and numerous camping options.
Unique Experience: Discover stunning mountain views, old-growth forests, and historic structures.

Amenities:
• Restrooms
• Picnic areas

Activities:
• Hiking
• Wildlife viewing

Carolina Beach State Park

Address: 1010 State Park Rd, Carolina Beach, NC 28428

Campground Description:
Located along the Cape Fear River, this state park offers excellent camping with easy access to the beach, trails, and fishing spots.
Unique Experience: Explore coastal ecosystems and the famous Venus flytrap in its natural habitat.

Amenities:
• Restrooms
• Boat ramp

Activities:
• Hiking
• Fishing

Boondocking

Pisgah National Forest

Address: 1600 Pisgah Hwy, Pisgah Forest, NC 28768

Campground Description:
Pisgah National Forest offers dispersed camping in a stunning forested area with waterfalls, trails, and beautiful mountain views.

Unique Experience: Camp near waterfalls and explore the iconic Blue Ridge Parkway.

Amenities:
• Primitive campsites
• Access to trails

Activities:
• Hiking
• Wildlife watching

Nantahala National Forest

Address: 160 Zillicoa St, Asheville, NC 28801

Campground Description:
Dispersed camping opportunities abound in the Nantahala National Forest, with access to rivers, trails, and scenic mountain views.

Unique Experience: Experience solitude and adventure in the Appalachian Mountains.

Amenities:
• Primitive campsites
• Access to rivers

Activities:
• Canoeing
• Hiking

Others Campgrounds

• Crosswinds Family Campground (Linwood, NC)
• Indian Springs Campground (Hickory, NC)
• Hiddenite Family Campground (Hiddenite, NC)
• Moonshine Creek Campground (Sylva, NC)
• Deep Creek Tube Center & Campground (Bryson City, NC)
• Yogi Bear's Jellystone Park™ Campground (Tabor City, NC)
• Julian Price Campground (Blowing Rock, NC)
• Jones Station RV Park (Mebane, NC)
• Holly Bluff Family Campground (Asheboro, NC)
• Goose Creek Resort (Newport, NC)

Others Boondocking

• Uwharrie National Forest (dispersed camping areas)
• Croatan National Forest (dispersed camping areas)
• Linville Gorge Wilderness Area
• Nantahala Gorge (dispersed camping)
• Badin Lake (Uwharrie National Forest, dispersed camping)

Others National Park

• Cape Hatteras National Seashore (Oregon Inlet Campground)
• Blue Ridge Parkway (Doughton Park Campground)

South Carolina: Southern Charm and Coastal Beauty

South Carolina, with its rich history, stunning coastlines, and Southern hospitality, offers RVers a mix of adventure and relaxation in one of the most beautiful states in the Southeast. Whether you're exploring the historic streets of **Charleston**, camping by the beaches of the **Grand Strand**, or hiking through the **Blue Ridge Mountains**, South Carolina is a destination that appeals to travelers looking for both natural beauty and cultural heritage.

The best season to RV in South Carolina is **spring and fall**, from **March to May** and **September to November**. **Spring** brings mild temperatures and blooming gardens, making it a perfect time to explore the state's coastal towns and scenic parks. **Fall** offers cooler weather and vibrant foliage, especially in the **Upstate** region near the mountains. **Summer** can be hot and humid, particularly along the coast, but if you enjoy warm beach days and water activities, it's a great time to visit. **Winter** is mild, particularly in the southern parts of the state, making it a popular off-season destination for RVers seeking to escape colder northern climates.

For coastal lovers, South Carolina's **Grand Strand** offers miles of sandy beaches and charming seaside towns. **Myrtle Beach**, one of the most popular destinations, has numerous RV parks that put you just steps away from the ocean, entertainment, and outdoor activities. For a quieter coastal experience, **Huntington Beach State Park** near **Murrells Inlet** offers pristine beaches, marshes, and hiking trails, providing a peaceful retreat with plenty of wildlife to observe.

History buffs will love exploring **Charleston**, a city known for its well-preserved architecture, cobblestone streets, and rich history. RVers can stay at nearby campgrounds and take day trips into the city to enjoy historical tours, Southern cuisine, and visits to sites like **Fort Sumter**, where the first shots of the Civil War were fired.

The **Upstate** region, in the northwestern part of South Carolina, offers a completely different landscape, with rolling hills, waterfalls, and access to the **Blue Ridge Mountains**. **Table Rock State Park** and **Caesars Head State Park** are popular spots for RVers who enjoy hiking, fishing, and camping in the mountains. The scenic byways and peaceful campgrounds in this region offer a serene escape from the busier coastal areas.

South Carolina's campgrounds are varied and welcoming, from full-service RV resorts along the coast to more rustic, nature-focused campgrounds in the mountains and forests. Whether you're camping by the beach, exploring historic towns, or enjoying the beauty of the state parks, South Carolina offers a perfect mix of culture and nature.

For RVers seeking Southern charm, coastal beauty, and outdoor adventure, South Carolina is a state that has it all. Whether you're basking in the sun on the Grand Strand or exploring the mountain trails of the Upstate, South Carolina offers an unforgettable RV experience that blends history, hospitality, and scenic beauty.

Lakewood Camping Resort

📍 5901 S Kings Hwy, Myrtle Beach, SC 29575

📞 (843) 238-5161　　　—　　$$

Campground Description:

Located along Myrtle Beach, this family-friendly resort offers beachfront camping with access to a waterpark, beach, and organized events, providing a perfect blend of relaxation and fun.

Types of Sites Available:
- RV sites with full hookups
- Tent camping sites
- Cabin and villa rentals

Amenities:
- Waterpark and pools
- Direct beach access
- Mini-golf course

Activities:
- Swimming at the beach and waterpark
- Playing mini-golf and attending family-friendly events
- Exploring Myrtle Beach attractions

Unique Experiences: With its beachfront access, waterpark, and organized events, this resort offers an ideal mix of entertainment and relaxation for families.

Feedback: Praised for its clean facilities, friendly staff, and variety of activities, it's a favorite for family vacations.

Ocean Lakes Family Campground

📍 6001 S Kings Hwy, Myrtle Beach, SC 29575

📞 (843) 238-5636　　　—　　$$

Campground Description:

This massive oceanfront campground offers direct beach access, multiple pools, and a range of amenities, making it one of the most popular destinations on the East Coast.

Types of Sites Available:
- RV sites with full hookups
- Tent camping sites
- Vacation home rentals

Amenities:
- Waterpark with lazy river
- Golf cart rentals
- Fishing lakes

Activities:
- Swimming in pools and waterpark
- Exploring Myrtle Beach boardwalk and local attractions
- Attending organized events like concerts and festivals

Unique Experiences: With beachfront access and family-friendly amenities, Ocean Lakes provides a fun-filled camping experience along the coast.

Feedback: Guests love the waterpark, beach access, and family-friendly atmosphere, making it a top choice for vacationers.

Carolina Pines RV Resort

📍 5800 SC-90, Conway, SC 29526

📞 (843) 896-0700 — $$

Campground Description:

This luxury RV resort in Conway offers a variety of upscale amenities, including a water park, mini-golf, and sports courts, with shuttle access to nearby Myrtle Beach.

Types of Sites Available:
- RV sites with full hookups
- Cabin rentals

Amenities:
- Waterpark and lazy river
- Fitness center and sports courts
- Shuttle service to Myrtle Beach

Activities:
- Swimming in the water park
- Playing mini-golf and attending events
- Exploring local attractions and beaches

Unique Experiences: Carolina Pines provides a luxurious camping experience with resort-style amenities and easy access to Myrtle Beach.

Feedback: Praised for its clean facilities and variety of activities, it's a favorite for families seeking both relaxation and adventure.

Hilton Head Harbor RV Resort & Marina

📍 43 Jenkins Rd, Hilton Head Island, SC 29926

📞 (843) 681-3256 — $$$

Campground Description:

This luxury RV resort on Hilton Head Island offers a waterfront setting with marina access, perfect for boating and fishing enthusiasts, while providing upscale amenities.

Types of Sites Available:
- RV sites with full hookups
- Waterfront and non-waterfront sites

Amenities:
- Marina with boat slips
- Two pools and a hot tub
- On-site restaurant

Activities:
- Boating and fishing from the marina
- Swimming and relaxing by the pools
- Exploring Hilton Head's beaches and golf courses

Unique Experiences: Offering waterfront views, marina access, and upscale facilities, this resort is perfect for a luxurious island getaway.

Feedback: Guests love the marina access, pools, and on-site dining, making it a top destination for a high-end RV experience.

HIDDEN GEMS

Little Cedar Creek Campground

Address: 1630 Cedar Creek Rd, Ridgeway, SC 29130

Campground Description:
A quiet, family-friendly campground surrounded by nature, offering a peaceful retreat away from the hustle and bustle.

Unique Experience: Enjoy serene camping near a picturesque creek, perfect for relaxing and enjoying the outdoors.

Amenities:
• Restrooms
• Fishing pond

Activities:
• Fishing
• Nature walks

Oak Plantation Campground

Address: 3540 Savannah Hwy, Charleston, SC 29455

Campground Description:
A charming campground close to Charleston, offering easy access to the city's attractions while nestled in a peaceful natural setting.

Unique Experience: Relax in a tranquil environment while being just minutes from Charleston's rich history and beaches.

Amenities:
• Full hookups
• Laundry facilities

Activities:
• Exploring Charleston
• Birdwatching

NATIONAL PARKS

Hunting Island State Park

Address: 2555 Sea Island Pkwy, Hunting Island, SC 29920

Campground Description:
A scenic coastal park offering beachfront camping with miles of sandy shores and lush forests.

Unique Experience: Camp right by the beach and enjoy the stunning sunrise over the Atlantic Ocean.

Amenities:
• Beach access
• Restrooms

Activities:
• Beachcombing
• Fishing

Paris Mountain State Park

Address: 2401 State Park Rd, Greenville, SC 29609

Campground Description:
A peaceful park located near Greenville, offering hiking trails, fishing spots, and beautiful views of the mountains.

Unique Experience: Hike through the scenic mountain trails and discover peaceful lakes nestled in the forest.

Amenities:
• Restrooms
• Picnic shelters

Activities:
• Hiking
• Fishing

Boondocking

Francis Marion National Forest

Address: 2967 Steed Creek Rd, Huger, SC 29450

Campground Description:
A large national forest offering plenty of dispersed camping opportunities amidst scenic woodlands and waterways.

Unique Experience: Camp in solitude surrounded by the diverse ecosystems of South Carolina's lowcountry.

Amenities:
• Primitive sites
• Hiking trails

Activities:
• Wildlife viewing
• Hiking

Sumter National Forest

Address: 4931 Broad River Rd, Columbia, SC 29212

Campground Description:
A vast national forest with designated boondocking areas, ideal for those seeking a quiet escape into nature.

Unique Experience: Explore miles of trails through forests and streams, perfect for primitive camping enthusiasts.

Amenities:
• Primitive sites
• Scenic trails

Activities:
• Hiking
• Birdwatching

Others Campgrounds

• Briarcliffe RV Resort (Myrtle Beach, SC)
• Apache Family Campground & Pier (Myrtle Beach, SC)
• Myrtle Beach KOA Resort (Myrtle Beach, SC)
• Lake Jasper RV Village (Hardeeville, SC)
• Barnyard RV Park (Lexington, SC)
• Magnolia RV Park and Campground (Kinards, SC)
• The Oaks at Point South RV Resort (Yemassee, SC)
• Cheraw State Park Campground (Cheraw, SC)
• Croft State Park Campground (Spartanburg, SC)
• Hamilton Branch State Park Campground (Plum Branch, SC)

Others Boondocking

• Santee Coastal Reserve WMA (McClellanville, SC)
• Wambaw Cycle Trail (Cordesville, SC)
• H. Cooper Black Jr. Memorial Field Trial Area (Cheraw, SC)
• Manchester State Forest (Wedgefield, SC)
• Pee Dee WMA (Florence, SC)

Georgia: Southern Charm and Scenic Beauty

Georgia is a state where hospitality, history, and natural beauty come together in perfect harmony. As an RVer, you'll find a warm welcome at every turn, along with some of the most scenic landscapes the South has to offer. From the rolling Blue Ridge Mountains in the north to the coastal marshlands along the Atlantic, Georgia is a state that offers a rich variety of experiences, all easily accessible by RV.

The best season to explore Georgia in an RV is **spring and fall**, from **March to May** and **September to November**. In the spring, Georgia bursts into bloom, with azaleas and dogwoods lining the roads and parks, making it a picture-perfect time to hit the road. **Fall** brings cooler temperatures and vibrant foliage, especially in the northern part of the state where the Blue Ridge Mountains put on a stunning display of color. **Summer**, particularly **June through August**, can be hot and humid, especially in the southern and coastal regions, so it's best to avoid the peak summer months unless you're staying near water or well-shaded areas. **Winter** is mild in most parts of the state, but the mountains can get quite chilly, so it's worth checking conditions if you plan to head north.

What I love about RVing in Georgia is the diversity of experiences available in one state. One day you can be exploring the historic streets of Savannah, where the Spanish moss drapes the trees, and the next day you're hiking through the misty mountains of northern Georgia. For those who love outdoor adventures, Georgia is full of surprises—whether it's camping by a peaceful lake, paddling down a winding river, or setting up camp in one of the many state parks that offer excellent RV facilities.

Georgia's campgrounds are as varied as the landscape itself. In the north, you'll find mountain retreats with stunning views, while along the coast, you can park your RV within walking distance of the beach. State parks like Tallulah Gorge and Cloudland Canyon offer some of the best RV camping in the region, with miles of hiking trails, waterfalls, and wildlife to enjoy. And if you're a history buff, don't miss a stop at some of Georgia's Civil War battlefields and historic towns.

For me, Georgia always feels like home. There's something about the laid-back pace, the warmth of the people, and the natural beauty that makes RVing here such a relaxing and rewarding experience. Whether you're chasing the changing leaves in the fall or soaking up the sun along the coast in the spring, Georgia is a state that welcomes RVers with open arms and endless opportunities for adventure.

Talona Ridge RV Resort

723 Highland Pkwy, East Ellijay, GA 30540

(706) 515-1120 — $$

Campground Description:

Located in the scenic mountains of East Ellijay, this luxury RV resort offers stunning views of the Appalachian foothills and spacious sites with top-tier amenities.

Types of Sites Available:

- Full hookup RV sites
- Premium and terrace sites

Amenities:

- Heated pool, Wi-Fi, fitness center
- Fire pits, clubhouse, dog park
- Laundry facilities

Activities:

- Hiking, fishing, and kayaking nearby
- Exploring apple orchards and wineries
- Relaxing by the heated pool

Unique Experiences: Breathtaking mountain views, modern amenities, and proximity to Ellijay's orchards and nature trails.

Feedback: Highly rated for its clean facilities, stunning views, and luxurious mountain escape.

River's End Campground and RV Resort

5 Fort Ave, Tybee Island, GA 31328

(912) 786-5518 — $$

Campground Description:

Located on Tybee Island, this coastal campground offers a friendly atmosphere, proximity to the beach, and easy access to nearby Savannah.

Types of Sites Available:

- Full hookup RV sites
- Tent camping and cabin rentals

Amenities:

- Swimming pool, Wi-Fi, dog park
- Camp store, laundry facilities
- Picnic areas with BBQ grills

Activities:

- Swimming and relaxing by the pool
- Beachcombing, biking, and exploring Tybee
- Visiting Fort Pulaski and Savannah
- Relaxing by the pool

Unique Experiences: Walking distance to the beach, with access to Tybee's history and Savannah's attractions.

Feedback: Loved for its clean facilities, friendly staff, and great location near the beach.

Pine Mountain RV Resort

📍 8804 Hamilton Rd, Pine Mountain, GA 31822

📞 (706) 663-4329 $$

Campground Description:

Situated near Callaway Gardens and F.D. Roosevelt State Park, this resort combines outdoor adventure with modern amenities for a peaceful getaway.

Types of Sites Available:

- Full hookup RV sites, glamping tents
- Tent camping and cabin rentals

Amenities:
- Heated pool, Wi-Fi, fitness center
- Dog park, outdoor fireplace
- Playground, laundry facilities

Activities:

- Hiking, fishing, and boating nearby
- Visiting Callaway Gardens and local trails
- Relaxing by the outdoor fireplace

Unique Experiences: Close proximity to Georgia's largest state park and the beautiful Callaway Gardens.

Feedback: Praised for its clean facilities, friendly staff, and access to nearby nature and attractions.

Coastal Georgia RV Resort

📍 287 South Port Pkwy, Brunswick, GA 31523

📞 (912) 264-3869 $$

Campground Description:

A luxurious RV resort located in Brunswick, providing easy access to the Golden Isles and scenic coastal marshes.

Types of Sites Available:
- Full hookup RV sites

Amenities:
- Heated pool, fishing pond, Wi-Fi
- Clubhouse, dog park, laundry
- Picnic areas with BBQ grills

Activities:

- Fishing and relaxing by the pool
- Exploring nearby Golden Isles beaches
- Visiting historic Brunswick

Unique Experiences: A blend of coastal charm and modern amenities, perfect for beach lovers and adventurers.

Feedback: Highly rated for its clean, spacious sites and excellent location near the Golden Isles.

McIntosh Manor RV Park and Campground

Address: 1066 GA-57, Townsend, GA 31331

Campground Description:
A quiet, family-owned campground nestled in the coastal region of Georgia, McIntosh Manor offers a peaceful stay with easy access to nearby nature reserves and historic sites.

Unique Experience: Enjoy the beauty of Georgia's Lowcountry with birdwatching and access to the Altamaha River.

Amenities:
• Full RV hookups
• Fishing pond

Activities:
• Birdwatching
• Fishing in the pond

Warthen RV Park

Address: 1413 GA-15, Warthen, GA 31094

Campground Description:
A small and lesser-known campground, Warthen RV Park provides a quiet, rural retreat perfect for relaxation and enjoying Georgia's countryside.

Unique Experience: Ideal for a secluded getaway, offering a rustic and simple camping experience.

Amenities:
• Full RV hookups
• Shaded sites

Activities:
• Nature walks
• Stargazing

Cloudland Canyon State Park

Address: 122 Cloudland Canyon Park Rd, Rising Fawn, GA 30738

Campground Description:
Cloudland Canyon State Park offers stunning views of rugged canyons, waterfalls, and scenic hiking trails, making it a favorite destination for nature lovers and hikers.

Unique Experience: Camp on the edge of a beautiful canyon with spectacular sunrises and access to waterfall trails.

Amenities:
• Scenic campsites
• Hiking trails

Activities:
• Hiking the canyon trails
• Waterfall viewing

Skidaway Island State Park

Address: 52 Diamond Causeway, Savannah, GA 31411

Campground Description:
Located near Savannah, Skidaway Island State Park offers coastal camping with Spanish moss-draped trees and access to salt marshes, ideal for both nature lovers and history buffs.

Unique Experience: Camp under ancient oak trees and explore the rich ecosystems of the Georgia coast.

Amenities:
• Spacious campsites
• Nature center

Activities:
• Hiking through maritime forests
• Birdwatching

Boondocking

Chattahoochee National Forest

Address: 1755 Cleveland Hwy, Gainesville, GA 30501

Campground Description:
Chattahoochee National Forest offers dispersed camping throughout its vast wilderness, perfect for those seeking solitude and natural beauty in northern Georgia's mountains.

Unique Experience: Enjoy free camping with access to hiking trails and peaceful, forested landscapes.

Amenities:
• Primitive campsites
• Hiking trails

Activities:
• Hiking and exploring forest trails
• Wildlife viewing

Oconee National Forest

Address: 1199 Madison Rd, Eatonton, GA 31024

Campground Description:
Oconee National Forest provides dispersed camping opportunities in a serene woodland setting, ideal for boondocking in central Georgia.

Unique Experience: Experience off-grid camping in the quiet forests of Georgia, surrounded by wildlife and scenic beauty.

Amenities:
• Primitive campsites
• Forest trails

Activities:
• Wildlife watching
• Nature walks

Others Campgrounds

• Red Gate Campground & RV Resort
• Riverbend Campground
• Bald Mountain Camping Resort
• Georgia Mountain Fairgrounds Campground
• Stone Mountain Park Campground
• Highland Marina Resort
• Southern Gates RV Park and Campground
• Lake Sinclair Recreation Area Campground
• Twin Oaks RV Park
• Elijah Clark State Park Campground

Others Boondocking

• Davenport Mountain OHV Trails Area
• Cohutta Wildlife Management Area
• Cedar Creek Wildlife Management Area
• Big Hammock Wildlife Management Area
• Dawson Forest Wildlife Management Area

Others National Park

• Cumberland Island National Seashore Campground

Florida: The Sunshine State, A Year-Round Paradise

Florida is, without a doubt, one of the most popular destinations for RVers, and it's easy to see why. Whether you're a snowbird escaping the winter chill or an adventurer looking to explore the tropical wilderness, Florida offers endless opportunities for fun, relaxation, and outdoor living. From the white sandy beaches of the Gulf Coast to the vibrant cities like Miami and Orlando, to the untouched beauty of the Everglades, Florida is a state that seems tailor-made for RVing.

The best season to visit Florida depends on where you're headed. For **North and Central Florida**, **fall through spring** (October to April) offers the most pleasant weather, with mild temperatures and less humidity. For **South Florida**, **winter** (December to February) is the prime time to enjoy the tropical climate without the intense summer heat. While **summer** can still be enjoyable, especially along the coasts, it's important to be prepared for high temperatures, humidity, and the possibility of afternoon thunderstorms. **The season to avoid**, especially for inland and southern areas, is **hurricane season**, which runs from **June through November**. Though not every year brings hurricanes, it's important to monitor the weather closely if you're RVing during this time.

What I love about RVing in Florida is the diversity of experiences packed into one state. You can park your RV steps away from a pristine beach and watch the sunrise over the Atlantic Ocean, or set up camp in the dense mangrove forests of the Everglades, where wildlife surrounds you. State parks like Bahia Honda in the Florida Keys and Grayton Beach along the Panhandle offer some of the most beautiful RV camping spots in the country. And let's not forget about Florida's freshwater springs—crystal-clear waters that are perfect for swimming, snorkeling, or just cooling off after a hot day.

Florida is also home to some of the best RV parks and resorts in the country. Whether you're looking for a luxurious resort with every amenity you can imagine or a more rustic experience surrounded by nature, Florida has something to offer every RVer. The state's welcoming, laid-back vibe and its endless sunshine make it easy to settle in and enjoy everything from the vibrant nightlife of Miami to the quiet, star-filled nights of the Panhandle.

RVing in Florida is more than just a vacation—it's an adventure that combines the best of nature, culture, and relaxation. From exploring the Florida Keys to driving through the historic towns of St. Augustine and Key West, this is a state that invites you to stay just a little longer.

Disney's Fort Wilderness Resort & Campground

📍 4510 Fort Wilderness Trail, Lake Buena Vista, FL 32830

📞 (407) 939-2273 $$$

Campground Description:

Set within Walt Disney World, this 750-acre campground combines the beauty of nature with Disney magic. Offers world-class amenities like pools, horseback riding, canoeing, and nightly campfires with Disney characters.

Types of Sites Available:

- RV sites with full hookups
- Tent camping, cabins

Amenities:

- Two heated pools, Wi-Fi, Disney transportation
- Dining options, horseback riding, canoeing
- Playground, arcade, and Disney character experiences

Activities:

- Horseback riding, swimming, canoeing
- Exploring Disney theme parks
- Campfires and outdoor movies with Disney characters

Unique Experiences: A unique Disney experience with outdoor adventure and close proximity to theme parks.

Feedback: Perfect for families and Disney fans looking to combine camping with the magic of Disney World.

Camp Gulf

📍 10005 Emerald Coast Parkway, Miramar Beach, FL 32550

📞 (850) 502-5282 $$$

Campground Description:

A premier beachside RV resort with direct access to the white sands of the Gulf of Mexico. Guests enjoy water sports, heated pools, and stunning beachfront views.

Types of Sites Available:

- Beachfront RV sites, standard RV sites
- Tent camping, beach cabins

Amenities:

- Two heated pools, waterslides
- Wi-Fi, laundry, fishing, water sports rentals
- On-site store, golf cart rentals

Activities:

- Swimming, sunbathing, kayaking
- Exploring Destin and local beaches
- Fishing and water sports

Unique Experiences: Beachfront RV sites right on the sand, offering a blend of relaxation and adventure.

Feedback: Ideal for beach lovers and families seeking a luxurious, coastal camping experience.

Bluewater Key RV Resort

2950 Overseas Hwy, Key West, FL 33040

(305) 745-2494 — $$$

Campground Description:

A luxury RV resort in Key West offering waterfront RV sites with private docks. Known for its high-end amenities, tropical landscaping, and serene setting.

Types of Sites Available:

- Waterfront RV sites with private docks
- Premium tropical sites

Amenities:

- Private docks, heated pool, Wi-Fi
- Laundry, dog park, clubhouse
- Fishing and boating access

Activities:

- Boating, kayaking, fishing
- Exploring Key West attractions
- Snorkeling and sunset viewing

RV Size Limits :
No specific size limits, but most sites are designed for larger Class A and luxury RVs.

Unique Experiences: Luxurious waterfront camping in the tropical paradise of Key West.

Feedback: Ideal for RV travelers seeking a high-end, waterfront camping experience in the Florida Keys.

Turtle Beach Campground

8862 Midnight Pass Rd, Sarasota, FL 34242

(941) 861-2267 — $$

Campground Description:

Located on the quieter side of Siesta Key, this beachfront campground offers RV and tent camping just steps from the Gulf of Mexico. Perfect for nature lovers and beachgoers.

Types of Sites Available:

- RV sites with full hookups
- Tent camping

Amenities:

- Direct beach access, Wi-Fi, picnic areas
- Laundry, kayak rentals nearby
- Boat ramp access

Activities:

- Swimming, sunbathing, kayaking
- Fishing, birdwatching
- Exploring nearby Siesta Key Village

Unique Experiences: Peaceful beachside camping with easy access to the Gulf of Mexico and quieter beaches.

Feedback: Perfect for beach lovers and nature enthusiasts seeking a serene coastal camping experience.

HIDDEN GEMS

NATIONAL PARKS

Tropical Palms Resort and Campground

Address: 2650 Holiday Trail, Kissimmee, FL 34746

Campground Description:
Tropical Palms Resort offers a tropical-themed, family-friendly camping experience just minutes from Orlando's attractions, including Disney World.

Unique Experience: A perfect blend of nature and theme park excitement, with plenty of activities for kids and families.

Amenities:
• Pool and splash zone
• Mini-golf

Activities:
• Relaxing by the pool
• Family-friendly events and mini-golf

Destin RV Beach Resort

Address: 362 Miramar Beach Dr, Destin, FL 32550

Campground Description:
Destin RV Beach Resort is a luxury RV campground located just steps from the beautiful beaches of Florida's Emerald Coast.

Unique Experience: Enjoy the convenience of beachside camping in a high-end resort atmosphere with stunning ocean views.

Amenities:
• Private beach access
• Heated pool

Activities:
• Beach lounging and swimming
• Exploring nearby shops and dining

Bahia Honda State Park

Address: 36850 Overseas Hwy, Big Pine Key, FL 33043

Campground Description:
Bahia Honda State Park offers oceanfront camping in the stunning Florida Keys, with some of the best snorkeling and diving opportunities in the state.

Unique Experience: Camp right by the turquoise waters of the Keys and explore the underwater world through snorkeling and diving.

Amenities:
• Oceanfront campsites
• Snorkeling gear rentals

Activities:
• Snorkeling and swimming
• Kayaking and boating

Fort Clinch State Park

Address: 2601 Atlantic Ave, Fernandina Beach, FL 32034

Campground Description:
Fort Clinch State Park offers a mix of history and nature, with camping near the Atlantic Coast and access to the historic Fort Clinch.

Unique Experience: Immerse yourself in history while camping near the beach, with tours of the historic Civil War-era fort.

Amenities:
• Historic fort tours
• Beach access

Activities:
• Touring Fort Clinch
• Beachcombing and swimming

Boondocking

Osceola National Forest

Address: 24874 US-90, Sanderson, FL 32087

Campground Description:
Osceola National Forest offers dispersed camping options for those seeking solitude in a natural, forested environment.

Unique Experience: Enjoy remote camping in the heart of Florida's wilderness, surrounded by pine forests and swamps.

Amenities:
• Primitive campsites
• Hiking trails

Activities:
• Wildlife viewing
• Hiking through pine forests

Big Cypress National Preserve

Address: 33100 Tamiami Trail E, Ochopee, FL 34141

Campground Description:
Big Cypress National Preserve allows boondocking in designated areas, offering a rugged camping experience in the Florida Everglades.

Unique Experience: Experience the wild beauty of the Everglades, with opportunities to spot alligators, wading birds, and other wildlife.

Amenities:
• Primitive campsites
• Scenic wetlands

Activities:
• Wildlife watching
• Kayaking through the preserve

Others Campgrounds

• Tampa East RV Resort
• Southern Comfort RV Resort
• Okeechobee KOA Resort
• Sugarloaf Key/Key West KOA Holiday
• Camp Venice Retreat
• Flamingo Campground (Everglades National Park)
• Jetty Park Campground
• North Beach Camp Resort
• Manatee Springs State Park Campground
• Myakka River State Park Campground

Others Boondocking

• Dupuis Wildlife Management Area
• Rotenberger Wildlife Management Area
• Big Bend Wildlife Management Area
• Picayune Strand State Forest
• Three Lakes Wildlife Management Area

Others National Park

• Everglades National Park (Long Pine Key Campground)
• Dry Tortugas National Park (Garden Key Campground)

Alabama: An Adventure of History and Nature

When I think of Alabama, I immediately recall the endless blue skies, rolling green landscapes, and those winding roads that beckon you to explore further. Alabama is a state that knows how to capture your heart, and for RVers, it's truly a hidden gem of the South.

One of the first things to consider when planning a trip to Alabama is the climate. **The best season** to visit in an RV is undoubtedly **spring**, from March to May, when the temperatures are mild, and the landscape bursts with color. Wildflowers paint the hills, and the weather is perfect for spending long days outdoors without the oppressive heat of summer. **The season to avoid**, if possible, is **summer**, especially **June through August**, when the humid heat can make your stay challenging, particularly if your RV isn't equipped with a strong air conditioning system.

But for those willing to brave the heat, Alabama offers surprises that more than make up for it. Its scenic byways, hidden campgrounds nestled in the mountains and along rivers, and the generous Southern hospitality make every stop memorable. There's something magical about parking your RV along the Gulf Coast, waking up to the sea breeze, and knowing the day holds a perfect mix of relaxation and adventure.

Another thing I learned during my travels here is how diverse Alabama truly is. You can go from the peace of tranquil rivers and beautiful lakes to the vibrant, history-filled cities like Montgomery and Birmingham in a short RV ride. This state knows how to satisfy everyone, whether you're seeking a nature getaway or a cultural deep dive.

Johnny's Lakeside RV Resort

📍 15810 AL-59, Foley, AL 36535

📞 (251) 970-3773 — $$

Campground Description:

Johnny's Lakeside RV Resort offers a peaceful lakeside retreat just minutes from Alabama's Gulf Coast beaches. Spacious RV sites with full hookups and family-friendly amenities, such as a pool and playground, make it ideal for a comfortable stay.

Types of Sites Available:
- RV sites with full hookups (water, electricity, sewer)
- Waterfront sites

Amenities:
- Swimming pool
- Free Wi-Fi
- Restrooms and showers
- Laundry facilities
- Fishing area

Activities:
- Fishing
- Swimming
- Walking around the lake
- Relaxing near the Gulf coast

Unique Experiences: Enjoy serene sunsets over the lake, or take a short drive to the Gulf Coast beaches for a perfect day of relaxation.

Feedback: Family-friendly and peaceful, ideal for a quiet getaway with well-maintained facilities.

Thousand Trails Hidden Cove RV Park

📍 687 County Road 3919, Arley, AL 35541

📞 (205) 221-7042 — $$

Campground Description:

Nestled near Lewis Smith Lake, Thousand Trails Hidden Cove RV Park offers a peaceful lakeside escape with access to fishing, boating, and swimming. With full hookup RV sites and a serene atmosphere, it's perfect for those seeking a relaxing nature retreat.

Types of Sites Available:
- RV sites with full hookups (water, electricity, sewer)
- Primitive tent sites

Amenities:
- Fishing dock
- Boat launch
- Restrooms and showers
- Laundry facilities
- Wi-Fi access

Activities:
- Fishing on Lewis Smith Lake
- Boating and kayaking
- Hiking and swimming

Unique Experiences: Hidden Cove's quiet lakeside setting offers stunning sunsets and peaceful mornings perfect for fishing or kayaking, making it feel like a private retreat in nature.

Feedback: Known for its peaceful, family-friendly atmosphere and well-maintained facilities, this campground is ideal for water lovers and anyone seeking a lakeside getaway.

Thousand Trails Hidden Cove RV Park

687 County Road 3919, Arley, AL 35541

(205) 221-7042   —— $$

Campground Description:

Tucked away near Lewis Smith Lake, this RV park offers a serene lakeside escape. With full hookup sites and access to fishing, boating, and swimming, Hidden Cove is perfect for those looking to relax in nature with modern amenities.

Types of Sites Available:

- RV sites with full hookups
- Primitive tent sites

Amenities:

- Swimming pool • Laundry facilities
- Fishing dock • Wi-Fi access
- Boat launch
- Restrooms and showers

Activities:

- Fishing and boating on Lewis Smith Lake
- Hiking and swimming
- Community events at the clubhouse

Unique Experiences: The peaceful atmosphere and stunning sunsets over Lewis Smith Lake offer the perfect backdrop for a quiet retreat in nature.

Feedback: Known for its relaxed, family-friendly environment, Hidden Cove is ideal for nature lovers and water activity enthusiasts seeking a quiet getaway.

Wales West RV Park & Light Railway

13670 Smiley St, Silverhill, AL 36576

(888) 569-5337   —— $$

Campground Description:

Wales West RV Park blends traditional camping with a unique light railway experience. Known for its family-friendly atmosphere, the park offers RV sites with full hookups and themed train rides, making it a perfect spot for families and railway enthusiasts.

Types of Sites Available:

- RV sites with full hookups
- Pull-through and back-in sites

Amenities:

- Light railway rides • Restrooms and showers
- Heated indoor pool • Laundry facilities
- Fishing pond
- Playground

Activities:

- Scenic train rides
- Swimming in the heated pool
- Fishing and playground fun

Unique Experiences: The park's light railway, with themed rides and holiday events, provides a unique experience for both children and adults.

Feedback: A family-friendly destination offering a mix of quiet relaxation and engaging activities. The light railway is a standout feature that guests love.

Mr. D's RV Park

Address: 1200 S Union Ave, Ozark, AL 36360

Campground Description:
Mr. D's RV Park is a peaceful, well-maintained campground located in the rural town of Ozark. Ideal for those seeking a quiet stop, it offers a more private and laid-back experience with spacious RV sites and a relaxed atmosphere.

Unique Experience: Enjoy the serene countryside of Alabama with easy access to local amenities.

Amenities:
• Full hookups for RVs
• Free Wi-Fi

Activities:
• Walking around nearby nature trails
• Exploring the historic town of Ozark

Camp Sherrye on the Coosa

Address: 247 Jordan Dam Rd, Wetumpka, AL 36092

Campground Description:
Nestled along the scenic Coosa River, Camp Sherrye is a hidden gem for water lovers. With direct river access, this less crowded campground provides a peaceful retreat for camping enthusiasts looking for an intimate riverside experience.

Unique Experience: Camp by the tranquil waters of the Coosa River, perfect for fishing and relaxation.

Amenities:
• Riverfront campsites
• Boat ramp access

Activities:
• Fishing on the Coosa River
• Boating and kayaking

Cheaha State Park

Address: 19644 AL-281, Delta, AL 36258

Campground Description:
Perched atop the highest point in Alabama, Cheaha State Park offers breathtaking views and a range of outdoor activities. The park is famous for its rugged mountain landscapes and well-maintained hiking trails.

Unique Experience: Camp on the highest peak in Alabama with stunning panoramic views and pristine hiking trails.

Amenities:
• Scenic campsites with hookups
• Hiking trails

Activities:
• Hiking to the highest point in Alabama
• Wildlife viewing

Oak Mountain State Park

Address: 200 Terrace Dr, Pelham, AL 35124

Campground Description:
Oak Mountain State Park is Alabama's largest state park, offering a variety of outdoor activities in a lush, forested setting. It is a perfect destination for campers who want to immerse themselves in nature while enjoying a host of recreational options.

Unique Experience: Experience Alabama's largest state park with picturesque lakes and miles of hiking and biking trails.

Amenities:
• RV and tent campsites with hookups
• Lake for swimming and fishing

Activities:
• Hiking and mountain biking
• Swimming in the park's lake

Talladega National Forest

Address: Near County Road 600-1, Talladega, AL 35160

Campground Description:
Talladega National Forest offers dispersed camping (boondocking) for those seeking solitude and a primitive camping experience. Surrounded by nature, this national forest is a perfect getaway for adventure-seekers who enjoy being off the grid.

Unique Experience: Boondock in the heart of a vast national forest, surrounded by pristine wilderness.

Amenities:
• Primitive campsites
• Access to nature trails

Activities:
• Hiking in the Talladega National Forest
• Wildlife watching

Tuskegee National Forest

Address: Forest Service Rd 949, Tuskegee, AL 36083

Campground Description:
Tuskegee National Forest offers a remote and peaceful boondocking experience for campers looking to escape into nature. It provides a quiet, wooded setting perfect for primitive camping enthusiasts.

Unique Experience: Camp in one of the smallest national forests in the U.S. while enjoying undisturbed nature.

Amenities:
• Primitive campsites
• Nearby hiking trails

Activities:
• Hiking through dense forest trails
• Birdwatching and wildlife observation

Others Campgrounds

• Parnell Creek RV Park
• DeSoto Caverns Family Fun Park & Campground
• River Country Campground
• Foley Oaks RV Resort
• Bluegrass RV Park
• Hidden Hollow RV Park
• Lake Guntersville State Park
• Raccoon Creek RV Park
• Shady Acres RV Park
• Hoover RV Park

Others Boondocking

• William B. Bankhead National Forest
• Conecuh National Forest
• Paint Rock River Free Dispersed Camping

Others National Park

• Gulf State Park Campground
• Little River Canyon National Preserve

Mississippi: Southern Hospitality and Riverfront Beauty

Mississippi, with its rich history, warm Southern hospitality, and scenic landscapes, is a destination that promises both relaxation and adventure for RVers. Whether you're exploring the banks of the mighty Mississippi River, camping by quiet lakes, or immersing yourself in the state's deep musical and cultural heritage, Mississippi offers an authentic Southern experience unlike any other. It's a place where the slow pace of life invites you to unwind and enjoy the beauty all around.

The best season to RV in Mississippi is **fall through spring**, from **October to April**. **Fall** brings cooler temperatures and beautiful autumn scenery, making it the perfect time to explore Mississippi's parks and outdoor spaces. **Spring** is equally pleasant, with blooming wildflowers and mild weather ideal for RVing. **Summer** can be hot and humid, particularly in southern Mississippi, so it's best to plan your visit for the cooler months if you prefer to avoid the intense heat. **Winter** is generally mild, especially in the southern part of the state, making it an ideal time for RVers looking to escape the colder climates up north.

What makes Mississippi so special is its rich blend of history, culture, and natural beauty. Driving along the **Natchez Trace Parkway**, one of the most scenic drives in the South, offers a glimpse into the state's history while also providing access to some of the best camping spots in Mississippi. Whether you're exploring the antebellum homes in **Natchez** or enjoying the serene beauty of the **Gulf Coast**, Mississippi has a little something for everyone.

RVers will find a wide range of campgrounds, from well-equipped state parks to more rustic options where you can enjoy the peace and quiet of Mississippi's forests and rivers. **Tishomingo State Park**, located in the northeastern part of the state, is a favorite for its scenic cliffs, hiking trails, and beautiful campgrounds nestled in the Appalachian foothills. For those who prefer the coast, **Gulf Islands National Seashore** offers stunning beaches and the opportunity to camp near the water, with plenty of activities like kayaking, fishing, and birdwatching.

Mississippi's slower pace, combined with its deep-rooted culture of music, history, and food, makes it a unique destination for RVers. Whether you're traveling along the river, exploring the blues heritage in the Delta, or simply relaxing by a quiet lake, Mississippi welcomes you with open arms and plenty of Southern charm.

Majestic Oaks RV Resort

1750 Pass Rd, Biloxi, MS 39531

(228) 436-4200   — $$

Campground Description:

Majestic Oaks RV Resort in Biloxi, Mississippi, offers a relaxing and upscale RV camping experience. Located minutes from the beach and Biloxi's top attractions, it provides a perfect balance of outdoor relaxation and city entertainment with spacious RV sites, a pool, and a clubhouse.

Types of Sites Available:
- RV sites with full hookups
- Pull-through and back-in sites

Amenities:
- Free Wi-Fi and cable TV
- Swimming pool, clubhouse
- Fire pits, dog park, shuttle service

Activities:
- Swimming, casino visits.
- Biking, BBQing in picnic areas
- Visiting nearby attractions like Biloxi Lighthouse and Ship Island

Unique Experiences: A peaceful setting with majestic oak trees close to Biloxi's beaches and casinos.

Feedback: Praised for clean facilities, friendly staff, and convenient location near Biloxi's attractions.

Cajun RV Park

1860 Beach Blvd, Biloxi, MS 39531

(228) 388-5590   — $$

Campground Description:

Located on Beach Boulevard in Biloxi, Mississippi, Cajun RV Park offers easy access to the beach, casinos, and local attractions. The park has spacious RV sites with modern amenities like a pool and a clubhouse, making it a perfect mix of relaxation and entertainment.

Types of Sites Available:
- RV sites with full hookups
- Pull-through and back-in sites

Amenities:
- Free Wi-Fi and cable TV
- Swimming pool, dog park
- Shuttle service to nearby casinos

Activities:
- Swimming, beach walks, casino visits
- BBQing, local sightseeing

Unique Experiences: Beachside relaxation with easy access to Biloxi's casinos and vibrant entertainment.

Feedback: Praised for its location near the beach, clean facilities, and friendly staff.

Percy Quin State Park

📍 2036 Percy Quin Dr, McComb, MS 39648

📞 (601) 684-3938 — $$

Campground Description:

Percy Quin State Park in McComb, Mississippi, offers a scenic camping experience by Percy Quin Lake. The park provides RV sites, tent camping, and cabins, with access to a golf course, hiking trails, and water activities.

Types of Sites Available:
- RV sites with water and electricity
- Tent camping sites, cabins

Amenities:
- Free Wi-Fi, golf course, pool
- Hiking trails, boat rentals

Activities:
- Fishing, kayaking, hiking
- Golf, swimming, picnicking

Unique Experiences: Peaceful lakeside camping with a mix of outdoor recreation and relaxation.

Feedback: Praised for its scenic beauty, well-maintained facilities, and variety of activities.

Reunion Lake RV Resort

📍 43234 LA-445, Ponchatoula, LA 70454

📞 (985) 520-6600 — $$$

Campground Description:

Reunion Lake RV Resort in Ponchatoula, Louisiana, offers a luxurious RV camping experience with upscale amenities like a lazy river, adult pool, and lake activities. It's perfect for those seeking relaxation and adventure, with easy access to New Orleans and Baton Rouge.

Types of Sites Available:
- RV sites with full hookups

Amenities:
- Free Wi-Fi, lazy river, adult pool
- Mini-golf, fitness center

Activities:
- Swimming, kayaking, mini-golf
- Day trips to New Orleans

Unique Experiences: Luxury camping with resort-style amenities, from lazy rivers to a swim-up bar.

Feedback: Highly praised for luxurious amenities, friendly staff, and a range of activities for all ages.

Whitten Park Campground

Address: 20014 N Access Rd, Fulton, MS 38843

Campground Description:
A peaceful campground along the Tennessee-Tombigbee Waterway, offering scenic views and water-based activities.
Unique Experience: Camp by the water and enjoy relaxing boat rides and fishing.

Amenities:
• Full hookups
• Boat ramp

Activities:
• Fishing
• Boating

Little Black Creek Campground

Address: 2159 Little Black Creek Rd, Lumberton, MS 39455

Campground Description:
This quiet, family-friendly campground surrounds a large lake, perfect for outdoor recreation and relaxation.
Unique Experience: Enjoy lakefront camping with opportunities for swimming and fishing.

Amenities:
• Full hookups
• Picnic areas

Activities:
• Swimming
• Fishing

Roosevelt State Park

Address: 2149 MS-13, Morton, MS 39117

Campground Description:
Located in central Mississippi, this park offers beautiful lake views and a wide range of outdoor activities.
Unique Experience: Hike to scenic overlooks or relax by the lake's edge.

Amenities:
• Restrooms
• Picnic areas

Activities:
• Hiking
• Swimming

Buccaneer State Park

Address: 1150 S Beach Blvd, Waveland, MS 39576

Campground Description:
Situated on the Gulf Coast, this park offers beachside camping with water-based activities and stunning coastal views.
Unique Experience: Camp along the Gulf of Mexico and enjoy the ocean breeze.

Amenities:
• Restrooms
• Water park

Activities:
• Beachcombing
• Swimming

Boondocking

Bienville National Forest

Address: 3473 MS-35, Forest, MS 39074

Campground Description:
A vast national forest offering dispersed camping in secluded spots, perfect for those looking to connect with nature.

Unique Experience: Explore dense forests and quiet trails in a peaceful wilderness setting.

Amenities:
• Dispersed campsites
• Hiking trails

Activities:
• Hiking
• Wildlife watching

Homochitto National Forest

Address: 1200 US-84, Meadville, MS 39653

Campground Description:
This forest provides remote boondocking opportunities amidst thick woods and rolling hills.

Unique Experience: Enjoy the quiet, remote campsites surrounded by untouched nature.

Amenities:
• Primitive campsites
• Fishing access

Activities:
• Fishing
• Hiking

Others Campgrounds

• LeFleur's Bluff State Park Campground (Jackson, MS)
• Tishomingo State Park Campground (Tishomingo, MS)
• Tombigbee State Park Campground (Tupelo, MS)
• Natchez State Park Campground (Natchez, MS)
• Paul B. Johnson State Park Campground (Hattiesburg, MS)
• Trace State Park Campground (Belden, MS)
• Lake Lincoln State Park Campground (Wesson, MS)
• Hugh White State Park Campground (Grenada, MS)
• J.P. Coleman State Park Campground (Iuka, MS)
• Legion State Park Campground (Louisville, MS)

Others Boondocking

• De Soto National Forest
• Tombigbee National Forest
• Holly Springs National Forest
• Sardis Lake (dispersed camping available)
• Ross Barnett Reservoir (specific areas allow boondocking)

Arkansas: The Natural State, A Hidden Gem

Arkansas often flies under the radar when people think of must-visit RV destinations, but for those of us who've had the privilege to explore it, we know just how special it is. Driving through the "Natural State," you're surrounded by lush forests, sparkling lakes, and winding rivers, making it an RVer's dream come true. It's a place where the outdoors is your constant companion, and each campground feels like a gateway to a new adventure.

The best season for RVing in Arkansas is in **spring and fall**, from **April to May** and **September to October**. The temperatures are mild, making it ideal for hiking through the Ozark or Ouachita Mountains, canoeing the Buffalo National River, or simply parking your RV by one of the state's many lakes. These seasons also show off the natural beauty of Arkansas at its best, with blooming wildflowers in the spring and vibrant foliage in the fall. **The season to avoid** is **summer**, especially **July and August**, as the heat and humidity can be quite intense, making outdoor activities more challenging, especially for those unaccustomed to the Southern summer.

What makes Arkansas stand out to me is the variety of experiences you can have in one state. One day you're hiking up to a breathtaking vista, and the next you're unwinding in a hot spring or fishing in a peaceful lake. RVers will also appreciate the range of campgrounds, from state parks nestled deep in the forests to lakeside spots with serene views. And if you're into wildlife, keep your eyes open—you might spot bald eagles, deer, or even a black bear during your travels.

RVing through Arkansas feels like discovering a hidden treasure. The roads lead you through charming small towns, past rolling hills, and into thick woodlands where the only sounds you hear are the rustle of the leaves and the call of birds. Whether you're chasing adventure or peace, Arkansas offers a little bit of everything, and it's one of those places that stays with you long after you've left.

Tom Sawyer's RV Park

1286 S 8th St, West Memphis, AR 72301

(870) 735-9770 — $$

Campground Description:

Tom Sawyer's RV Park offers peaceful riverfront camping along the Mississippi River. Its spacious sites and scenic views of the river provide a serene setting, while its proximity to Memphis makes it convenient for day trips to the city's attractions.

Types of Sites Available:

- RV sites with full hookups
- Waterfront sites

Amenities:

- Free Wi-Fi
- Laundry facilities
- Walking trails along the river

Activities:

- Walking and biking along the river
- Fishing and watching river traffic
- Exploring nearby Memphis

Unique Experiences: The park offers unique views of the Mississippi River, where guests can watch barges float by and enjoy scenic sunsets.

Feedback: Ideal for those seeking a relaxing riverside experience with easy access to Memphis attractions.

Catherine's Landing RV Resort

1700 Shady Grove Rd, Hot Springs, AR 71901

(501) 262-2550 — $$

Campground Description:

Set on a 400-acre peninsula along Lake Catherine, Catherine's Landing offers a luxurious RV experience with access to boating, fishing, and hiking, just minutes from Hot Springs.

Types of Sites Available:

- RV sites with full hookups
- Waterfront sites

Amenities:

- Swimming pool and splash pad
- Marina with boat rentals
- Fitness center

Activities:

- Boating and fishing on Lake Catherine
- Hiking and zip-lining
- Exploring Hot Springs National Park

Unique Experiences: Guests can enjoy lakefront activities and the resort's upscale amenities, while also having the option to explore historic Hot Springs.

Feedback: A perfect mix of nature and luxury, ideal for families and adventurers.

Treasure Isle RV Park

📍 205 Treasure Isle Rd, Hot Springs, AR 71913

📞 (501) 767-6852 $$

Campground Description:

Located on the shores of Lake Hamilton, Treasure Isle RV Park offers lakeside camping with access to boating, fishing, and water activities, all in a tranquil setting near Hot Springs.

Types of Sites Available:

- RV sites with full hookups
- Waterfront sites

Amenities:
- Boat dock and fishing pier
- Picnic tables and BBQ grills

Activities:

- Boating and fishing on Lake Hamilton
- Swimming and relaxing by the lake

Unique Experiences: Guests can enjoy lakeside camping with access to water activities and nearby Hot Springs attractions.

Feedback: A relaxing lakeside spot, ideal for water lovers and those seeking peaceful surroundings.

Murfreesboro RV Park

📍 1410 S Washington Ave, Murfreesboro, AR 71958

📞 (870) 285-4058 $

Campground Description:

Located near Crater of Diamonds State Park, Murfreesboro RV Park offers a quiet, affordable stay with full hookups and a friendly atmosphere, perfect for exploring the local area.

Types of Sites Available:

- RV sites with full hookups
- Tent camping available

Amenities:
- Fishing pond
- Laundry facilities
- General store

Activities:

- Digging for diamonds at Crater of Diamonds State Park
- Fishing at the on-site pond

Unique Experiences: Located near the unique Crater of Diamonds State Park, where visitors can dig for real diamonds, offering a fun and educational experience.

Feedback: Ideal for budget-conscious travelers and families looking to visit Crater of Diamonds State Park.

Ramblin' Hills RV Park

Address: 1922 AR-7, Harrison, AR 72601

Campground Description:
Ramblin' Hills RV Park offers a quiet and peaceful camping experience in the Ozark Mountains. Perfect for those seeking a low-key, scenic getaway with all the essentials.

Unique Experience: Enjoy breathtaking views of the Ozarks while staying in a serene, uncrowded park.

Amenities:
• Full RV hookups
• Laundry facilities

Activities:
• Exploring the Ozark Mountains
• Birdwatching and wildlife viewing

JB's RV Park & Campground

Address: 12322 I-30, Benton, AR 72015

Campground Description:
Located off I-30, JB's RV Park & Campground provides a convenient stopover with clean facilities and a friendly atmosphere, ideal for travelers passing through or seeking a quiet stay.

Unique Experience: Enjoy the welcoming, family-run environment and peaceful surroundings.

Amenities:
• Full RV hookups
• Free Wi-Fi

Activities:
• Relaxing on-site
• Exploring nearby Benton attractions

Lake Catherine State Park

Address: 1200 Catherine Park Rd, Hot Springs, AR 71913

Campground Description:
Lake Catherine State Park offers beautiful lakeside camping and access to outdoor recreation in the Ouachita Mountains. It's a perfect spot for families and nature lovers.

Unique Experience: Camp by the lake with opportunities for fishing and boating in a picturesque natural setting.

Amenities:
• Restrooms and showers
• Boat launch

Activities:
• Boating and fishing on Lake Catherine
• Hiking on the Falls Branch Trail

Petit Jean State Park

Address: 1285 Petit Jean Mountain Rd, Morrilton, AR 72110

Campground Description:
As Arkansas' first state park, Petit Jean offers incredible views, rich history, and plenty of outdoor adventures. It's known for its unique rock formations and hiking trails.

Unique Experience: Hike to Cedar Falls, one of Arkansas' tallest waterfalls, and explore the park's rich history.

Amenities:
• Restrooms and showers
• Picnic areas

Activities:
• Hiking the Cedar Falls Trail
• Exploring the historic Mather Lodge

Boondocking

Ozark National Forest

Address: Ozark National Forest, AR (Dispersed camping available throughout the forest)

Campground Description:
Ozark National Forest offers dispersed camping in a stunning wilderness area filled with mountains, rivers, and trails. Ideal for off-grid campers seeking solitude and adventure.

Unique Experience: Camp in the heart of the Ozarks and enjoy breathtaking views and rugged landscapes.

Amenities:
• Primitive campsites
• Access to trails and rivers

Activities:
• Hiking and exploring forest trails
• Fishing in streams and rivers

Ouachita National Forest

Address: Ouachita National Forest, AR (Dispersed camping available throughout the forest)

Campground Description:
Ouachita National Forest offers boondocking in a vast, rugged landscape, surrounded by mountains and lakes. It's a great spot for those looking for a remote, natural camping experience.

Unique Experience: Enjoy the quiet solitude of the Ouachitas, with access to scenic drives and hidden trails.

Amenities:
• Primitive campsites
• Scenic forest views

Activities:
• Hiking and wildlife watching
• Exploring scenic byways

Others Campgrounds

• Gulpha Gorge Campground
• Delta Ridge RV Park
• Millwood State Park
• Shady Oaks Campground & RV Park
• Mount Magazine State Park
• Downtown Riverside RV Park (North Little Rock)
• Indian Lakes Resort
• Young's Lakeshore RV Resort
• Springhill Park
• Cowhide Cove Campground

Others Boondocking

• Bell Slough State Wildlife Management Area
• Sylamore Creek Road (BLM land)
• Little Rock District BLM Land
• Brock Creek (motorized trails area)
• Henry Gray Hurricane Lake Wildlife Management Area

Others National Park

• Buffalo National River (Steel Creek Campground)
• Buffalo National River (Tyler Bend Campground)

Louisiana: A Cultural and Natural Feast

Louisiana is a state like no other, where vibrant culture, rich history, and stunning natural landscapes come together to create an unforgettable experience for RVers. From the bayous and swamps filled with cypress trees to the lively streets of New Orleans, Louisiana offers a journey through its unique blend of French, Creole, and Cajun influences. This is a state where you can park your RV under ancient oak trees draped in Spanish moss one day and explore the bustling music and food scene the next.

The best season to RV in Louisiana is **fall through spring**, from **October to April**. During these months, the temperatures are milder, making it the perfect time to enjoy outdoor activities and explore the state's many parks and wildlife areas. **Summer** can be extremely hot and humid, particularly in southern Louisiana, and the state's notorious mosquito population makes camping less enjoyable. **Hurricane season**, from **June to November**, is also something to be aware of, so it's best to avoid those months if possible, or keep a close eye on the weather if you do plan to visit.

What makes Louisiana such a special destination for RVers is the combination of culture and nature. One day you can be taking a swamp tour, gliding through still waters while spotting alligators and exotic birds, and the next you're strolling through the streets of the French Quarter, tasting gumbo, jambalaya, and beignets while the sound of jazz fills the air. The campgrounds in Louisiana often reflect this mix, with locations nestled in serene natural settings not far from vibrant cities and towns.

One of my favorite places to camp is in the bayou region, where the water glistens between towering cypress trees and the air feels alive with the sounds of nature. For RVers looking for unique experiences, the state parks, like Fontainebleau and Chicot State Park, offer beautiful, quiet spots to set up camp and enjoy Louisiana's natural beauty. And if you're interested in history, you can follow the Mississippi River Road, where old plantations stand as reminders of Louisiana's storied past.

Louisiana is more than just a place to visit—it's a state you experience with all your senses. From the sounds of zydeco music to the smell of a crawfish boil, every corner of Louisiana is alive with flavor, rhythm, and beauty. For RVers seeking a mix of cultural immersion and outdoor adventure, Louisiana is the perfect destination.

Reunion Lake RV Resort

📍 43234 Highway 445, Ponchatoula, LA 70454

📞 (844) 336-4214   ___ $$$

Campground Description:

A luxurious lakeside RV resort offering high-end amenities, including a lazy river, pools, and lakeside water sports. Ideal for families and couples seeking both relaxation and adventure near New Orleans and Baton Rouge.

Types of Sites Available:

- RV sites with full hookups
- Pull-through and back-in sites

Amenities:

- Lazy river, swimming pools, adult-only pool
- Fitness center, water sports
- Playground, dog park

Activities:

- Swimming, water sports, mini-golf
- Exploring nearby Ponchatoula and day trips to New Orleans

Unique Experiences: Combines resort-style luxury with outdoor fun, featuring water activities and proximity to Louisiana's top attractions.

Feedback: Praised for its clean facilities, luxurious atmosphere, and range of activities, making it a top pick for premium RV camping.

Jude Travel Park of New Orleans
(now known as Sun Outdoors New Orleans North Shore)

📍 7400 Chef Menteur Hwy, New Orleans, LA 70126

📞 (504) 241-0632   ___ $$

Campground Description:

A convenient urban RV park near New Orleans, offering full hookups and a quiet retreat just a short drive from the city's famous attractions, including the French Quarter and Bourbon Street.

Types of Sites Available:
- RV sites with full hookups

Amenities:
- Swimming pool, hot tub
- Shuttle service to downtown New Orleans
- Dog park, laundry facilities

Activities:

- Exploring New Orleans, swamp tours
- Relaxing by the pool

Unique Experiences: A great base for exploring the culture and cuisine of New Orleans, with a shuttle service for easy access to the city.

Feedback: Guests love the convenient location, clean facilities, and friendly staff, making it a great choice for visitors to New Orleans.

River View RV Park & Resort

📍 100 River View Pkwy, Vidalia, LA 71373

📞 (318) 336-1400 — $$

Campground Description:

A peaceful and picturesque RV park along the Mississippi River with modern amenities and stunning river views, perfect for both short-term and extended stays. Its proximity to historic Natchez, Mississippi, adds to the charm of the riverside setting.

Types of Sites Available:

- RV sites with full hookups
- Pull-through and back-in sites
- Tent camping sites

Amenities:

- Swimming pool, hot tub
- Walking trails, picnic areas
- Dog park, fitness center

Activities:

- Fishing, walking along riverfront trails
- Exploring nearby Natchez and its historic sites

Unique Experiences: This campground offers a tranquil riverside retreat with scenic views and access to both riverfront activities and historical attractions.

Feedback: Highly praised for its scenic location, clean facilities, and relaxing atmosphere, making it a top pick for both history lovers and those seeking a peaceful stay.

Poche's RV Park & Fish-N-Camp

📍 1080 Sawmill Hwy, Breaux Bridge, LA 70517

📞 (337) 332-0326 — $$

Campground Description:

A serene RV park in Cajun Country, offering a unique camping experience centered around fishing with access to four stocked ponds. Ideal for anglers and families looking to enjoy the outdoors in a peaceful, rural setting.

Types of Sites Available:

- RV sites with full hookups
- Tent camping sites
- Cabin rentals

Amenities:

- Swimming pool, stocked fishing ponds
- Picnic areas, playground
- Boat rentals, camp store

Activities:

- Fishing in stocked ponds
- Swimming, hiking, and exploring nearby Breaux Bridge

Unique Experiences: A peaceful fishing retreat with Cajun hospitality, offering a family-friendly atmosphere and excellent fishing opportunities.

Feedback: Praised for its clean facilities, friendly staff, and relaxing environment, making it a favorite for anglers and families seeking a quiet getaway.

HIDDEN GEMS

Hidden Treasure RV Resort

Address: 1799 LA-121, Boyce, LA 71409

Campground Description:
A peaceful RV resort nestled near the Red River, offering visitors a quiet retreat with scenic views and modern amenities.

Unique Experience: Relax by the river and enjoy fishing or birdwatching in this tranquil environment.

Amenities:
• Full RV hookups
• Picnic areas

Activities:
• Fishing
• Birdwatching

Flagon Creek RV Park

Address: 2608 LA-28 E, Pineville, LA 71360

Campground Description:
A family-friendly RV park located near Pineville, providing a convenient and quiet base for exploring nearby attractions.

Unique Experience: Stay close to local trails and the Kisatchie National Forest while enjoying the peaceful creekside setting.

Amenities:
• Full RV hookups
• Restrooms and showers

Activities:
• Hiking
• Relaxing by the creek

NATIONAL PARKS

Chicot State Park

Address: 3469 Chicot Park Rd, Ville Platte, LA 70586

Campground Description:
A large state park with RV and tent camping, offering visitors opportunities to explore the park's trails, lake, and rich wildlife.

Unique Experience: Hike through hardwood forests and enjoy a peaceful paddle on the lake.

Amenities:
• Restrooms and showers
• Boat rentals

Activities:
• Hiking
• Fishing

Lake Fausse Pointe State Park

Address: 5400 Levee Rd, St. Martinville, LA 70582

Campground Description:
Located in the heart of Louisiana's bayou, this state park provides a true swamp experience with camping and water activities.

Unique Experience: Explore the bayou by canoe or hike the trails that wind through cypress trees and marshes.

Amenities:
• Restrooms and showers
• Boat ramps

Activities:
• Canoeing
• Hiking

Boondocking

Kisatchie National Forest

Address: 2500 Shreveport Hwy, Pineville, LA 71360

Campground Description:
Louisiana's only national forest offers dispersed camping in its peaceful and diverse wilderness, with plenty of hiking trails and scenic views.
Unique Experience: Enjoy the solitude of the forest, camping under the stars in one of Louisiana's most scenic regions.

Amenities:
• Primitive campsites
• Vault toilets

Activities:
• Hiking
• Wildlife watching

Atchafalaya National Wildlife Refuge

Address: 1741 Main St, Franklin, LA 70538

Campground Description:
The Atchafalaya Basin offers boondocking options in this vast wildlife refuge, known for its rich biodiversity and stunning wetlands.
Unique Experience: Immerse yourself in the heart of Louisiana's wetlands and spot a variety of bird species and wildlife.

Amenities:
• Primitive campsites
• Boat ramps

Activities:
• Birdwatching
• Fishing

Others Campgrounds

• Bayou Segnette State Park Campground (Westwego, LA)
• Grand Isle State Park Campground (Grand Isle, LA)
• Fontainebleau State Park Campground (Mandeville, LA)
• Jimmie Davis State Park Campground (Chatham, LA)
• Fairview-Riverside State Park Campground (Madisonville, LA)
• Lake Bistineau State Park Campground (Doyline, LA)
• Tickfaw State Park Campground (Springfield, LA)
• Palmetto Island State Park Campground (Abbeville, LA)
• South Toledo Bend State Park Campground (Anacoco, LA)
• Poverty Point Reservoir State Park Campground (Delhi, LA)

Others Boondocking

• Clear Creek Wildlife Management Area
• Dewey W. Wills Wildlife Management Area
• Pearl River Wildlife Management Area
• Sabine National Wildlife Refuge
• Bayou Teche National Wildlife Refuge

Texas: The Lone Star State's Vast Adventure

Texas is a state of superlatives, offering RVers a vast array of landscapes and experiences, from the deserts of **West Texas** to the rolling hills of the **Hill Country**, the vibrant cities, and the coastal beauty along the **Gulf of Mexico**. Known for its wide-open spaces, cowboy culture, and rich history, Texas is a place where you can roam freely and experience the true essence of the American West. Whether you're looking to explore rugged canyons, relax on a sunny beach, or dive into the history of the Old West, Texas delivers in a big way.

The best season to RV in Texas depends on the region. **Fall through spring** (from **October to April**) is the ideal time for exploring **West Texas** and the **Hill Country**, where the temperatures are milder, and the wildflowers bloom. **Summer** can be extremely hot, particularly in central and southern parts of the state, but it's also a great time to explore Texas' coastlines and lakes. **Winter** is generally mild, especially in the southern regions, making it a popular season for RVers escaping colder climates to enjoy the warmth of Texas.

For outdoor lovers, **Big Bend National Park** in **West Texas** is a must-visit destination. Known for its dramatic desert landscapes, towering canyons, and the winding **Rio Grande**, Big Bend offers a unique and remote camping experience. The park's RV campgrounds are surrounded by spectacular scenery, making it a perfect base for hiking, river rafting, and stargazing under some of the darkest skies in the country.

Another gem for RVers is the **Texas Hill Country**, a beautiful region of rolling hills, rivers, and quaint small towns. Popular spots like **Fredericksburg** and **Luckenbach** offer a mix of history, music, and charm, while **Garner State Park** and **Pedernales Falls State Park** provide RV-friendly campgrounds nestled in natural beauty, ideal for hiking, swimming, and fishing. Springtime in the Hill Country is especially stunning, with bluebonnets and other wildflowers blanketing the hillsides.

For a coastal experience, Texas' **Gulf Coast** offers miles of sandy beaches, wildlife refuges, and charming seaside towns. **Galveston Island** and **Padre Island National Seashore** are popular destinations for RVers seeking beachside camping, where you can park your RV just steps from the ocean, enjoy fishing, birdwatching, or simply relax by the Gulf's warm waters.

Texas is also home to some of the most vibrant cities in the U.S., including **Austin**, known for its live music scene and laid-back vibe, and **San Antonio**, with its famous **River Walk** and historic **Alamo**. RVers can find campgrounds just outside the city limits, allowing easy access to urban exploration while still enjoying the peace of nature.

Texas' campgrounds are as diverse as the state itself, ranging from full-service RV resorts with modern amenities to more rustic, remote spots in state parks and natural areas. Whether you're looking to camp in the desert, by the coast, or in the hills, Texas offers a variety of options for every type of RVer.

For RVers seeking wide-open spaces, diverse landscapes, and a taste of true Texan culture, Texas is a state that offers endless possibilities. Whether you're camping in the remote beauty of Big Bend, enjoying the charm of the Hill Country, or relaxing on a Gulf Coast beach, Texas invites you to experience the freedom and adventure that only the Lone Star State can provide.

Texas Hill Country RV Resort

📍 1965 FM 2673, Canyon Lake, TX 78133

📞 (830) 256-0088 —— $$

Campground Description:

Nestled near Canyon Lake, this resort offers a peaceful escape in the Texas Hill Country with access to boating, fishing, and tubing on the Guadalupe River. Perfect for families and nature lovers.

Types of Sites Available:

- RV sites with full hookups
- Cabin rentals

Amenities:

- Swimming pool and hot tub
- Playground and dog park
- Boat ramp access

Activities:

- Boating and tubing on the Guadalupe River
- Exploring local wineries and hiking trails
- Relaxing by the pool and campfire

Unique Experiences: With easy access to Canyon Lake and the scenic Hill Country, this resort offers a serene setting for outdoor activities and relaxation.

Feedback: Guests love the clean facilities, scenic location, and proximity to outdoor recreation, making it a favorite for peaceful getaways.

Guadalupe River RV Resort

📍 14130 River Rd, New Braunfels, TX 78132

📞 (830) 964-3613 —— $$

Campground Description:

Located along the Guadalupe River, this upscale RV resort provides direct access to tubing, kayaking, and fishing. It's ideal for nature lovers and those looking to explore New Braunfels' attractions.

Types of Sites Available:

- RV sites with full hookups
- Cabin rentals

Amenities:

- Swimming pool and hot tub
- Fitness center and clubhouse
- River access for water activities

Activities:

- Tubing and kayaking on the river
- Exploring nearby attractions like Gruene and Schlitterbahn
- Enjoying live music and cultural events

Unique Experiences: The resort's riverside location and access to water sports make it a great base for adventure and relaxation in the Texas Hill Country.

Feedback: Guests praise the peaceful riverside setting, clean facilities, and friendly staff, making it a popular choice for outdoor enthusiasts.

Lake Tawakoni State Park

10822 FM 2475, Wills Point, TX 75169

(903) 560-7123 $

Campground Description:

This lakeside state park offers a quiet retreat with scenic views and opportunities for fishing, swimming, and hiking. Ideal for families and nature lovers seeking a peaceful getaway.

Types of Sites Available:
- RV sites with water and electricity hookups
- Tent camping sites

Amenities:
- Fishing piers and boat ramps
- Swimming beach and hiking trails
- Playgrounds and picnic areas

Activities:
- Boating, fishing, and swimming in Lake Tawakoni
- Hiking and wildlife watching on scenic trails
- Picnicking by the lakeside

Unique Experiences: With easy access to water-based activities and beautiful wooded surroundings, this state park is a perfect escape for outdoor recreation.

Feedback: Praised for its clean facilities, friendly staff, and serene atmosphere, it's a top destination for fishing and hiking enthusiasts.

Creekside Campground

Address: 10482 Ranch Rd 12, Wimberley, TX 78676

Campground Description:
A charming riverside campground in the Texas Hill Country, offering shaded sites and access to Cypress Creek.

Unique Experience: Enjoy peaceful camping by the creek with opportunities for kayaking and exploring the natural beauty of Wimberley.

Amenities:
• Creek access
• Picnic tables

Activities:
• Kayaking
• Wildlife watching

Choke Canyon State Park Campground

Address: 358 Recreation Rd 8, Calliham, TX 78007

Campground Description:
A spacious lakeside campground perfect for fishing, boating, and birdwatching in South Texas.

Unique Experience: Camp by the reservoir and enjoy some of the best fishing and birding opportunities in the region.

Amenities:
• Electric hookups
• Restrooms

Activities:
• Fishing
• Boating

Palo Duro Canyon State Park Campground

Address: 11450 State Hwy Park Rd 5, Canyon, TX 79015

Campground Description:
Located in the "Grand Canyon of Texas," this campground offers stunning views of the canyon and access to scenic trails.

Unique Experience: Explore breathtaking canyon landscapes and enjoy starry skies while camping in one of Texas' most iconic natural wonders.

Amenities:
• Electric hookups
• Restrooms

Activities:
• Hiking
• Mountain biking

Enchanted Rock State Natural Area

Address: 16710 Ranch Rd 965, Fredericksburg, TX 78624

Campground Description:
A popular spot for rock climbers and hikers, offering primitive camping near the massive pink granite dome.

Unique Experience: Climb the granite dome for panoramic views of the Texas Hill Country and camp beneath the stars.

Amenities:
• Picnic tables
• Primitive sites

Activities:
• Rock climbing
• Hiking

Boondocking

Sam Houston National Forest

Address: 394 FM 1375 W, New Waverly, TX 77358

Campground Description:

A vast forest with dispersed camping options, perfect for those seeking solitude and outdoor adventure.

Unique Experience: Camp in the heart of the forest, with access to hiking trails and quiet, secluded spots.

Amenities:
• Primitive sites
• Hiking trails

Activities:
• Hiking
• Wildlife viewing

Palo Duro Canyon State Park (free areas)

Address: 11450 State Hwy Park Rd 5, Canyon, TX 79015

Campground Description:

Offering dispersed camping in the stunning Palo Duro Canyon, perfect for boondockers looking for scenic views and isolation.

Unique Experience: Free camping in one of Texas' most beautiful landscapes, with miles of hiking trails and dramatic canyon vistas.

Amenities:
• Primitive sites
• Scenic overlooks

Activities:
• Hiking
• Stargazing

Others Campgrounds

• North Texas Jellystone Park (Burleson, TX)
• Rayford Crossing RV Resort (Spring, TX)
• Bluebonnet Ridge RV Park (Terrell, TX)
• South Padre Island KOA Holiday (South Padre Island, TX)
• Fredericksburg RV Park (Fredericksburg, TX)
• Mill Creek Ranch Resort (Canton, TX)
• Bentsen Palm Village RV Resort (Mission, TX)
• Buckhorn Lake Resort (Kerrville, TX)
• Brazos Bend State Park (Needville, TX)
• Mustang Island State Park (Port Aransas, TX)

Others Boondocking

• Big Bend National Park (various areas)
• Padre Island National Seashore (North Beach)
• Laredo District BLM Land (Laredo, TX)
• Black Gap Wildlife Management Area (Terlingua, TX)
• Amistad National Recreation Area (Del Rio, TX)

Oklahoma: The Land of Diverse Landscapes

Oklahoma, often referred to as the "Sooner State," offers RVers a surprising mix of landscapes that range from rolling prairies and lush forests to rugged mountains and sparkling lakes. For those seeking outdoor adventure or simply a quiet retreat in nature, Oklahoma provides a perfect blend of open spaces and hidden gems, from the sweeping views of the **Great Plains** to the unique beauty of the **Ouachita Mountains**. Whether you're exploring the state's rich Native American history, enjoying a peaceful night by a lake, or hiking through scenic forests, Oklahoma is an ideal destination for RVers.

The best season to RV in Oklahoma is **spring and fall**, from **April to June** and **September to October**. **Spring** brings mild temperatures and vibrant wildflowers, making it a perfect time for exploring Oklahoma's parks and countryside. **Fall** is equally beautiful, with cooler weather and the leaves changing color in the forests. **Summer** can be quite hot, especially in the central and western parts of the state, while **winter** brings colder temperatures, though milder compared to northern states, making it possible for RVers who are prepared for cooler weather.

One of Oklahoma's most scenic regions is the **Wichita Mountains Wildlife Refuge**, where RVers can camp surrounded by stunning granite peaks, grasslands, and lakes. The refuge is home to a variety of wildlife, including bison, elk, and longhorn cattle, and offers excellent hiking, rock climbing, and fishing opportunities. For those looking for a peaceful retreat, camping near **Lake Murray** or **Broken Bow Lake** offers beautiful waterfront spots where you can enjoy kayaking, fishing, or simply relaxing by the water.

For history enthusiasts, Oklahoma has a rich Native American heritage that you can explore at sites like the **Cherokee Heritage Center** and **Chickasaw National Recreation Area**. The **Route 66** corridor through Oklahoma is another popular destination for RVers, offering a nostalgic trip through small towns and iconic landmarks along America's "Mother Road."

Oklahoma's campgrounds are as diverse as its landscapes, offering a range of options from fully equipped RV parks with modern amenities to more rustic, nature-focused sites in state parks and forests. **Beavers Bend State Park**, located in the southeastern part of the state, is a favorite for RVers who enjoy hiking, boating, and fishing amidst the beauty of the **Ouachita National Forest**. For those seeking more solitude, Oklahoma's wide-open spaces provide plenty of opportunities for boondocking and off-the-grid camping.

For RVers who appreciate wide-open landscapes, diverse outdoor activities, and a connection to both history and nature, Oklahoma is a state that offers a little bit of everything. Whether you're enjoying a sunset over the prairies or exploring the mountains and forests, Oklahoma invites you to experience the beauty and adventure of the American heartland.

Twin Fountains RV Resort

📍 2727 NE 63rd St, Oklahoma City, OK 73111

📞 (405) 475-5514 — $$

Campground Description:

This luxurious resort in Oklahoma City offers top-tier amenities and easy access to the city's attractions, providing a perfect mix of relaxation and urban exploration.

Types of Sites Available:
- RV sites with full hookups
- Pull-through and back-in sites
- Cabin rentals

Amenities:
- Heated pool and hot tub
- Mini-golf course
- Fitness center
- Shuttle service

Activities:
- Swimming and relaxing in the pool
- Playing mini-golf
- Visiting the Oklahoma City Zoo and National Cowboy Museum
- Exploring Bricktown for dining and entertainment

Unique Experiences: A blend of resort-style amenities and proximity to Oklahoma City's top attractions makes this campground ideal for both relaxation and adventure.

Feedback: Praised for its clean facilities, family-friendly atmosphere, and convenient location, Twin Fountains is a favorite among both short-term and extended stay guests.

Wanderlust Crossings RV Park

📍 1038 Airport Rd, Weatherford, OK 73096

📞 (580) 772-2800 — $$

Campground Description:

Set in a peaceful environment, this upscale RV park in Weatherford provides a modern, luxurious experience for travelers, with easy access to Route 66 and the Stafford Air & Space Museum.

Types of Sites Available:
- RV sites with full hookups
- Pull-through and back-in sites

Amenities:
- Clubhouse with kitchen
- Fitness center
- Walking trails

Activities:
- Walking and biking on scenic trails
- Exploring Route 66 attractions
- Visiting the Stafford Air & Space Museum

Unique Experiences: This park offers a high-end RV experience with resort-level amenities, perfect for both cross-country travelers and local adventurers.

Feedback: Guests love the modern amenities, clean facilities, and peaceful atmosphere, making it a popular choice for luxury RV camping.

Lake Thunderbird State Park

13101 Alameda Dr, Norman, OK 73026

(405) 360-3572 — $$

Campground Description:

Located along the shores of Lake Thunderbird, this state park offers nature lovers a wide range of outdoor activities, from boating and fishing to hiking and wildlife watching.

Types of Sites Available:

- RV sites with full hookups
- Tent camping sites
- Primitive sites

Amenities:

- Boat ramps and marinas
- Hiking and biking trails
- Fishing docks

Activities:

- Boating and fishing on Lake Thunderbird
- Hiking and wildlife viewing
- Swimming and picnicking by the lake

Unique Experiences: The scenic beauty of Lake Thunderbird and its abundant outdoor activities make this park a perfect retreat for families and nature enthusiasts.

Feedback: Praised for its natural beauty and variety of activities, guests appreciate the park's peaceful atmosphere and well-maintained facilities.

Fun Town RV Park at Winstar

21902 Merle Wolfe Rd, Thackerville, OK 73459

(580) 276-8900 — $$

Campground Description:

Located at Winstar World Casino and Resort, this RV park offers easy access to gaming, concerts, and resort amenities while providing a peaceful camping environment.

Types of Sites Available:

- RV sites with full hookups
- Pull-through and back-in sites

Amenities:

- Free Wi-Fi and cable TV
- Shuttle service to the casino
- Dog park

Activities:

- Gaming and entertainment at Winstar Casino
- Relaxing at the resort's pools and spa
- Playing golf at Winstar Golf Club

Unique Experiences: Fun Town RV Park combines the excitement of Winstar's casino and resort amenities with the tranquility of RV camping, offering the best of both worlds.

Feedback: Guests love the convenience of being near the casino and appreciate the clean facilities and helpful staff, making it a popular destination for entertainment and relaxation.

HIDDEN GEMS

Big Cedar RV Park & Cabins
Address: 21823 US-259, Hodgen, OK 74939

Campground Description:
A cozy RV park nestled in the heart of the Ouachita National Forest, offering a peaceful retreat with cabin options.
Unique Experience: Enjoy the quiet of the forest and the rustic charm of the nearby mountains.

Amenities:
• Full hookups
• Cabins available

Activities:
• Hiking
• Wildlife viewing

Country Home Estates RV Park
Address: 18644 Hogback Rd, Luther, OK 73054

Campground Description:
A quiet and friendly RV park located in a rural setting, providing a relaxing environment with easy access to Oklahoma City.
Unique Experience: Stay in a tranquil country setting while still being close to city amenities.

Amenities:
• Full hookups
• Wi-Fi access

Activities:
• Fishing
• Biking

NATIONAL PARKS

Lake Murray State Park
Address: 3323 Lodge Rd, Ardmore, OK 73401

Campground Description:
Oklahoma's largest state park offers a variety of recreational activities, including water sports on Lake Murray.
Unique Experience: Camp by the lake and enjoy stunning sunsets over the water.

Amenities:
• Restrooms
• Boat ramps

Activities:
• Boating
• Fishing

Robbers Cave State Park
Address: 2084 NW 146th Rd, Wilburton, OK 74578

Campground Description:
A historic park famous for its scenic beauty and rock formations, perfect for hiking and exploring caves.
Unique Experience: Explore the legendary caves once used by outlaws like Jesse James.

Amenities:
• Restrooms
• Picnic areas

Activities:
• Hiking
• Rock climbing

Boondocking

Wichita Mountains Wildlife Refuge

Address: 32 Refuge HQ Rd, Indiahoma, OK 73552

Campground Description:
Boondocking in this wildlife refuge provides a unique experience with access to stunning mountain landscapes and diverse wildlife.

Unique Experience: Camp near roaming bison, elk, and prairie dogs while surrounded by rugged mountains.

Amenities:
• Primitive campsites
• Access to trails

Activities:
• Wildlife watching
• Hiking

Osage Hills State Park

Address: 2131 Osage Hills State Park Rd, Pawhuska, OK 74056

Campground Description:
Boondocking available in this serene park, known for its rolling hills, wooded trails, and lakes.

Unique Experience: Enjoy peaceful camping in the park's remote areas, perfect for nature enthusiasts.

Amenities:
• Primitive campsites
• Lake access

Activities:
• Fishing
• Hiking

Others Campgrounds

• Little Sahara State Park Campground (Waynoka, OK)
• Keystone State Park (Sand Springs, OK)
• Red Rock Canyon Adventure Park (Hinton, OK)
• Arrowhead State Park (Canadian, OK)
• Elk City / Clinton KOA Journey (Foss, OK)
• Belle Starr Campground (Eufaula, OK)
• Twin Bridges State Park (Wyandotte, OK)
• Roman Nose State Park (Watonga, OK)
• Honey Creek State Park (Grove, OK)
• Cherokee Landing State Park (Park Hill, OK)

Others Boondocking

• Black Kettle National Grassland (dispersed camping)
• Ouachita National Forest (dispersed camping areas)
• McClellan-Kerr Wildlife Management Area
• Spavinaw Hills Wildlife Management Area
• Cimarron River area (public lands)

Others National Park

• Chickasaw National Recreation Area

Montana: The Big Sky Country

Montana, famously known as "Big Sky Country," is a destination that every RVer dreams of. With its vast open spaces, towering mountains, and crystal-clear rivers, Montana offers some of the most breathtaking landscapes in the United States. Whether you're exploring the wild beauty of **Glacier National Park**, the rolling plains, or the stunning **Yellowstone National Park**, Montana is a state where nature truly takes center stage.

The best season to RV in Montana is **late spring through early fall**, from **May to October**. **Summer** is the perfect time to experience the great outdoors, with long, warm days that are ideal for hiking, fishing, and exploring the state's many parks and wilderness areas. **Fall** is another beautiful time to visit, as the weather cools and the landscape is painted in vibrant autumn colors. **Winter**, while breathtaking in its own way, brings heavy snow and freezing temperatures, particularly in the mountainous regions, making RV travel more challenging unless you're well-prepared for winter camping.

Montana's crown jewel for RVers is **Glacier National Park**, a place where the mountains seem to touch the sky, and the wildlife roams freely. The iconic **Going-to-the-Sun Road** offers one of the most scenic drives in the world, and camping near the park gives you easy access to its stunning alpine lakes, glaciers, and endless hiking trails. For those seeking even more adventure, **Yellowstone National Park**, which extends into southern Montana, is another must-visit, offering geothermal wonders, spectacular waterfalls, and abundant wildlife.

Montana's campgrounds offer a mix of rugged wilderness camping and more comfortable, well-equipped sites. You'll find beautiful campgrounds along the **Yellowstone River**, nestled in the forests of **Flathead National Forest**, or along the shores of the state's many lakes. For RVers looking to get off the beaten path, Montana's public lands provide plenty of opportunities for boondocking, where you can enjoy the peace and solitude of the wide-open wilderness.

What makes Montana so special for RVers is the sense of freedom and vastness you feel as you travel through its landscapes. Whether you're taking in the sweeping views of the Rocky Mountains or camping under a sky filled with stars, Montana offers a connection to nature that's hard to find elsewhere. And with its friendly small towns, rich Native American history, and endless outdoor activities, Montana is a state that invites you to explore and savor every moment.

Yellowstone Grizzly RV Park

📍 210 S Electric St, West Yellowstone, MT 59758

📞 (406) 646-4466 — $$

Campground Description:

Yellowstone Grizzly RV Park is a premium RV destination located minutes from the west entrance of Yellowstone National Park. Surrounded by the scenic beauty of the Rocky Mountains, this park offers spacious RV sites, cabins, and tent camping, perfect for families and adventurers looking to explore the natural wonders of Yellowstone.

Types of Sites Available:

- RV sites with full hookups
- Tent camping sites
- Cabin rentals

Amenities:

- Free Wi-Fi, restrooms, laundry, playground
- Clubhouse, picnic areas, and walking paths

Activities:

- Exploring Yellowstone, wildlife viewing
- Fishing, hiking, visiting West Yellowstone

Unique Experiences: A scenic gateway to Yellowstone National Park with modern amenities, making it a perfect base for adventure.

Feedback: Highly praised for its clean facilities, excellent location, and peaceful atmosphere.

Jim & Mary's RV Park

📍 9800 US-93 N, Missoula, MT 59808

📞 (406) 549-4416 — $$

Campground Description:

Jim & Mary's RV Park, just outside Missoula, offers a peaceful and scenic experience, surrounded by beautifully landscaped gardens. Known for its welcoming atmosphere and modern amenities, this park provides an ideal base for both short-term stays and extended visits while exploring Missoula and the surrounding natural beauty.

Types of Sites Available:

- RV sites with full hookups

Amenities:

- Free Wi-Fi, restrooms, laundry
- Picnic areas, walking paths, dog park

Activities:

- Exploring Missoula, hiking, fishing
- Relaxing in the park's landscaped gardens

Unique Experiences: Renowned for its stunning flower gardens and tranquil atmosphere, offering both nature and convenience near Missoula.

Feedback: Praised for beautiful gardens, clean facilities, and a quiet, relaxing environment.

Outback Montana RV Park & Campground

13772 Outback Ln, Bigfork, MT 59911

(406) 837-6973 $$

Campground Description:

Outback Montana RV Park, located in Bigfork, Montana, provides a rustic camping experience in the heart of the Flathead Valley. Minutes from Flathead Lake and Glacier National Park, this family-owned park offers spacious RV sites, tent camping, and cabins, making it a great destination for outdoor enthusiasts.

Types of Sites Available:
- RV sites with full hookups
- Tent camping sites
- Cabin rentals

Amenities:
- Free Wi-Fi, restrooms, laundry
- Playground, picnic areas, fire pits

Activities:
- Exploring Glacier National Park, boating on Flathead Lake
- Visiting Bigfork's shops and galleries

Unique Experiences: Rustic charm combined with proximity to Glacier National Park and Flathead Lake, perfect for outdoor lovers.

Feedback: Praised for its friendly owners, clean facilities, and peaceful setting near Flathead Lake.

Mountain Meadow RV Park and Cabins

9125 US Highway 2 E, Hungry Horse, MT 59919

(406) 387-9125 $$

Campground Description:

Mountain Meadow RV Park, located in Hungry Horse, Montana, offers a serene camping experience surrounded by pine trees and meadows. Just minutes from Glacier National Park, this park provides spacious RV sites, tent camping, and cabins, ideal for nature lovers seeking both relaxation and adventure.

Types of Sites Available:
- RV sites with full hookups
- Tent camping sites
- Cabin rentals

Amenities:
- Free Wi-Fi, restrooms, laundry
- Picnic areas, playground, fire pits

Activities:
- Hiking in Glacier National Park, fishing, kayaking
- Relaxing in the park's peaceful surroundings

Unique Experiences: A tranquil retreat near Glacier National Park, offering beautiful natural surroundings and easy access to outdoor adventures.

Feedback: Praised for its scenic setting, clean facilities, and close proximity to Glacier National Park.

7th Ranch RV Park

Address: 662 Reno Creek Rd, Garryowen, MT 59031

Campground Description:
A peaceful RV park near the historic Little Bighorn Battlefield, offering beautiful views of Montana's rolling plains.
Unique Experience: Stay in a spot filled with history, with scenic views of the Big Sky Country.

Amenities:
• Full hookups
• Laundry facilities

Activities:
• Historical tours nearby
• Birdwatching

Granite Peak RV Resort

Address: 10680 US-93, Frenchtown, MT 59834

Campground Description:
Located in Frenchtown, this RV resort offers modern amenities in a serene natural setting, perfect for families and adventurers alike.
Unique Experience: Relax in a quiet, beautifully landscaped park surrounded by Montana's mountains.

Amenities:
• Full hookups
• Clubhouse

Activities:
• Hiking nearby
• Fishing

Glacier National Park - Apgar Campground

Address: Apgar Campground Rd, West Glacier, MT 59936

Campground Description:
The largest campground in Glacier National Park, near Lake McDonald and surrounded by stunning mountain views.
Unique Experience: Wake up to the beauty of Glacier National Park and explore trails and crystal-clear lakes.

Amenities:
• Restrooms
• Picnic areas

Activities:
• Hiking
• Lake access

Yellowstone National Park - Mammoth Campground

Address: Grand Loop Rd, Yellowstone National Park, WY 82190

Campground Description:
The only campground in Yellowstone open year-round, Mammoth Campground provides an ideal base for exploring geothermal wonders and wildlife.
Unique Experience: Camp in a geothermal hotspot, with views of wildlife like bison and elk.

Amenities:
• Restrooms
• Picnic tables

Activities:
• Wildlife viewing
• Exploring hot springs

Boondocking

Beartooth Highway
(dispersed camping)

Address: Beartooth Hwy, Red Lodge, MT 59068

Campground Description:
Dispersed camping along the scenic Beartooth Highway offers unparalleled views of the rugged mountain terrain.

Unique Experience: Experience solitude with sweeping vistas along one of America's most beautiful drives.

Amenities:
• Primitive campsites
• Scenic views

Activities:
• Scenic driving
• Hiking

Flathead National Forest

Address: 650 Wolfpack Way, Kalispell, MT 59901

Campground Description:
Dispersed camping in the Flathead National Forest offers remote campsites surrounded by dense forests and mountain peaks.

Unique Experience: Immerse yourself in the wilderness with ample opportunities for outdoor adventure.

Amenities:
• Dispersed campsites
• Hiking trails

Activities:
• Hiking
• Wildlife viewing

Others Campgrounds

• Lewis & Clark Caverns State Park Campground (Whitehall, MT)
• Missouri Headwaters State Park Campground (Three Forks, MT)
• Fort Peck Campground (Fort Peck, MT)
• Bannack State Park Campground (Dillon, MT)
• Tongue River State Park Campground (Decker, MT)
• Medicine Rocks State Park Campground (Ekalaka, MT)
• Whitefish Lake State Park Campground (Whitefish, MT)
• Makoshika State Park Campground (Glendive, MT)
• Placid Lake State Park Campground (Seeley Lake, MT)
• Giant Springs State Park Campground (Great Falls, MT)

Others Boondocking

• Bridger-Teton National Forest (various dispersed sites)
• Gallatin National Forest (dispersed camping areas)
• Lewis and Clark National Forest (dispersed camping in designated spots)
• Ruby Reservoir (dispersed camping allowed in some areas)
• Clearwater National Forest (dispersed camping spots near rivers and trails)

Wyoming: The Wild West and Natural Wonders

Wyoming, known for its vast open spaces, rugged mountains, and iconic national parks, is a paradise for RVers seeking adventure and breathtaking natural beauty. Whether you're exploring the geothermal wonders of **Yellowstone National Park**, hiking through the majestic **Grand Tetons**, or camping under the star-filled skies of the **Great Plains**, Wyoming offers an unparalleled RV experience where nature reigns supreme.

The best season to RV in Wyoming is **late spring through early fall**, from **May to September**. **Summer** is the ideal time to explore the state's stunning landscapes, with warm days perfect for hiking, wildlife viewing, and outdoor activities. **Fall** brings cooler temperatures and fewer crowds, making it a great time to visit Wyoming's national parks and scenic byways. **Winter**, while beautiful in its own right, can be harsh, especially in the mountains and remote areas, making RV travel challenging unless you're well-prepared for cold-weather camping.

For RVers, **Yellowstone National Park** is the crown jewel of Wyoming. Famous for its geysers, hot springs, and abundant wildlife, Yellowstone offers an unforgettable experience for those looking to immerse themselves in one of the most unique ecosystems in the world. The park's RV-friendly campgrounds put you close to attractions like **Old Faithful**, **Mammoth Hot Springs**, and **Grand Prismatic Spring**, while also providing access to miles of hiking trails, fishing spots, and scenic drives.

Adjacent to Yellowstone is **Grand Teton National Park**, another must-see destination for RVers. The dramatic peaks of the **Teton Range** create a stunning backdrop for camping, hiking, and wildlife watching. Whether you're kayaking on **Jenny Lake**, spotting bison and elk in the valleys, or taking in the breathtaking views from **Signal Mountain**, the Tetons offer a true wilderness experience. RV campgrounds in and around the park provide a comfortable base for exploring this rugged and iconic landscape.

For those who prefer the quieter, more remote parts of Wyoming, the **Wind River Range** and the **Bighorn Mountains** offer solitude and beauty. The **Wind River Range**, with its jagged peaks and alpine lakes, is perfect for experienced hikers and backcountry explorers. The **Bighorn National Forest** offers a more accessible escape into nature, with scenic byways, waterfalls, and peaceful campgrounds where you can unwind and take in the beauty of the surrounding wilderness.

Wyoming's wide-open plains and cowboy culture are also a big draw for RVers. The state's western heritage is celebrated in towns like **Cody**, where you can visit the **Buffalo Bill Center of the West** and experience a rodeo, or in **Jackson Hole**, a gateway to the parks that combines rustic charm with upscale amenities. RVers can enjoy the balance of outdoor adventure and the classic Wild West atmosphere that makes Wyoming so unique.

Wyoming's campgrounds range from national park campgrounds with stunning views to more remote sites in state parks and forests. Whether you're camping near Yellowstone, in the shadow of the Tetons, or in the quiet plains, Wyoming's campgrounds offer unparalleled access to some of the most beautiful landscapes in the country.

For RVers seeking wide-open spaces, dramatic mountains, and an authentic Wild West experience, Wyoming is the ultimate destination. Whether you're exploring geothermal wonders, hiking through majestic peaks, or simply enjoying the peace and quiet of the great outdoors, Wyoming offers an RV journey like no other.

Fishing Bridge RV Park

1 East Entrance Rd, Yellowstone National Park, WY 82190

(307) 344-7311 — $$$

Campground Description:

Located in Yellowstone National Park, this RV-only campground offers full hookups and modern amenities, perfect for exploring Yellowstone's geothermal wonders and wildlife.

Types of Sites Available:

- RV sites with full hookups (water, electricity, sewer)
- Pull-through and back-in sites

Amenities:

- Restrooms and showers
- Laundry facilities
- Bear-proof storage boxes

Activities:

- Exploring geysers, hot springs, and wildlife
- Fishing and boating on Yellowstone Lake

Unique Experiences: Stay in the heart of Yellowstone with full hookups and easy access to iconic landmarks like Old Faithful and the Grand Canyon of Yellowstone.

Feedback: Guests love the modern facilities and convenient location for exploring Yellowstone's main attractions.

Jenny Lake Campground

Teton Park Rd, Moose, WY 83012

(307) 543-3100 — $

Campground Description:

A tent-only campground in Grand Teton National Park, offering stunning views and immediate access to popular hiking trails near Jenny Lake.

Types of Sites Available:

- Tent camping sites (first-come, first-served)

Amenities:

- Restrooms with flush toilets
- Bear-proof storage lockers
- Fire rings

Activities:

- Hiking to Inspiration Point and Hidden Falls
- Canoeing and kayaking on Jenny Lake

Unique Experiences: Experience breathtaking views of the Tetons and easy access to some of the park's best trails in a quiet, rustic setting.

Feedback: Guests rave about the stunning scenery and peaceful, no-RV atmosphere, making it perfect for tent campers.

Curt Gowdy State Park Campground

1264 Granite Springs Rd, Cheyenne, WY 82009

(307) 632-7946 — $

Campground Description:

A scenic park between Cheyenne and Laramie, offering camping, hiking, and mountain biking, with access to beautiful reservoirs and rock formations.

Types of Sites Available:
- RV sites with electrical hookups
- Tent camping sites

Amenities:
- Restrooms and showers
- Fire pits and picnic areas
- Boat ramps

Activities:
- Boating and fishing on Granite and Crystal Reservoirs
- Hiking and mountain biking on 35 miles of trails

Unique Experiences: Explore stunning trails and rock formations while enjoying water sports and nature in a picturesque Wyoming setting.

Feedback: Guests love the well-maintained trails, scenic views, and variety of outdoor activities for all ages.

Buffalo Bill State Park Campground

4192 Northfork Hwy, Cody, WY 82414

(307) 587-9227 — $

Campground Description:

Located near Cody, this campground offers stunning views of the Absaroka Mountains and access to Buffalo Bill Reservoir for boating and fishing.

Types of Sites Available:
- RV sites with electrical hookups
- Tent camping sites

Amenities:
- Restrooms and showers
- Fire pits and picnic areas
- Boat ramps

Activities:
- Boating and fishing on Buffalo Bill Reservoir
- Hiking with mountain views

Unique Experiences: Enjoy lakeside camping with mountain views, close to Cody and Yellowstone National Park for an adventure-filled getaway.

Feedback: Guests love the peaceful setting, clean facilities, and proximity to Yellowstone and Cody.

Hot Springs State Park Campground

Address: 220 Park St, Thermopolis, WY 82443

Campground Description:
A relaxing campground located in Thermopolis, home to natural hot springs and scenic landscapes.
Unique Experience: Soak in the world's largest mineral hot springs while surrounded by beautiful park views.

Amenities:
• Restrooms
• Hot springs pool access

Activities:
• Soaking in hot springs
• Hiking

Bighorn National Forest Campground

Address: Bighorn National Forest, Buffalo, WY 82834

Campground Description:
A hidden gem within the stunning Bighorn Mountains, offering peaceful forested campsites.
Unique Experience: Camp amid pine forests with access to scenic trails and high mountain lakes.

Amenities:
• Restrooms
• Picnic areas

Activities:
• Hiking
• Fishing

Devil's Tower National Monument Campground

Address: WY-110, Devils Tower, WY 82714

Campground Description:
A unique camping spot near the iconic Devil's Tower, a geological wonder and sacred Native American site.
Unique Experience: Camp near the striking monolith and enjoy stunning views of the night sky.

Amenities:
• Restrooms
• Picnic areas

Activities:
• Hiking
• Wildlife viewing

Sinks Canyon State Park Campground

Address: 3079 Sinks Canyon Rd, Lander, WY 82520

Campground Description:
A beautiful campground located near the mysterious Sinks and Rise, where the river disappears underground.
Unique Experience: Explore the fascinating geology and enjoy scenic views of the canyon.

Amenities:
• Restrooms
• Picnic areas

Activities:
• Hiking
• Fishing

Boondocking

BLM Land around the Red Desert

Address: Red Desert, WY (various dispersed camping locations)

Campground Description:
Remote and quiet boondocking in the vast Red Desert, offering solitude and rugged beauty.

Unique Experience: Enjoy off-grid camping in Wyoming's high desert, with wide-open spaces and desert wildlife.

Amenities:
• Primitive sites
• Scenic views

Activities:
• Wildlife viewing
• Stargazing

Shoshone National Forest

Address: Northern Wyoming (various dispersed camping locations)

Campground Description:
A peaceful boondocking area within one of the oldest national forests, offering access to pristine wilderness.

Unique Experience: Camp in a remote location with access to rivers, hiking trails, and stunning mountain landscapes.

Amenities:
• Primitive sites
• Water access

Activities:
• Hiking
• Fishing

Others Campgrounds

• Teton Valley Campground (Victor, WY)
• Laramie KOA Journey (Laramie, WY)
• Bear Lodge Resort Campground (Dayton, WY)
• Colter Bay Village RV Park (Grand Teton National Park, WY)
• Greys River Cove Campground (Alpine, WY)
• Canyon Campground (Yellowstone National Park, WY)
• Ten Sleep Rock Ranch Campground (Ten Sleep, WY)
• Little America RV Park (Little America, WY)
• Keyhole State Park Campground (Moorcroft, WY)
• Snowy Range RV Park (Saratoga, WY)

Others Boondocking

• Wind River Range (dispersed camping areas)
• Bridger-Teton National Forest (dispersed camping near Jackson, WY)
• Big Horn Mountains (dispersed camping)
• Greys River Road (dispersed camping spots)
• Medicine Bow National Forest (dispersed camping)

Others National Park

• Yellowstone National Park (Madison Campground)
• Grand Teton National Park (Colter Bay Campground)

Colorado: A Mountain Paradise

If there's one place that feels like it was designed with RVers in mind, it's Colorado. The sheer beauty of the Rocky Mountains, the endless open skies, and the crisp mountain air make it a dream destination for anyone traveling by RV. Every time I roll into Colorado, I'm struck by how effortlessly nature and adventure come together here. Whether you're looking to hike, fish, ski, or just enjoy the breathtaking scenery, Colorado offers it all.

The best season to RV in Colorado really depends on what kind of adventure you're after. For outdoor enthusiasts who love hiking, camping, and fishing, **summer and early fall**, from **June to September**, are ideal. The weather is warm but not too hot, and the mountains are alive with wildflowers, wildlife, and crystal-clear streams. **Fall**, in particular, is spectacular, with the aspens turning brilliant shades of yellow and gold. **The season to avoid**, for most RVers, is **winter**, from **December to February**, unless you're prepared for snowy conditions. While winter RVing is possible, especially if you're a fan of skiing or snowboarding, the mountain roads can be treacherous, and many campgrounds are closed due to the snow.

What makes Colorado stand out is the sheer variety of experiences you can have in one state. In the summer, you can camp at high altitudes surrounded by towering peaks and alpine lakes, or you can explore the red rock landscapes in the western part of the state. The drive through Rocky Mountain National Park is one of the most scenic in the country, and there's something incredibly special about waking up in your RV to the sight of elk grazing just outside your window.

For RVers, the campgrounds here are some of the best, ranging from well-equipped state parks to more rustic, off-the-beaten-path spots where you can truly disconnect. And no matter where you park, the beauty of Colorado is never far. Whether you're into mountain biking, kayaking, or just soaking in a hot spring after a long day of exploring, Colorado offers a little something for everyone. It's a state that's hard to leave, and even harder to forget.

Tiger Run RV Resort

85 Revett Dr, Breckenridge, CO 80424

(970) 453-9690 $$$

Campground Description:

A luxurious RV resort in the Rocky Mountains, offering access to skiing, hiking, and year-round outdoor activities near Breckenridge. Perfect for adventure lovers and those looking to relax in mountain scenery.

Types of Sites Available:

- RV sites with full hookups
- Vacation chalets for rent

Amenities:
- Indoor heated pool and hot tubs
- Fitness center
- Clubhouse with social events

Activities:

- Skiing and snowboarding
- Hiking and mountain biking
- Fishing in the Blue River

Unique Experiences: Enjoy the breathtaking beauty of the Rockies while staying in a resort-style environment with easy access to Breckenridge's outdoor attractions.

Feedback: Perfect for families and adventure seekers looking for a year-round mountain getaway.

Garden of the Gods RV Resort

3704 W Colorado Ave, Colorado Springs, CO 80904

(719) 475-9450 $$

Campground Description:

Nestled near the famous Garden of the Gods in Colorado Springs, this RV resort offers stunning red rock views and easy access to nearby attractions like Pikes Peak. Ideal for outdoor enthusiasts.

Types of Sites Available:
- RV sites with full hookups
- Cabins and cottages for rent

Amenities:
- Heated swimming pools
- Dog park and playground
- Clubhouse with game room

Activities:

- Hiking in Garden of the Gods
- Exploring Pikes Peak
- Scenic drives and local attractions

Unique Experiences: A front-row seat to one of Colorado's natural wonders, with family-friendly amenities and access to world-class hiking.

Feedback: Popular among families and nature lovers looking for a scenic and comfortable base near Colorado Springs.

Palisade Basecamp RV Resort

985 N River Rd, Palisade, CO 81526

(970) 462-9712 $$

Campground Description:

Located in Colorado's wine country, this riverside resort offers access to vineyards, orchards, and outdoor recreation. A tranquil spot for wine lovers and outdoor enthusiasts.

Types of Sites Available:

- RV sites with full hookups
- Riverside and vineyard-adjacent sites

Amenities:
- Swimming pool
- Riverside access
- Event pavilion

Activities:

- Wine tasting tours
- Hiking and mountain biking
- Fishing and kayaking

Unique Experiences: A peaceful riverside retreat surrounded by vineyards and orchards, offering a perfect blend of relaxation and adventure.

Feedback: Ideal for those seeking a serene getaway with access to wine country and outdoor activities.

Mountaindale Cabins & RV Resort

2000 Barrett Rd, Colorado Springs, CO 80926

(719) 576-0619 $$

Campground Description:

A tranquil retreat in the foothills near Colorado Springs, Mountaindale offers a peaceful, nature-focused experience with spacious RV sites and easy access to major attractions like Pikes Peak.

Types of Sites Available:

- RV sites with full hookups
- Cabins for rent

Amenities:
- On-site hiking trails
- Clubhouse with social activities
- Playground and picnic areas

Activities:

- Hiking and wildlife viewing
- Exploring Colorado Springs
- Birdwatching and nature photography

Unique Experiences: A peaceful escape into the Colorado wilderness, with on-site hiking and proximity to major attractions, providing a perfect balance of adventure and relaxation.

Feedback: A favorite for families and outdoor enthusiasts looking for a quiet, nature-filled getaway near Colorado Springs.

CanyonSide Campground

Address: 33040 Poudre Canyon Rd, Bellvue, CO 80512

Campground Description:
Located along the scenic Poudre River, CanyonSide Campground offers a peaceful escape with easy access to fishing, hiking, and wildlife viewing in a tranquil mountain setting.
Unique Experience: Camp near the river, surrounded by the rugged beauty of the Poudre Canyon.

Amenities:
• Full RV hookups
• On-site camp store

Activities:
• Fishing on the Poudre River
• Hiking the surrounding trails

Wolf Creek Run Motorcoach Resort

Address: 1742 E Hwy 160, Pagosa Springs, CO 81147

Campground Description:
This luxury motorcoach resort is set in the picturesque town of Pagosa Springs, offering premium amenities and stunning views of the San Juan Mountains.
Unique Experience: Relax in a high-end motorcoach resort with easy access to the nearby hot springs.

Amenities:
• Full RV hookups with concrete pads
• Clubhouse and dog park

Activities:
• Visiting Pagosa Springs Hot Springs
• Exploring nearby mountain trails

Ranger Lakes Campground

Address: 56750 CO-14, Walden, CO 80480 (State Forest State Park)

Campground Description:
Ranger Lakes Campground is nestled in State Forest State Park, offering beautiful views of the Rockies and easy access to serene lakes.
Unique Experience: Camp near peaceful lakes and explore the vast landscapes of one of Colorado's most diverse parks.

Amenities:
• Restrooms and showers
• Fishing pier

Activities:
• Fishing and kayaking on Ranger Lakes
• Wildlife viewing in the park

Moraine Park Campground

Address: 848 Moraine Park Rd, Estes Park, CO 80517 (Rocky Mountain National Park)

Campground Description:
Moraine Park Campground offers breathtaking views of Rocky Mountain National Park, with easy access to some of the park's best hiking trails and wildlife watching spots.
Unique Experience: Wake up to stunning mountain views and watch elk roam through the meadows.

Amenities:
• Restrooms and showers
• Bear-proof food storage

Activities:
• Hiking in Rocky Mountain National Park
• Wildlife viewing, including elk and bighorn sheep

Boondocking

San Luis State Wildlife Area

Address: San Luis State Wildlife Area, CO (near Great Sand Dunes National Park)

Campground Description:
This wildlife area offers dispersed camping near the Great Sand Dunes, providing a quiet, off-grid camping experience with stunning views of the dunes and mountains.

Unique Experience: Camp in seclusion with incredible views of the Great Sand Dunes and Sangre de Cristo Mountains.

Amenities:
• Primitive campsites
• Scenic mountain and dune views

Activities:
• Hiking in Great Sand Dunes National Park
• Wildlife viewing in the San Luis Valley

Gunnison National Forest

Address: Various dispersed camping locations near Crested Butte, CO

Campground Description:
Gunnison National Forest offers dispersed camping in a rugged wilderness setting with access to some of Colorado's most beautiful landscapes, including alpine meadows and aspen groves.

Unique Experience: Enjoy off-grid camping with stunning mountain views and access to world-class hiking and biking trails.

Amenities:
• Primitive campsites
• Wide-open wilderness access

Activities:
• Hiking and mountain biking near Crested Butte
• Exploring the wilderness of Gunnison National Forest

Others Campgrounds

• Elk Meadow Lodge & RV Resort
• Clear Creek RV Park
• St. Vrain State Park Campground
• Arkansas River Rim Campground & RV Park
• Yogi Bear's Jellystone Park at Larkspur
• Winding River Resort
• Colorado Heights Camping Resort
• Elk Creek Campground & RV Park
• Royal Gorge/Canon City KOA
• Snowy Peaks RV Park

Others Boondocking

• Arapaho National Forest (dispersed camping)
• San Isabel National Forest (dispersed camping)
• Pike National Forest (dispersed camping)
• Uncompahgre National Forest (dispersed camping)
• Flat Tops Wilderness (dispersed camping)

Others National Park

• Black Canyon of the Gunnison National Park (South Rim Campground)
• Great Sand Dunes National Park (Pinyon Flats Campground)

New Mexico: The Land of Enchantment

New Mexico, often referred to as the "Land of Enchantment," lives up to its name with its stunning desert landscapes, rich Native American culture, and vibrant art scene. For RVers, New Mexico offers a mix of adventure and tranquility, where you can explore everything from ancient cliff dwellings and sprawling deserts to high mountain peaks and hot springs. Whether you're captivated by the red rock formations or the endless blue skies, New Mexico is a destination that promises unique experiences at every turn.

The best season to RV in New Mexico is **spring and fall**, from **April to June** and **September to October**. During these months, the weather is mild, making it ideal for outdoor activities like hiking, exploring national parks, and visiting the state's many cultural sites. **Summer** can be hot, especially in the desert regions, but the higher elevations, like **Taos** and **Santa Fe**, offer cooler temperatures. **Winter**, while cold in the northern mountains, is perfect for those looking to enjoy snow sports or the festive charm of Santa Fe during the holiday season. However, winter can bring snow and cold to higher elevations, making it less ideal for RVing unless you're prepared for colder conditions.

One of the highlights of RVing in New Mexico is the access to its rich cultural history and natural wonders. You can explore ancient sites like **Bandelier National Monument**, where you'll find cliff dwellings and petroglyphs, or visit the **Gila Cliff Dwellings** for a glimpse into the lives of the Mogollon people. For those who enjoy otherworldly landscapes, **White Sands National Park** offers miles of rolling, white gypsum dunes that look like something from another planet. And don't miss **Carlsbad Caverns National Park**, where you can descend into a massive underground cave system.

New Mexico's diverse landscapes provide a range of camping experiences. You can park your RV in the desert under a canopy of stars, enjoy the cooler forests in **Lincoln National Forest**, or camp by the rivers and hot springs of the **Rio Grande Valley**. For a truly unique experience, you can camp near **Taos** or **Santa Fe**, two towns that are rich in art, culture, and history, offering a mix of Southwestern charm and mountain beauty.

The state's blend of Native American, Spanish, and Anglo influences makes for a rich cultural experience that you can feel in the art, architecture, and cuisine. From the vibrant adobe buildings of Santa Fe to the colorful hot air balloons dotting the sky during Albuquerque's International Balloon Fiesta, New Mexico's cultural richness adds another layer of magic to your RV adventure.

For RVers seeking a mix of stunning natural beauty, rich cultural history, and peaceful desert serenity, New Mexico is a destination that never disappoints. Whether you're watching the sunset over the desert or exploring hidden mountain gems, this state offers a unique and unforgettable experience.

Santa Fe Skies RV Park

14 Browncastle Ranch, Santa Fe, NM 87508

(505) 473-5946 $$

Campground Description:

Santa Fe Skies RV Park offers a peaceful camping experience with panoramic views of the Sangre de Cristo and Jemez Mountains. Located on the southwest side of Santa Fe, this RV park combines modern amenities with the charm of the Southwest, serving as an excellent base for exploring the rich cultural history, art, and outdoor recreation that Santa Fe offers.

Types of Sites Available:
- RV sites with full hookups
- Pull-through and back-in sites

Amenities:
- Dog park and pet-friendly areas
- On-site propane and RV supplies
- Picnic areas with BBQ grills
- Free Wi-Fi
- Walking trails

Activities:
- Exploring historic Santa Fe
- Hiking and biking
- Scenic drives through the surrounding mountains
- Visiting local attractions like Santa Fe Plaza and Georgia O'Keeffe Museum
- Relaxing by campfires with sunset views

Unique Experiences: This park offers breathtaking mountain views and easy access to Santa Fe's world-renowned art scene and cultural attractions, providing both relaxation and city exploration.

Feedback: Guests appreciate the clean facilities, peaceful atmosphere, and stunning views, making it a popular choice for visitors to Santa Fe.

American RV Resort

13500 Central Ave SW, Albuquerque, NM 87121

(505) 831-3545 $$

Campground Description:

Located just outside Albuquerque, American RV Resort offers a comfortable and well-equipped RV camping experience. Known for its friendly atmosphere and proximity to local attractions like Old Town Albuquerque and the Sandia Mountains, this resort provides a relaxing stay for travelers looking to explore the rich culture and outdoor activities of the area.

Types of Sites Available:
- RV sites with full hookups
- Pull-through and back-in sites

Amenities:
- Free Wi-Fi and cable TV
- Restrooms and showers
- Heated swimming pool
- Picnic areas with BBQ grills
- Camp store
- Dog park
- Fitness center

Activities:
- Exploring Albuquerque's attractions
- Swimming and relaxing by the pool
- Attending the Albuquerque Balloon Fiesta
- Hiking and biking nearby

Unique Experiences: The resort offers both relaxation and adventure, with easy access to the Albuquerque International Balloon Fiesta and the Sandia Mountains.

Feedback: Guests love the friendly staff, clean facilities, and convenient location for exploring Albuquerque.

Elephant Butte Lake RV Resort

📍 402 NM-195, Elephant Butte, NM 87935

📞 (575) 744-5996   — $$

Campground Description:

Elephant Butte Lake RV Resort is located near one of New Mexico's largest lakes, offering a spacious and comfortable RV camping experience. The resort provides modern amenities and is ideal for water sports enthusiasts and nature lovers. With panoramic views of the lake and desert, it's a perfect spot for both relaxation and outdoor adventure.

Types of Sites Available:
- RV sites with full hookups
- Pull-through and back-in sites

Amenities:
- Free Wi-Fi
- Swimming pool and hot tub
- Clubhouse
- Dog park
- Picnic areas

Activities:
- Boating, fishing, and swimming at Elephant Butte Lake
- Hiking and biking nearby
- Day trips to local attractions

Unique Experiences: Guests enjoy lakeside adventures paired with modern amenities, making this a great spot for outdoor recreation.

Feedback: Praised for its clean facilities and friendly staff, the resort is a popular choice for those seeking lakeside fun and relaxation.

Alamogordo / White Sands KOA Journey

📍 412 24th St, Alamogordo, NM 88310

📞 (575) 437-3003   — $$

Campground Description:

Alamogordo KOA offers a scenic camping experience with views of the Sacramento Mountains. Located near White Sands National Park, this KOA is ideal for travelers wanting to explore the stunning natural beauty of southern New Mexico. The campground offers a range of amenities, providing comfort and convenience for a memorable stay.

Types of Sites Available:
- RV sites with full hookups
- Tent camping sites
- Cabin rentals

Amenities:
- Swimming pool
- Playground
- Camp store
- Fire pits

Activities:
- Exploring White Sands National Park
- Hiking and biking in the nearby forest
- Visiting the Space History Museum

Unique Experiences: This KOA offers easy access to White Sands and other regional attractions, with stargazing opportunities in the desert sky.

Feedback: Guests appreciate the family-friendly atmosphere and proximity to White Sands, making it a popular destination for outdoor enthusiasts.

HIDDEN GEMS

NATIONAL PARKS

Rusty's RV Ranch

Address: 22 Border Rd, Rodeo, NM 88056

Campground Description:
Rusty's RV Ranch is a peaceful, remote campground located near the Arizona border, offering expansive mountain views and dark skies for stargazing.
Unique Experience: Perfect for astronomy lovers, with some of the darkest skies in the country for stargazing.

Amenities:
• Full hookups
• Stargazing pads

Activities:
• Stargazing
• Hiking

Along the River RV Park

Address: 127 NM-246, Capitan, NM 88316

Campground Description:
A tranquil RV park located along the Rio Bonito, offering shaded sites and a peaceful, natural environment.
Unique Experience: Relax by the river and enjoy nature in a serene, wooded setting.

Amenities:
• Full hookups
• River access

Activities:
• Fishing
• Birdwatching

Brantley Lake State Park

Address: 33 E Brantley Lake Rd, Carlsbad, NM 88221

Campground Description:
Located on the shores of Brantley Lake, this state park offers scenic water views, excellent fishing opportunities, and desert landscapes.
Unique Experience: Camp near the water's edge and enjoy spectacular sunsets over the desert.

Amenities:
• Restrooms
• Boat ramp

Activities:
• Fishing
• Boating

White Sands National Park

Address: 19955 US-70, Alamogordo, NM 88310

Campground Description:
White Sands National Park offers surreal landscapes of rolling white gypsum sand dunes, perfect for day visits and backcountry camping.
Unique Experience: Walk among the striking white dunes in one of the most unique natural settings in the world.

Amenities:
• Picnic areas
• Restrooms

Activities:
• Sand sledding
• Hiking

Boondocking

Gila National Forest

Address: 3005 E Camino del Bosque, Silver City, NM 88061

Campground Description:
Gila National Forest offers vast boondocking opportunities amid rugged terrain, including rivers, hot springs, and wilderness areas.

Unique Experience: Discover remote wilderness with access to the Gila Cliff Dwellings and natural hot springs.

Amenities:
• Primitive campsites
• Access to hiking trails

Activities:
• Hiking
• Hot springs soaking

Carson National Forest

Address: 208 Cruz Alta Rd, Taos, NM 87571

Campground Description:
Carson National Forest provides dispersed camping in a scenic forested area with views of the Sangre de Cristo Mountains.

Unique Experience: Camp beneath towering pines with access to beautiful mountain trails and alpine lakes.

Amenities:
• Primitive campsites
• Mountain access

Activities:
• Hiking
• Wildlife watching

Others Campgrounds

• Rancheros de Santa Fe Campground (Santa Fe, NM)
• Silver City KOA Holiday (Silver City, NM)
• Enchanted Trails RV Park & Trading Post (Albuquerque, NM)
• Hidden Valley RV Park (Deming, NM)
• Sky Mountain Resort RV Park (Chama, NM)
• Kiva RV Park & Horse Motel (Bernalillo, NM)
• Rose Valley RV Ranch (Silver City, NM)
• Las Cruces KOA Journey (Las Cruces, NM)
• Angel Fire RV Resort (Angel Fire, NM)
• Bluewater Lake State Park (Prewitt, NM)

Others Boondocking

• El Malpais National Conservation Area
• Rio Grande National Forest (designated areas)
• Ojo Caliente Area (dispersed camping)
• Wild Rivers Recreation Area
• Caja del Rio (dispersed camping)

Arizona: A Desert Paradise

Arizona has a way of leaving you speechless. Driving through its vast deserts, with the sun setting behind towering red rock formations, is something that stays with you. For RVers, Arizona is an absolute dream—offering a unique combination of rugged wilderness and modern conveniences, perfect for both adventure seekers and those looking to unwind in nature.

The best season for RVing in Arizona is definitely **fall through spring**, from **October to April**. The desert temperatures are mild, making it the ideal time to explore places like the Grand Canyon, Monument Valley, and the incredible saguaro-dotted landscapes of Saguaro National Park. The weather is perfect for outdoor activities, whether you're hiking, biking, or simply soaking in the beauty of the desert. **The season to avoid**, unless you're well-prepared, is **summer**, especially **June through August**, when the temperatures in places like Phoenix can reach well over 100°F. The heat can be intense, and without adequate cooling in your RV, it can become quite uncomfortable.

But beyond the desert heat, Arizona offers a stunning variety of landscapes and experiences. You could be marveling at the red rocks of Sedona one day and walking among pine forests in Flagstaff the next. One of my favorite things about RVing in Arizona is the ability to park your RV in remote spots, far from the crowds, where the night sky is so clear that you can see the Milky Way stretching across the heavens. And for those who enjoy a bit of luxury, the state also boasts some incredibly well-equipped campgrounds with all the amenities you could need.

The diversity of Arizona's terrain, from the low desert to high mountain ranges, makes every drive an adventure. And whether you're visiting its iconic national parks, exploring Native American ruins, or simply relaxing by a crystal-clear lake, there's always something new to discover in this beautiful desert state.

Desert's Edge RV Village

2398 W Williams Dr, Phoenix, AZ 85027

(623) 587-0940 — $$

Campground Description:

Known as "The Purple Park," Desert's Edge RV Village is a vibrant RV community in Phoenix, AZ, offering a welcoming atmosphere and easy access to nearby attractions.

Types of Sites Available:

- RV sites with full hookups

Amenities:

- Heated pool and hot tub
- Fitness center
- Dog park and pet wash
- Free Wi-Fi

Activities:

- Swimming and relaxing by the pool
- Fitness center
- Social events at the clubhouse

Unique Experiences: Desert's Edge offers a colorful and friendly atmosphere with stunning desert sunsets and great proximity to Phoenix's top attractions.

Feedback: Ideal for families and solo travelers seeking comfort, convenience, and a unique RV experience.

Superstition Sunrise RV Resort

702 S Meridian Rd, Apache Junction, AZ 85120

(480) 986-4524 — $$

Campground Description:

A 55+ luxury resort with exceptional amenities, Superstition Sunrise offers an active and vibrant community with stunning views of the Superstition Mountains.

Types of Sites Available:

- RV sites with full hookups

Amenities:

- Indoor/outdoor pools
- Fitness center
- Tennis and pickleball courts
- Ballroom and entertainment center

Activities:

- Fitness classes and sports
- Social events and concerts
- Hiking nearby

Unique Experiences: A vibrant 55+ community with endless activities and a scenic desert backdrop, perfect for active adults and retirees.

Feedback: Ideal for those seeking an active lifestyle with luxury amenities in a stunning Arizona desert setting.

Grand Canyon Railway RV Park

📍 601 W Franklin Ave, Williams, AZ 86046

📞 (800) 843-8724   — $$

Campground Description:

Located in Williams, AZ, this RV park provides easy access to the Grand Canyon Railway and the scenic wonders of the Grand Canyon.

Types of Sites Available:

- RV sites with full hookups

Amenities:

- Pet resort
- Laundry facilities
- Access to Grand Canyon Railway Hotel amenities

Activities:

- Ride the Grand Canyon Railway
- Explore Williams and nearby attractions
- Hiking and sightseeing in the Grand Canyon

Unique Experiences: A convenient base to explore the Grand Canyon with the option to take a scenic train ride from Williams to the South Rim.

Feedback: Perfect for families and travelers looking for a comfortable and unique way to visit the Grand Canyon.

Palm Creek Golf & RV Resort

📍 1110 N Henness Rd, Casa Grande, AZ 85122

📞 (888) 647-6614   — $$$

Campground Description:

Palm Creek Golf & RV Resort is a luxury 55+ resort offering an active, vibrant community with a professional 18-hole golf course and extensive amenities.

Types of Sites Available:
- RV sites with full hookups

Amenities:
- 18-hole golf course
- Swimming pools and hot tubs
- Tennis and pickleball courts
- Clubhouse with dining and events

Activities:

- Golfing
- Tennis, pickleball, and social events
- Arts and crafts workshops

Unique Experiences: Luxurious amenities combined with an active community make this resort perfect for retirees seeking a fulfilling, sun-soaked lifestyle.

Feedback: A favorite among snowbirds and retirees looking for luxury, community, and an active lifestyle in a beautiful desert setting.

HIDDEN GEMS

Leaf Verde RV Resort

Address: 1500 S Apache Rd, Buckeye, AZ 85326

Campground Description:
Leaf Verde RV Resort offers a peaceful desert escape with easy access to Phoenix. This well-maintained resort is perfect for those looking for a relaxing stay with modern amenities.

Unique Experience: Relax in the serene desert surroundings with views of the Sonoran Desert while being close to city conveniences.

Amenities:
- Full RV hookups
- Swimming pool

Activities:
- Relaxing by the pool
- Exploring nearby hiking trails

White Mountain RV Park

Address: 448 N White Mountain Rd, Show Low, AZ 85901

Campground Description:
White Mountain RV Park is nestled in Arizona's high country, offering cooler temperatures and easy access to outdoor recreation. A perfect spot for nature lovers seeking a quiet retreat.

Unique Experience: Enjoy cool mountain air and proximity to hiking and fishing in the White Mountains.

Amenities:
- Full RV hookups
- Free Wi-Fi

Activities:
- Fishing in nearby lakes
- Hiking in the White Mountains

NATIONAL PARKS

Lost Dutchman State Park

Address: 6109 N Apache Trail, Apache Junction, AZ 85119

Campground Description:
Lost Dutchman State Park is located near the Superstition Mountains, offering stunning desert landscapes and access to scenic hiking trails. It's an ideal spot for adventure enthusiasts.

Unique Experience: Hike through the majestic Superstition Mountains and enjoy spectacular desert sunsets.

Amenities:
- Restrooms and showers
- Picnic tables and fire rings

Activities:
- Hiking the Siphon Draw Trail
- Stargazing in the desert

Catalina State Park

Address: 11570 N Oracle Rd, Tucson, AZ 85737

Campground Description:
Catalina State Park is a desert oasis near Tucson, offering easy access to the Santa Catalina Mountains. It's known for its desert flora and fauna, including saguaros and wildlife.

Unique Experience: Camp in the shadow of the Santa Catalina Mountains and explore the beautiful desert landscape.

Amenities:
- Restrooms and showers
- Picnic areas

Activities:
- Hiking the Romero Canyon Trail
- Birdwatching

Boondocking

Quartzsite

Address: Quartzsite, AZ 85346 (Various dispersed camping spots around town)

Campground Description:
Quartzsite is a well-known destination for boondockers, offering vast areas of desert land for dispersed camping. It's famous for its winter RV gatherings and rock and gem shows.
Unique Experience: Experience the desert lifestyle with wide-open spaces and vibrant RV communities during winter months.

Amenities:
• Primitive campsites
• Dump stations available nearby

Activities:
• Rock and gem shows
• Off-roading in the desert

Kofa National Wildlife Refuge

Address: Yuma County, AZ (Along US-95, north of Yuma)

Campground Description:
Kofa National Wildlife Refuge offers remote boondocking in a stunning desert landscape, surrounded by rugged mountains and unique wildlife. It's ideal for those looking for solitude and adventure.
Unique Experience: Enjoy off-grid camping with opportunities to see bighorn sheep and explore desert canyons.

Amenities:
• Primitive campsites
• Scenic desert views

Activities:
• Hiking and wildlife viewing
• Photography of desert landscapes

Others Campgrounds

• Butterfield RV Resort & Observatory
• Tombstone RV Park & Campground
• Meteor Crater RV Park
• Bonita Campground (Safford, AZ)
• Pioneer RV Resort
• Pine Flat Campground (Sedona, AZ)
• River Island State Park
• Distant Drums RV Resort
• Lo Lo Mai Springs Outdoor Resort
• Verde Ranch RV Resort

Others Boondocking

• Saddle Mountain BLM Land
• Craggy Wash (Lake Havasu City)
• Plomosa Road (Quartzsite area)
• Vulture Peak Road (Wickenburg)
• Harquahala Mountain Summit

Others National Park

• Mather Campground (Grand Canyon National Park)
• Desert View Campground (Grand Canyon National Park)
• Bonita Canyon Campground (Chiricahua National Monument)

Utah: A Land of Red Rock Wonders and Outdoor Adventure

Utah is a state that captivates RVers with its otherworldly landscapes, dramatic canyons, and towering red rock formations. Known for its iconic national parks and boundless outdoor activities, Utah offers a playground for those seeking adventure in some of the most breathtaking scenery in the United States. From the awe-inspiring **Mighty 5** national parks to the vast, open desert of the **Great Basin**, Utah is a destination that promises unforgettable experiences for RVers.

The best season to RV in Utah is **spring and fall**, from **April to June** and **September to October**. **Spring** brings comfortable temperatures and blooming wildflowers, making it a great time to explore the national parks and scenic byways. **Fall** offers cooler weather and fewer crowds, making it ideal for hiking, camping, and sightseeing. **Summer**, particularly in the southern desert regions, can be extremely hot, but the higher elevations and northern areas offer relief from the heat. **Winter**, though cold in some areas, can be beautiful, especially in Utah's ski regions and for those who enjoy snow sports.

For RVers, Utah's **Mighty 5** national parks—**Zion**, **Bryce Canyon**, **Arches**, **Canyonlands**, and **Capitol Reef**—are the crown jewels of the state. Each park offers unique landscapes and experiences, from the towering red cliffs of Zion to the surreal hoodoos of Bryce Canyon. The RV campgrounds in and around these parks provide easy access to hiking trails, scenic viewpoints, and opportunities for photography and wildlife spotting. Zion and Bryce Canyon, in particular, are popular for their breathtaking overlooks and well-maintained campgrounds, making them a must-visit for any RVer.

The **Moab** region, home to both **Arches National Park** and **Canyonlands National Park**, is another favorite for RVers. Moab offers a blend of adventure and natural beauty, with RV parks located just minutes from world-famous arches, canyons, and rock formations. This area is perfect for hiking, off-roading, mountain biking, and exploring Utah's vast desert landscapes. The nearby **Dead Horse Point State Park** offers some of the most stunning views of the Colorado River and the surrounding canyons.

For those seeking a more peaceful experience, **Capitol Reef National Park** offers rugged beauty with fewer crowds, where you can camp in the quiet desert surrounded by towering cliffs and historic orchards. **Goblin Valley State Park**, with its unique, mushroom-shaped rock formations, is another hidden gem that offers RV-friendly camping in a surreal, Martian-like landscape.

Utah's higher elevations also provide incredible opportunities for RVers. **Bear Lake**, often called the "Caribbean of the Rockies," offers crystal-clear waters and sandy beaches, perfect for a summer getaway. **Park City**, known for its world-class skiing in winter, transforms into a haven for hiking, biking, and fishing during the summer and fall months, offering RVers access to mountain trails and alpine beauty.

Utah's campgrounds range from fully equipped RV parks to more remote, rustic spots in national and state parks. Whether you're camping near the iconic red rocks, in a desert valley, or by a mountain lake, Utah's campgrounds offer spectacular views and easy access to outdoor activities.

For RVers seeking adventure, awe-inspiring landscapes, and endless opportunities for exploration, Utah is a state that delivers in every way. Whether you're exploring the red rock canyons of the Mighty 5, hiking in remote desert landscapes, or relaxing by a mountain lake, Utah offers an unforgettable experience for those traveling by RV.

Zion Canyon Campground

📍 479 Zion Park Blvd, Springdale, UT 84767

📞 (435) 772-3237   — $$

Campground Description:

Located near Zion National Park, this campground offers stunning views and direct access to park trails and the Virgin River, making it an ideal base for hiking and exploring the area.

Types of Sites Available:

- RV sites with full hookups
- Tent camping sites

Amenities:

- Free Wi-Fi
- Swimming pool (seasonal)
- Picnic areas and BBQ grills

Activities:

- Hiking Zion's famous trails
- Relaxing by the Virgin River
- Exploring Springdale's shops and dining

Unique Experiences: Enjoy the breathtaking red rock views and easy access to Zion National Park's iconic hikes like Angel's Landing.

Feedback: Praised for its location and convenience, guests love the clean facilities and proximity to the park entrance.

Ruby's Inn RV Park and Campground

📍 300 S Main Hwy 63, Bryce Canyon City, UT 84764

📞 (866) 878-9373   — $$

Campground Description:

Just a mile from Bryce Canyon National Park, Ruby's Inn provides a convenient base with modern amenities for exploring the park's famous hoodoos and stunning viewpoints.

Types of Sites Available:

- RV sites with full hookups
- Tent camping sites
- Cabin rentals

Amenities:

- Free Wi-Fi
- Pool and hot tub (at nearby hotel)
- Shuttle to Bryce Canyon

Activities:

- Hiking Bryce Canyon trails
- Horseback riding and ATV rentals
- Stargazing and ranger-led programs

Unique Experiences: With access to the park's shuttle and nearby activities like horseback riding, Ruby's Inn provides a perfect mix of adventure and relaxation.

Feedback: Guests love the proximity to Bryce Canyon, the variety of activities, and the convenience of the free shuttle.

Moab Valley RV Resort & Campground

📍 1773 N Highway 191, Moab, UT 84532

📞 (888) 599-6622 — $$

Campground Description:

Close to Arches and Canyonlands National Parks, Moab Valley offers modern amenities and scenic views, making it an ideal spot for adventure-seekers and those looking to relax after exploring Utah's red rock landscapes.

Types of Sites Available:

- RV sites with full hookups
- Tent camping sites
- Cabin rentals

Amenities:

- Free Wi-Fi and cable TV
- Pool and hot tub
- Playground

Activities:

- Hiking Arches and Canyonlands
- Biking on Moab's famous trails
- Exploring downtown Moab

Unique Experiences: Perfectly situated for outdoor adventures, this resort provides easy access to Utah's stunning national parks and offers a relaxing environment after a day of exploring.

Feedback: Guests appreciate the location, clean facilities, and proximity to both national parks and downtown Moab.

Fish Springs National Wildlife Refuge

📍 Fish Springs Refuge Road, Delta, UT 84624

📞 (435) 831-5353 — Free

Campground Description:

Located in Utah's remote west desert, Fish Springs offers a peaceful boondocking experience surrounded by wetlands and desert landscapes. It's ideal for birdwatchers and nature lovers seeking solitude.

Types of Sites Available:

- Primitive camping (boondocking)

Amenities:

- Vault toilets
- Wildlife viewing platforms

Activities:

- Birdwatching and wildlife photography
- Exploring the historic Pony Express Trail
- Stargazing in clear desert skies

Unique Experiences: Experience the tranquility of Utah's desert and wetlands, perfect for birdwatching and connecting with nature in an isolated, undisturbed setting.

Feedback: Visitors enjoy the solitude and opportunity to observe diverse wildlife in a peaceful, off-the-grid environment.

Sand Hollow State Park Campground

Address: 3351 Sand Hollow Rd, Hurricane, UT 84737

Campground Description:
A scenic desert campground by a vibrant red rock reservoir, ideal for water sports and off-roading.
Unique Experience: Camp beside the stunning Sand Hollow Reservoir, where you can enjoy boating and ATV adventures on the nearby sand dunes.

Amenities:
• Electric hookups
• Restrooms

Activities:
• Boating
• Off-roading

Goblin Valley State Park Campground

Address: Hwy 24, Green River, UT 84525

Campground Description:
A unique campground surrounded by whimsical rock formations, perfect for stargazing and photography.
Unique Experience: Camp amongst the "goblins," incredible rock formations that create a surreal landscape in this hidden desert gem.

Amenities:
• Restrooms
• Picnic tables

Activities:
• Hiking
• Stargazing

Arches National Park Campground
Address: Arches Entrance Rd, Moab, UT 84532

Campground Description:
Located inside the park, this campground offers incredible views and access to world-famous sandstone arches.
Unique Experience: Wake up to the sight of iconic red rock arches and explore the park's trails directly from your campsite.

Amenities:
• Picnic tables
• Restrooms

Activities:
• Hiking
• Photography

Canyonlands National Park Campground (Isle in the Sky)
Address: Grand View Point Rd, Moab, UT 84532

Campground Description:
A remote campground in the Island in the Sky district, offering breathtaking canyon vistas.
Unique Experience: Experience camping on the rim of a canyon with stunning views of the vast Canyonlands below.

Amenities:
• Picnic tables
• Restrooms

Activities:
• Scenic drives
• Hiking

Boondocking

BLM Land near Moab
Address: Moab, UT

Campground Description:
Free dispersed camping near Moab, offering seclusion and proximity to Arches and Canyonlands National Parks.

Unique Experience: Enjoy boondocking with views of red rock landscapes and easy access to popular national parks.

Amenities:
• Primitive sites
• Scenic views

Activities:
• Hiking
• Off-roading

Fish Springs Flat (West Desert)
Address: Fish Springs National Wildlife Refuge, UT

Campground Description:
A remote boondocking spot in Utah's West Desert, perfect for solitude and wildlife viewing.

Unique Experience: Camp in Utah's West Desert, where vast, open spaces meet a peaceful, wildlife-rich environment.

Amenities:
• Primitive sites
• Wildlife viewing

Activities:
• Wildlife watching
• Stargazing

Others Campgrounds

• Green River State Park (Green River, UT)
• Dead Horse Point State Park (Moab, UT)
• East Zion Riverside RV Park (Orderville, UT)
• Bear Lake State Park (Garden City, UT)
• Escalante Petrified Forest State Park (Escalante, UT)
• Jordanelle State Park (Heber City, UT)
• Red Fleet State Park (Vernal, UT)
• Starvation State Park (Duchesne, UT)
• Antelope Island State Park (Syracuse, UT)
• Deer Creek State Park (Heber City, UT)

Others Boondocking

• Valley of the Gods (Bluff, UT)
• BLM Land near Cottonwood Canyon (near Bryce Canyon, UT)
• Muley Point (Mexican Hat, UT)
• Lone Rock Beach (Lake Powell, UT)
• Grand Staircase-Escalante National Monument (dispersed areas)

Nevada: The Desert Playground

Nevada is a state of contrasts, offering RVers everything from vibrant cities to vast, quiet deserts. Known as the "Silver State," Nevada is a playground for those seeking adventure, with its stunning landscapes, wide-o-pen spaces, and opportunities for off-the-grid exploration. Whether you're drawn to the bright lights of **Las Vegas** or the rugged beauty of the **Great Basin**, Nevada is a state that promises excitement, discovery, and plenty of room to roam.

The best season to RV in Nevada is **fall through spring**, from **October to April. Fall** and **spring** bring pleasant temperatures, making it the perfect time to explore Nevada's deserts, canyons, and mountains. **Winter** can be ideal for southern Nevada, where mild weather makes outdoor activities comfortable, especially in areas like **Red Rock Canyon** and **Death Valley**. However, northern Nevada, particularly around the **Sierra Nevada Mountains**, can experience cold and snowy conditions. **Summer** in Nevada's desert regions can be brutally hot, especially in southern areas like Las Vegas and the Mojave Desert, so it's best to avoid RVing in these regions during the hottest months unless you're well-prepared for the extreme heat.

One of the best parts of RVing in Nevada is the sense of freedom and adventure that comes with the state's vast, open landscapes. Whether you're camping in the remote wilderness of **Great Basin National Park**, with its towering peaks and ancient bristlecone pines, or exploring the vast desert stretches along **Highway 50**, known as the "Loneliest Road in America," Nevada offers a sense of solitude and discovery that's hard to match.

For those seeking a bit of luxury alongside nature, **Lake Tahoe**, located on the Nevada-California border, offers stunning lakeside campgrounds with crystal-clear waters, perfect for kayaking, swimming, or simply relaxing. And, of course, no trip to Nevada would be complete without experiencing **Las Vegas**, where RV parks offer proximity to the city's world-famous entertainment, casinos, and nightlife, while still providing a retreat from the neon-lit hustle of the Strip.

Nevada's campgrounds range from fully equipped RV resorts near cities like Las Vegas and Reno to more primitive sites in the state's expansive deserts and mountains. **Valley of Fire State Park**, with its striking red rock formations, offers a unique desert camping experience, while the cooler mountain areas of the **Ruby Mountains** provide a peaceful, scenic escape.

For RVers, Nevada is a state of endless possibilities. Whether you're looking to gamble under the bright lights of Las Vegas, hike through remote wilderness areas, or camp beneath a canopy of stars in the desert, Nevada has something to offer every kind of traveler.

Oasis Las Vegas RV Resort

📍 2711 W Windmill Ln, Las Vegas, NV 89123
📞 (702) 260-2000   ___ $$$

Campground Description:

Oasis Las Vegas RV Resort offers a luxurious camping experience near the Las Vegas Strip, featuring top-tier amenities like a swimming pool, spa, fitness center, and on-site restaurant. Perfect for travelers seeking both relaxation and excitement, the resort provides spacious RV sites, desert landscaping, and recreational options for a tranquil yet vibrant stay.

Types of Sites Available:

- RV sites with full hookups
- Pull-through and back-in sites

Amenities:

- Free Wi-Fi, cable TV, pool, spa
- On-site restaurant, fitness center, mini-golf

Activities:

- Dining at the on-site restaurant
- Exploring the Las Vegas Strip and local attractions

Unique Experiences: Oasis Las Vegas combines luxury amenities with proximity to the Strip, offering a peaceful desert retreat minutes from entertainment and dining.

Feedback: Praised for upscale facilities, excellent location, and a relaxing atmosphere close to the excitement of Las Vegas.

Lake Mead RV Village

📍 268 Lakeshore Rd, Boulder City, NV 89005
📞 (702) 293-2540   ___ $$

Campground Description:

Lake Mead RV Village offers a scenic retreat at Boulder Beach within the Lake Mead National Recreation Area. The campground provides stunning lake views and easy access to activities like boating, fishing, hiking, and swimming, making it perfect for outdoor enthusiasts. Located near Hoover Dam and a short drive from Las Vegas, this RV park offers a peaceful balance between nature and city life.

Types of Sites Available:

- RV sites with full hookups
- Pull-through and back-in sites

Amenities:

- Free Wi-Fi, restrooms, laundry
- Picnic areas, boat launch nearby

Activities:

- Boating, fishing, hiking around Lake Mead
- Exploring Hoover Dam and Boulder City

Unique Experiences: A serene lakefront escape with outdoor activities, combined with proximity to Hoover Dam and Las Vegas.

Feedback: Guests appreciate the scenic views, access to Lake Mead, and clean, quiet facilities, making it a popular choice for outdoor relaxation.

Valley of Fire State Park - Atlatl Rock Campground

📍 29450 Valley of Fire Hwy, Overton, NV 89040

📞 (702) 397-2088   — $$

Campground Description:

Atlatl Rock Campground in Valley of Fire State Park offers a unique desert camping experience surrounded by red sandstone formations and ancient petroglyphs. This scenic campground is perfect for outdoor enthusiasts seeking adventure, with hiking trails, rock climbing, and wildlife viewing opportunities. The park's striking landscapes make it an ideal spot for photography and stargazing.

Types of Sites Available:

- RV sites with water and electrical hookups
- Tent camping sites

Amenities:

- Restrooms, showers, dump station
- Picnic tables, fire rings, shaded ramadas

Activities:

- Hiking, exploring petroglyphs
- Rock climbing and wildlife viewing

RV Size Limits (if any):

Accommodates RVs up to 35 feet in length.

Unique Experiences: Atlatl Rock offers unforgettable desert vistas, ancient petroglyphs, and proximity to hiking trails, creating a perfect mix of natural beauty and outdoor adventure.

Feedback: Highly praised for its scenic beauty, peaceful atmosphere, and access to trails and ancient petroglyphs, this campground is a favorite for nature lovers.

New Frontier RV Park

📍 4360 Rim Rock Rd, Winnemucca, NV 89445

📞 (775) 621-5277   — $$

Campground Description:

New Frontier RV Park in Winnemucca, Nevada, provides a modern and comfortable camping experience with state-of-the-art facilities and scenic desert views. Perfect for both short-term and long-term stays, the park offers spacious RV sites, a fitness center, and easy access to hiking and biking trails. Located conveniently near I-80, New Frontier is ideal for travelers exploring northern Nevada or passing through on a road trip.

Types of Sites Available:

- RV sites with full hookups
- Pull-through and back-in sites

Amenities:

- Free Wi-Fi, fitness center, laundry
- Fire pits, dog park, picnic areas

Activities:

- Walking and biking scenic trails
- Exploring local outdoor recreation areas

Unique Experiences: New Frontier offers modern comfort and convenience, with easy access to outdoor activities and local attractions, providing a perfect blend of relaxation and adventure.

Feedback: Guests enjoy the clean, spacious sites and modern amenities, with friendly staff and a convenient location for road trips or exploring northern Nevada.

Silver City RV Resort

Address: 3165 US-395, Minden, NV 89423

Campground Description:
A well-kept RV resort near Lake Tahoe, offering modern amenities in a peaceful setting with mountain views.

Unique Experience: Relax in a convenient, scenic spot with proximity to Lake Tahoe and Carson City.

Amenities:
• Full hookups
• Pool and spa

Activities:
• Hiking nearby
• Fishing at Lake Tahoe

Boulder Oaks RV Resort

Address: 1015 NV-160, Pahrump, NV 89048

Campground Description:
A desert oasis for RVers, offering spacious sites and easy access to nearby attractions like Death Valley National Park.

Unique Experience: Stay in the heart of the Nevada desert, perfect for those exploring nearby national parks.

Amenities:
• Full hookups
• Laundry facilities

Activities:
• Day trips to Death Valley
• Casino gaming nearby

Great Basin National Park (Upper Lehman Creek Campground)

Address: Lehman Caves Rd, Baker, NV 89311

Campground Description:
A serene mountain campground in Great Basin National Park, nestled among pinyon pine and juniper trees.

Unique Experience: Camp in the shadow of Wheeler Peak, with easy access to stargazing and cave tours.

Amenities:
• Restrooms
• Picnic tables

Activities:
• Stargazing
• Cave tours

Washoe Lake State Park

Address: 4855 Eastlake Blvd, Carson City, NV 89704

Campground Description:
A quiet campground between Carson City and Reno, perfect for birdwatching and outdoor activities around Washoe Lake.

Unique Experience: Enjoy stunning views of the Sierra Nevada and water recreation on Washoe Lake.

Amenities:
• Electric hookups
• Boat launch

Activities:
• Birdwatching
• Fishing

Boondocking

Spring Mountains - Lovell Canyon

Address: Lovell Canyon Rd, Las Vegas, NV 89124

Campground Description:
Dispersed camping in the Spring Mountains with beautiful forested landscapes, just a short drive from Las Vegas.

Unique Experience: Escape the heat and bustle of Vegas with quiet, scenic camping in the cool mountain air.

Amenities:
• Primitive campsites
• Fire rings

Activities:
• Hiking
• Wildlife viewing

Humboldt-Toiyabe National Forest

Address: Multiple dispersed camping areas throughout the forest

Campground Description:
A vast forest offering dispersed camping opportunities with varied landscapes from mountains to desert basins.

Unique Experience: Camp in one of the most diverse national forests in the U.S., with endless options for outdoor adventure.

Amenities:
• Primitive campsites
• Fire pits (in designated areas)

Activities:
• Hiking
• Off-roading

Others Campgrounds

• Cathedral Gorge State Park (Panaca, NV)
• Echo Canyon State Park (Pioche, NV)
• Wildhorse Reservoir State Recreation Area (Elko, NV)
• Berlin-Ichthyosaur State Park (Gabbs, NV)
• Rye Patch State Recreation Area (Lovelock, NV)
• Cave Lake State Park (Ely, NV)
• South Fork State Recreation Area (Spring Creek, NV)
• Walker Lake State Recreation Area (Hawthorne, NV)
• Lahontan State Recreation Area (Silver Springs, NV)
• Beaver Dam State Park (Caliente, NV)

Others Boondocking

• Pahrump BLM Land
• Eldorado Canyon (Nelson, NV)
• Walker Lake BLM Land
• Winnemucca Dry Lake
• Amargosa Valley BLM Land

Idaho: The Wilderness Playground

Idaho is one of those states that often gets overlooked, but for RVers who love the outdoors, it's an absolute paradise. Known for its rugged landscapes, towering mountains, and crystal-clear lakes, Idaho offers endless opportunities for adventure. Every time I drive through Idaho, I'm struck by how untouched and vast the wilderness feels—this is a place where nature truly takes center stage.

The best season to RV in Idaho is **summer through early fall**, from **June to September**. During these months, the weather is warm and perfect for hiking, fishing, and exploring the state's many outdoor wonders. The temperatures in the mountains are cooler, making summer the ideal time to visit the high-altitude areas. **Fall** is also stunning, especially in the northern part of the state, where the forests turn brilliant shades of gold and red. **The season to avoid** is **winter**, unless you're equipped for snow and love cold-weather activities like skiing or snowmobiling. Idaho's winters can be harsh, particularly in the mountains, and many campgrounds close for the season due to snow.

What makes Idaho stand out to RVers is its diversity. You can go from the rugged Sawtooth Mountains, where alpine lakes shimmer under snow-capped peaks, to the wide-open plains of southern Idaho, where vast farmlands stretch to the horizon. One of my favorite places to camp is near the Salmon River, where you can park your RV right next to the water and spend your days fishing or rafting through the rapids. And if you're looking for something truly unique, Idaho's Craters of the Moon National Monument offers an otherworldly landscape of ancient lava flows that make for a one-of-a-kind camping experience.

Idaho's campgrounds are as varied as its landscapes. You'll find everything from remote, rustic spots deep in the wilderness to well-maintained state parks with all the amenities you need for a comfortable stay. And if you're into off-the-grid camping, Idaho is full of opportunities for boondocking in some of the most peaceful and remote areas in the country. Whether you're exploring the scenic byways, hiking to hidden hot springs, or simply enjoying a quiet evening by the campfire, Idaho is a place that invites you to slow down and take in the beauty around you.

For RVers who crave adventure and solitude, Idaho is a state that delivers in spades. It's a destination where you can truly disconnect from the hustle of everyday life and reconnect with the wild. Whether you're navigating mountain passes or relaxing by a serene lake, Idaho's rugged charm will keep you coming back for more.

McCall RV Resort

200 Scott St, McCall, ID 83638

(208) 634-5646 $$

Campground Description:

Luxurious camping along the Payette River in McCall, Idaho, offering spacious RV sites, cabins, and access to outdoor activities year-round, including hiking, fishing, and skiing.

Types of Sites Available:
- RV sites with full hookups
- Pull-through and back-in sites
- Cabins

Amenities:
- Heated indoor pool and hot tub
- Free Wi-Fi, restrooms, showers
- Fitness center, playground
- Camp store

Activities:
- Fishing, kayaking, hiking
- Skiing at Brundage Mountain
- Exploring Ponderosa State Park
- Relaxing in the pool and hot tub

Unique Experiences: The resort's riverside location and luxury amenities make it a perfect base for outdoor adventures in Idaho's scenic wilderness.

Feedback: Highly rated for its clean facilities, scenic location, and friendly staff.

Ravenwood RV Resort

9300 N. Ravenwood Ln, Athol, ID 83801

(208) 561-5735 $$

Campground Description:

Family-friendly RV resort near Silverwood Theme Park, offering modern amenities and access to North Idaho's forests and lakes.

Types of Sites Available:
- RV sites with full hookups
- Tent camping

Amenities:
- Swimming pool, free Wi-Fi
- Restrooms, showers, laundry
- Playground, dog park

Activities:
- Visiting Silverwood Theme Park and Boulder
- Visiting Silverwood Theme Park
- Exploring Farragut State Park
- Hiking, biking, swimming

Unique Experiences: A convenient location near Silverwood Theme Park combined with a peaceful atmosphere for families and outdoor enthusiasts.

Feedback: Popular with families visiting Silverwood, praised for its clean facilities and friendly atmosphere.

Mountain View RV Park

📍 705 W Grand Ave, Arco, ID 83213

📞 (208) 527-3707 — $$

Campground Description:

Scenic RV park in Arco, Idaho, with stunning views of the Lost River Range and easy access to Craters of the Moon National Monument.

Types of Sites Available:
- RV sites with full hookups
- Tent camping

Amenities:
- Free Wi-Fi, restrooms, showers
- Picnic areas, BBQ grills
- On-site restaurant (Pickle's Place)

Activities:
- Visiting Craters of the Moon
- Hiking in the Lost River Range
- Stargazing

Unique Experiences: Perfect base for exploring Craters of the Moon and enjoying quiet mountain views.

Feedback: Loved for its friendly staff, clean facilities, and excellent location near Craters of the Moon.

Silverwood RV Park

📍 27843 N US-95, Athol, ID 83801

📞 (208) 683-3400 — $$

Campground Description:

Convenient RV park next to Silverwood Theme Park, offering full-service camping with easy access to roller coasters, water slides, and entertainment.

Types of Sites Available:
- RV sites with full hookups
- Tent camping

Amenities:
- Free Wi-Fi, restrooms, showers
- Laundry facilities, picnic areas
- Playground

Activities:
- Spending the day at Silverwood Theme Park
- Hiking at Farragut State Park
- Relaxing by the pool at Boulder Beach

Unique Experiences: Stay just steps away from Silverwood Theme Park for fun-filled family adventures.

Feedback: Highly rated for its proximity to Silverwood and family-friendly facilities.

Meadow Lake Resort & Campground

Address: 254 Theriault Rd, St. Maries, ID 83861

Campground Description:
A peaceful lakeside campground surrounded by lush forest, Meadow Lake Resort offers scenic views and fishing opportunities.
Unique Experience: Camp by the water and enjoy quiet moments while fishing or paddling on the lake.

Amenities:
• Picnic areas
• Restrooms with showers

Activities:
• Fishing and boating on Meadow Lake
• Hiking in nearby forests

Moose Crossing RV Park

Address: 2999 Gibbonsville Rd, Salmon, ID 83467

Campground Description:
Located near the Idaho-Montana border, Moose Crossing RV Park provides a quiet, rustic retreat in a scenic mountain setting.
Unique Experience: Stay in a tranquil location known for wildlife sightings and serene mountain views.

Amenities:
• Full RV hookups
• Picnic tables

Activities:
• Hiking and wildlife watching
• Relaxing by the Salmon River

Henry's Lake State Park

Address: 3917 E 5100 N, Island Park, ID 83429

Campground Description:
A beautiful campground on the shores of Henry's Lake, known for its excellent fishing and panoramic views of the surrounding mountains.
Unique Experience: Fish for trophy trout while enjoying the stunning high-desert landscape.

Amenities:
• Restrooms and showers
• Picnic areas

Activities:
• Fishing for trophy trout
• Boating and kayaking on the lake

Bruneau Dunes State Park

Address: 27608 Bruneau Sand Dunes Rd, Bruneau, ID 83604

Campground Description:
Home to the tallest single-structured sand dune in North America, Bruneau Dunes State Park offers a unique desert camping experience.
Unique Experience: Explore giant sand dunes and stargaze at Idaho's only public observatory.

Amenities:
• Restrooms and showers
• Picnic areas

Activities:
• Sandboarding on the dunes
• Stargazing at the observatory

Boondocking

Boise National Forest

Address: 1249 S Vinnell Way, Boise, ID 83709

Campground Description:
Offering dispersed camping opportunities in a pristine forest setting, Boise National Forest is perfect for those seeking solitude in nature.

Unique Experience: Camp in secluded spots surrounded by towering pines and mountain streams.

Amenities:
• Primitive campsites
• Vault toilets

Activities:
• Hiking and fishing in remote areas
• Off-roading and wildlife watching

Sawtooth National Forest

Address: 5 N Fork Canyon Rd, Ketchum, ID 83340

Campground Description:
Sawtooth National Forest is known for its dramatic mountain peaks, alpine lakes, and wilderness areas, offering incredible boondocking experiences.

Unique Experience: Wake up to breathtaking views of rugged peaks and crystal-clear lakes in complete isolation.

Amenities:
• Primitive campsites
• Vault toilets

Activities:
• Hiking to alpine lakes
• Mountain biking and rock climbing

Others Campgrounds

• Blue Lake RV Resort
• Water's Edge RV Resort
• Teton Valley Resort
• Bear Den RV Resort
• Wagonhammer RV Park
• Challis Hot Springs Campground
• Deer Run RV Park
• Clearwater Crossing RV Park
• Three Island Crossing State Park
• Priest Lake State Park

Others Boondocking

• Craters of the Moon National Monument (dispersed camping areas)
• Salmon-Challis National Forest (dispersed camping)
• Magic Reservoir (dispersed camping)
• Sawtooth Wilderness (dispersed camping zones)
• Clearwater National Forest (various dispersed camping spots)

Others National Park

• Craters of the Moon National Monument Campground

Washington: Pacific Northwest Adventure

Washington State, with its towering mountains, lush forests, and dramatic coastline, is a paradise for RVers looking for adventure and natural beauty. Known for its diverse landscapes, from the snow-capped peaks of the **Cascade Mountains** to the rugged shores of the **Olympic Peninsula**, Washington offers endless opportunities for exploration. Whether you're hiking through alpine meadows, exploring the vibrant city of **Seattle**, or camping by a pristine lake, Washington invites RVers to discover the wild beauty of the Pacific Northwest.

The best season to RV in Washington is **late spring through early fall**, from **May to October**. **Summer** is the prime time to explore the state's national parks and outdoor attractions, with warm, dry weather perfect for hiking, camping, and sightseeing. **Spring** is equally beautiful, with blooming wildflowers and snow-capped mountains creating stunning scenery. **Fall** offers cooler temperatures and colorful foliage, especially in the forests and mountain regions. **Winter** can be cold and rainy, particularly in the western part of the state, but it's also the season for snow sports in the mountains, making it ideal for RVers looking to ski, snowboard, or snowshoe.

For RVers, Washington's **national parks** are must-see destinations. **Mount Rainier National Park**, with its iconic 14,410-foot peak, offers breathtaking vistas, alpine meadows, and waterfalls. The park's campgrounds are nestled in the shadow of the mountain, providing a serene and scenic base for hiking and wildlife viewing. **North Cascades National Park** is another gem, offering rugged wilderness, glacial lakes, and some of the most dramatic mountain scenery in the country.

The **Olympic Peninsula**, home to **Olympic National Park**, offers a completely different experience. Here, you can explore lush rainforests, rugged coastlines, and alpine peaks all in one park. The **Hoh Rain Forest**, one of the largest temperate rainforests in the U.S., is a must-visit for its moss-draped trees and serene atmosphere. Coastal campgrounds in the park offer the chance to camp near the Pacific Ocean, with the sound of crashing waves in the background.

Washington's cities also offer plenty of attractions for RVers. **Seattle**, the state's largest city, is known for its vibrant arts scene, world-class dining, and iconic landmarks like the **Space Needle** and **Pike Place Market**. RVers can stay in campgrounds just outside the city, allowing easy access to Seattle's urban offerings while still being close to nature. For a quieter experience, **San Juan Islands** offer a peaceful retreat with opportunities for kayaking, whale watching, and camping by the water.

The **Columbia River Gorge**, with its towering cliffs and cascading waterfalls, is another favorite for RVers. The scenic drive along the gorge offers stunning views, hiking trails, and campsites with river access, making it a perfect destination for outdoor lovers.

Washington's campgrounds range from full-service RV parks to more rustic, off-the-grid options in national and state parks. Whether you're camping in the mountains, by the coast, or near one of the state's many lakes and rivers, Washington's campgrounds offer plenty of opportunities to immerse yourself in the state's natural beauty.

For RVers seeking a mix of adventure, serene landscapes, and vibrant city life, Washington offers an unforgettable experience. Whether you're hiking to a glacier, strolling through a bustling market, or camping by the ocean, Washington delivers a Pacific Northwest adventure that's hard to beat.

Kalaloch Campground

157151 US-101, Forks, WA 98331

(360) 962-2271 — $

Campground Description:

Located within Olympic National Park, Kalaloch Campground offers stunning ocean views and a peaceful coastal setting. Ideal for nature lovers, it provides easy access to beaches, tide pools, and hiking trails.

Types of Sites Available:

- Tent camping
- RV sites (no hookups)
- Group camping

Amenities:
- Restrooms
- Picnic tables
- Fire rings
- Beach access
- Bump station (seasonal)

Activities:

- Exploring tide pools
- Hiking coastal trails,
- Wildlife watching
- Visiting nearby Olympic National Park attractions.

Unique Experiences: Enjoy oceanfront camping with breathtaking views of the Pacific, access to pristine beaches, and proximity to iconic Olympic National Park landmarks.

Feedback: Guests rave about the scenic beauty, peaceful atmosphere, and access to tide pools and trails.

Lake Sammamish State Park Campground

2000 NW Sammamish Rd, Issaquah, WA 98027

(425) 649-4275 — $$

Campground Description:

This lakeside campground near Issaquah offers peaceful camping with access to swimming, boating, and hiking in a scenic park setting, just minutes from the city.

Types of Sites Available:
- Tent camping
- RV sites (no hookups)

Amenities:
- Restrooms   • Swim beaches
- Picnic areas • Playground
- Boat launch

Activities:

- Swimming
- Boating
- Fishing
- Hiking
- Picnicking
- Wildlife watching

Unique Experiences: Campers can enjoy Lake Sammamish's beaches and water activities while remaining close to Issaquah's local attractions.

Feedback: Praised for its family-friendly environment, clean facilities, and beautiful lake access, offering a perfect mix of nature and convenience.

Scenic Beach State Park Campground

Address: 9565 Scenic Beach Rd NW, Seabeck, WA 98380

Campground Description:
A picturesque waterfront campground offering stunning views of the Olympic Mountains and Hood Canal.

Unique Experience: Camp near the shore and enjoy breathtaking sunsets over the mountains.

Amenities:
• Restrooms
• Picnic areas

Activities:
• Beachcombing
• Hiking

Camano Island State Park Campground

Address: 2269 Lowell Point Rd, Camano, WA 98282

Campground Description:
A peaceful forested campground with easy access to Puget Sound, ideal for nature lovers and outdoor enthusiasts.

Unique Experience: Camp surrounded by lush forests with access to quiet beach walks along the Sound.

Amenities:
• Restrooms
• Fire pits

Activities:
• Hiking
• Beach exploration

Mount Rainier National Park (Cougar Rock Campground)

Address: Paradise Rd E, Ashford, WA 98304

Campground Description:
A popular campground near the base of Mount Rainier, offering magnificent views and easy access to the park's hiking trails.

Unique Experience: Camp with panoramic views of Mount Rainier and explore alpine meadows and scenic trails.

Amenities:
• Restrooms
• Picnic areas

Activities:
• Hiking
• Wildlife viewing

North Cascades National Park (Newhalem Campground)

Address: 810 State Route 20, Rockport, WA 98283

Campground Description:
A tranquil campground located in the lush forests of North Cascades National Park, perfect for adventurers.

Unique Experience: Explore rugged mountains and pristine lakes while camping in one of the country's most beautiful wilderness areas.

Amenities:
• Restrooms
• Fire pits

Activities:
• Hiking
• Scenic drives

Boondocking

Mount Baker-Snoqualmie National Forest

Address: Washington (various dispersed camping locations)

Campground Description:
Boondocking options in a vast forest, offering diverse landscapes from towering mountains to dense woodlands.

Unique Experience: Enjoy secluded camping with access to hiking, fishing, and scenic drives through stunning mountain terrain.

Amenities:
• Primitive sites
• Scenic views

Activities:
• Hiking
• Fishing

Okanogan-Wenatchee National Forest

Address: Washington (various dispersed camping locations)

Campground Description:
A vast forest offering dispersed camping with access to rugged mountain landscapes and scenic river valleys.

Unique Experience: Explore remote wilderness areas with stunning views and enjoy the tranquility of the forest.

Amenities:
• Primitive sites
• Scenic views

Activities:
• Hiking
• Wildlife viewing

Others Campgrounds

• Deception Pass State Park Campground (Oak Harbor, WA)
• Sun Lakes-Dry Falls State Park Campground (Coulee City, WA)
• Fort Worden State Park Campground (Port Townsend, WA)
• Kitsap Memorial State Park Campground (Poulsbo, WA)
• Cape Disappointment State Park Campground (Ilwaco, WA)
• Blake Island State Park Campground (Blake Island, WA)
• Dosewallips State Park Campground (Brinnon, WA)
• Twanoh State Park Campground (Union, WA)
• Wenatchee Confluence State Park Campground (Wenatchee, WA)
• Battle Ground Lake State Park Campground (Battle Ground, WA)

Others Boondocking

• Gifford Pinchot National Forest (dispersed camping in various locations, WA)
• Colville National Forest (dispersed sites near water bodies, WA)
• Ahtanum State Forest (Yakima area, WA)
• Capitol State Forest (Olympia area, WA)
• Green Mountain State Forest (Silverdale area, WA)

Others National Park

• Olympic National Park (Hoh Campground)
• Mount Rainier National Park (White River Campground)
• North Cascades National Park (Goodell Creek Campground)

Oregon: A Pacific Wonderland

Oregon is a state that offers RVers an incredible variety of landscapes and outdoor experiences, from the rugged Pacific coastline to the towering peaks of the **Cascade Mountains**, and the vast, serene deserts of the east. Known for its lush forests, pristine rivers, and diverse natural beauty, Oregon is a dream destination for those looking to immerse themselves in nature. Whether you're exploring the volcanic wonders of **Crater Lake National Park**, hiking along the majestic **Columbia River Gorge**, or relaxing in a peaceful forest campground, Oregon invites you to discover its wild and scenic beauty.

The best season to RV in Oregon is **late spring through early fall**, from **May to October**. **Summer** is the perfect time to enjoy Oregon's great outdoors, with warm, dry weather that makes hiking, camping, and exploring the coast ideal. **Spring** is beautiful, with blooming wildflowers and lush greenery, while **fall** brings cooler temperatures and spectacular foliage, particularly in the forests and mountain regions. **Winter** can be cold and wet, especially along the coast and in the western part of the state, but for those who enjoy winter sports, the mountains offer excellent skiing and snowboarding opportunities.

Oregon's **Pacific Coast** is one of the most stunning drives in the country, with dramatic cliffs, sandy beaches, and charming coastal towns that make it a favorite destination for RVers. **Cape Perpetua**, **Cannon Beach**, and **Tillamook** are just a few of the highlights along the scenic **Highway 101**, where you can camp with ocean views and explore tide pools, lighthouses, and seaside forests. For a quieter coastal experience, the southern part of the coast offers fewer crowds and pristine, rugged beauty.

Inland, the **Cascade Mountains** and the **Columbia River Gorge** are must-see destinations for RVers. The **Columbia River Gorge** is famous for its stunning waterfalls, such as **Multnomah Falls**, and offers excellent hiking, biking, and camping opportunities with breathtaking views of the river and cliffs. Further south, **Crater Lake National Park**, with its deep blue volcanic lake, is a true natural wonder and one of the most awe-inspiring places to camp in the state.

Eastern Oregon provides a completely different landscape, with wide-open deserts, dramatic rock formations, and plenty of solitude. **Smith Rock State Park** is a favorite for rock climbers and hikers, while the **Alvord Desert** and the **Steens Mountain Wilderness** offer remote and peaceful camping experiences for those who want to escape the crowds.

Oregon's campgrounds are as diverse as its landscapes, with options ranging from full-service RV resorts to more rustic, wilderness spots in state and national parks. Whether you're camping by a river, in the forest, or along the coast, Oregon's well-maintained campgrounds make it easy to enjoy the state's natural beauty.

For RVers seeking adventure, tranquility, and a deep connection with nature, Oregon is a destination that offers it all. From its misty forests and rushing rivers to its serene deserts and oceanfront vistas, Oregon provides endless opportunities for exploration and relaxation.

Sea and Sand RV Park

4985 N Hwy 101, Depoe Bay, OR 97341

(541) 764-2313 — **$$**

Campground Description:

Located on the Oregon Coast, this RV park offers direct beach access and stunning ocean views. It's the perfect base for coastal adventures like whale watching, hiking, and exploring Depoe Bay.

Types of Sites Available:
- RV sites with full hookups
- Ocean view and standard sites

Amenities:
- Direct beach access
- Restrooms and showers
- Dog park

Activities:
- Beachcombing
- Whale watching
- Exploring coastal trails

Unique Experiences: Guests can enjoy panoramic ocean views and direct access to sandy beaches, perfect for a relaxing coastal retreat.

Feedback: Praised for its peaceful atmosphere, ocean views, and proximity to the beach, making it ideal for nature lovers.

Harris Beach State Park

1655 Hwy 101 N, Brookings, OR 97415

(800) 551-6949 — **$**

Campground Description:

This scenic coastal campground offers stunning views of sea stacks and sandy beaches, providing easy access to tide pools and wildlife along the Oregon Coast.

Types of Sites Available:
- RV sites with full hookups
- Tent camping sites
- Yurts available

Amenities:
- Beach access
- Hiking trails
- Fire rings

Activities:
- Beachcombing and tide pooling
- Whale watching
- Hiking along coastal trails

Unique Experiences: Harris Beach offers guests a chance to explore tide pools, spot wildlife, and enjoy dramatic ocean views, making it a top coastal destination.

Feedback: Loved for its scenic beauty, clean facilities, and rich wildlife viewing opportunities, it's perfect for nature lovers.

Fort Stevens State Park

📍 100 Peter Iredale Rd, Hammond, OR 97121

📞 (800) 551-6949 $$

Campground Description:

A historic and scenic park with expansive beaches, hiking trails, and military fortifications to explore, including the famous Peter Iredale shipwreck.

Types of Sites Available:
- RV sites with full hookups
- Tent camping sites
- Yurts available

Amenities:
- Historic sites
- Restrooms and showers
- Hiking and biking trails

Activities:
- Exploring the historic fort and shipwreck
- Hiking and biking
- Wildlife watching

Unique Experiences: Fort Stevens offers a unique blend of history and nature, with historic military sites and miles of scenic coastline to explore.

Feedback: Guests appreciate the park's historical significance and variety of outdoor activities, making it a popular spot for families and history enthusiasts.

Mt. Hood Village RV Resort

📍 65000 E. Hwy 26, Welches, OR 97067

📞 (503) 622-4011 $$

Campground Description:

Nestled in the Mount Hood National Forest, this resort offers year-round access to outdoor activities like hiking, skiing, and fishing, making it a great spot for nature lovers.

Types of Sites Available:
- RV sites with full hookups
- Cabins and yurts available

Amenities:
- Indoor heated pool
- Fitness center
- Hiking trails

Activities:
- Hiking and skiing in Mount Hood National Forest
- Fishing and kayaking on local lakes
- Relaxing in the pool and hot tub

Unique Experiences: Guests enjoy year-round outdoor adventures, from hiking in summer to skiing in winter, with the comforts of a well-equipped resort.

Feedback: Praised for its excellent amenities and proximity to Mount Hood's recreational activities, it's a favorite among adventurers and families.

Sunny Valley RV Park and Campground

Address: 140 Old Stage Rd, Sunny Valley, OR 97497

Campground Description:
A peaceful RV park located in a beautiful valley, offering easy access to nearby rivers and trails.

Unique Experience: Enjoy quiet camping surrounded by nature with opportunities for river walks and fishing.

Amenities:
- Full hookups
- Camp store

Activities:
- Fishing
- Hiking

Belknap Hot Springs RV Park

Address: 59296 N Belknap Springs Rd, McKenzie Bridge, OR 97413

Campground Description:
A tranquil RV park nestled near the McKenzie River, featuring natural hot springs and lush forest surroundings.

Unique Experience: Relax in the soothing hot springs while enjoying the peaceful riverside setting.

Amenities:
- Hot springs pool
- Restrooms

Activities:
- Soaking in hot springs
- Hiking nearby trails

Wallowa Lake State Park

Address: 72214 Marina Ln, Joseph, OR 97846

Campground Description:
Located at the foot of the Wallowa Mountains, this scenic state park offers lakeside camping with stunning mountain views.

Unique Experience: Camp near a crystal-clear lake with access to boat rentals and mountain hikes.

Amenities:
- Boat ramp
- Restrooms

Activities:
- Boating
- Hiking

Nehalem Bay State Park

Address: 34600 Gary St, Nehalem, OR 97131

Campground Description:
A coastal state park offering beachfront camping with easy access to sand dunes and ocean views.

Unique Experience: Fall asleep to the sound of waves and explore scenic coastal trails and beaches.

Amenities:
- Restrooms
- Picnic areas

Activities:
- Beachcombing
- Fishing

Boondocking

Deschutes National Forest
Address: Deschutes National Forest, OR

Campground Description:
Boondocking is available in the vast wilderness of Deschutes National Forest, offering remote camping amidst towering pines and clear mountain lakes.

Unique Experience: Disconnect from the world in this beautiful forested area, ideal for peaceful solitude and nature immersion.

Amenities:
• Primitive campsites
• Lake access

Activities:
• Hiking
• Wildlife watching

Umpqua National Forest
Address: Umpqua National Forest, OR

Campground Description:
This expansive forest offers numerous boondocking opportunities, featuring rivers, waterfalls, and rugged wilderness.

Unique Experience: Explore the remote beauty of the Umpqua Forest with opportunities for fishing and river adventures.

Amenities:
• Primitive campsites
• River access

Activities:
• Fishing
• Hiking

Others Campgrounds

• Silver Spur RV Park (Silverton, OR)
• Seven Feathers RV Resort (Canyonville, OR)
• Big Pines RV Park (Rogue River, OR)
• Crown Villa RV Resort (Bend, OR)
• Hee Hee Illahee RV Resort (Salem, OR)
• Bend/Sisters Garden RV Resort (Sisters, OR)
• South Beach State Park (Newport, OR)
• Beverly Beach State Park (Newport, OR)
• Joseph H. Stewart State Recreation Area (Trail, OR)
• Clyde Holliday State Recreation Site (Mount Vernon, OR)

Others Boondocking

• BLM Land near Burns, OR
• Mount Hood National Forest (dispersed camping areas)
• Ochoco National Forest (dispersed camping areas)
• Fremont-Winema National Forest (dispersed camping areas)
• Deschutes River Recreation Area

Others National Park

• Crater Lake National Park (Mazama Village Campground)

California: The Ultimate Playground

California is a state like no other. From the moment you hit the road, it feels like you're embarking on the adventure of a lifetime. I've driven through California many times, and each journey brings something new—whether it's the coastal breeze along Highway 1, the towering redwoods of the north, or the vast deserts stretching out under a blanket of stars. For RVers, California is nothing short of paradise, offering an endless variety of landscapes, climates, and experiences that can't be matched.

The best season for RVing in California depends largely on where you're headed. For **coastal areas and Northern California**, **spring and fall** are the ideal times, offering mild temperatures and fewer crowds, making places like Big Sur, Mendocino, and the Redwood National and State Parks even more magical. For **Southern California**, the weather is favorable almost year-round, although **summer** can get quite hot in inland areas like Death Valley and the Mojave Desert. For those areas, it's best to visit in **winter** or **early spring**. **The season to avoid** largely depends on where you're going, but **summer** in desert regions like **Death Valley** can be dangerously hot, while **winter** in the Sierra Nevada can bring heavy snow, closing roads and limiting access to some of the state's most iconic parks.

California's diversity is what makes it so special. One moment you're basking in the sun along the Pacific Coast, and the next, you're winding through the awe-inspiring Sierra Nevada or hiking in the desert canyons. The state is home to some of the most famous national parks in the world, like Yosemite, Sequoia, and Joshua Tree, each offering a unique experience for RVers. Whether you're looking to camp among the world's tallest trees or park your RV near a serene alpine lake, there's no shortage of unforgettable spots.

One of my favorite parts of RVing in California is the endless options for adventure. In a single trip, you can go from surfing in the morning to snowboarding in the afternoon. And the campgrounds? They range from luxurious RV resorts with every amenity you can imagine to remote, peaceful spots where it's just you and the wilderness. No matter where you go, California promises unforgettable views, endless activities, and that perfect blend of natural beauty and laid-back culture.

Newport Dunes Waterfront Resort & Marina

📍 1131 Back Bay Dr, Newport Beach, CA 92660

📞 (949) 729-3863 $$$

Campground Description:

A luxury RV resort with stunning waterfront views in Newport Beach, CA. Offers water sports, a heated pool, and resort-style relaxation with easy access to local beaches and attractions.

Types of Sites Available:
- RV sites with full hookups
- Beachfront and non-beachfront sites

Amenities:
- Marina and waterfront access
- Heated pool and spa
- On-site restaurant
- Water sports rentals

Activities:
- Kayaking, paddleboarding, and boating
- Swimming and beach activities
- Exploring Newport Beach

Unique Experiences: Combines luxury and adventure with water sports and beach access, making it the perfect upscale RV getaway in Southern California.

Feedback: Ideal for families and travelers seeking a high-end resort experience with beach and water activities.

Flying Flags RV Resort & Campground

📍 180 Avenue of the Flags, Buellton, CA 93427

📞 (877) 783-5247 $$

Campground Description:

Located in California's wine country, Flying Flags RV Resort offers a family-friendly experience with luxury amenities, including pools, dog parks, and access to nearby wineries and outdoor activities.

Types of Sites Available:
- RV sites with full hookups
- Cottages and glamping tents

Amenities:
- Pools and hot tubs
- Dog parks
- On-site dining and market

Activities:
- Wine tasting and hiking
- Swimming and on-site events
- Exploring the nearby town of Solvang

Unique Experiences: A perfect blend of comfort and adventure in California's wine country, offering relaxing amenities with close proximity to outdoor fun and cultural exploration.

Feedback: Popular among families and groups looking to enjoy the scenic beauty of wine country with upscale amenities.

Palm Canyon Hotel & RV Resort

📍 221 Palm Canyon Dr, Borrego Springs, CA 92004

📞 (760) 767-5341 — $$

Campground Description:

Located in Borrego Springs, this RV resort combines Old West charm with modern amenities, offering easy access to Anza-Borrego Desert State Park for hiking and desert exploration.

Types of Sites Available:

- RV sites with full hookups
- Hotel rooms available

Amenities:

- Heated pools and hot tubs
- On-site restaurant
- Retro-themed hotel rooms

Activities:

- Hiking in Anza-Borrego Desert State Park
- Stargazing and desert wildlife viewing

Unique Experiences:
Offers a unique Old West atmosphere with access to stunning desert landscapes, perfect for nature lovers and adventure seekers.

Feedback:
A favorite for those wanting to explore the desert with the comfort of a modern resort and historic flair.

Ocean Mesa at El Capitan

📍 100 El Capitan Terrace Ln, Goleta, CA 93117

📞 (866) 410-5783 — $$$

Campground Description:

A luxurious coastal RV resort with panoramic ocean views and access to El Capitan State Beach. Features resort-style amenities like a heated pool, hiking trails, and fire pits for a perfect mix of adventure and relaxation.

Types of Sites Available:

- RV sites with full hookups
- Cabins for rent

Amenities:
- Heated pool and hot tub
- On-site store
- Hiking trails

Activities:

- Hiking and wildlife viewing
- Swimming and beach exploration

Unique Experiences: A coastal paradise offering oceanfront camping with the luxury of resort-style amenities and access to California's stunning coastline.

Feedback: Perfect for travelers seeking luxury and tranquility by the ocean with top-notch facilities and breathtaking views.

Parkway RV Resort & Campground

Address: 6330 County Road 200, Orland, CA 95963

Campground Description:
Parkway RV Resort & Campground offers a peaceful and relaxing atmosphere surrounded by orchards in Northern California. It's an ideal base for exploring nearby nature reserves and parks.

Unique Experience: Enjoy a serene, family-friendly environment with easy access to the Sacramento River.

Amenities:
• Full RV hookups
• Swimming pool

Activities:
• Exploring local nature reserves
• Relaxing by the pool and picnicking

Sierra Skies RV Park

Address: 100 Sierra Skies Rd, Sierra City, CA 96125

Campground Description:
Nestled in the Sierra Nevada Mountains, Sierra Skies RV Park provides a scenic and tranquil retreat with a small-town charm, perfect for those seeking adventure and relaxation.

Unique Experience: Camp along the Yuba River, with easy access to the Pacific Crest Trail and nearby alpine lakes.

Amenities:
• Full RV hookups
• River access

Activities:
• Hiking the Pacific Crest Trail
• Fishing and swimming in the Yuba River

Jedediah Smith Redwoods State Park

Address: 1461 US-199, Crescent City, CA 95531

Campground Description:
Jedediah Smith Redwoods State Park is renowned for its towering ancient redwoods and lush forest landscapes. This park offers a peaceful escape surrounded by nature's giants.

Unique Experience: Camp under the world's tallest trees and explore the pristine Smith River.

Amenities:
• Restrooms and showers
• Picnic areas

Activities:
• Hiking among the redwoods
• Fishing and kayaking on the Smith River

Pfeiffer Big Sur State Park

Address: 47225 Highway 1, Big Sur, CA 93920

Campground Description:
Located along California's famous Big Sur coast, Pfeiffer Big Sur State Park offers stunning views, towering redwoods, and access to scenic hiking trails.

Unique Experience: Enjoy dramatic coastal views and explore nearby waterfalls in this iconic park.

Amenities:
• Restrooms and showers
• Picnic areas

Activities:
• Hiking in the redwoods
• Exploring McWay Falls and the coastline

Boondocking

Bureau of Land Management (BLM) Land

Address: Various locations near Joshua Tree National Park, CA

Campground Description:
BLM land near Joshua Tree National Park offers dispersed camping in a rugged desert landscape. Perfect for off-grid campers seeking solitude and stunning night skies.

Unique Experience: Camp under the stars in the Mojave Desert, just minutes from Joshua Tree's famous boulders and trails.

Amenities:
• Primitive campsites
• Wide-open desert views

Activities:
• Stargazing in the dark desert skies
• Hiking and bouldering in Joshua Tree

Anza-Borrego Desert State Park

Address: 200 Palm Canyon Dr, Borrego Springs, CA 92004

Campground Description:
Anza-Borrego Desert State Park is California's largest state park, offering dispersed camping in a vast desert landscape filled with rugged beauty and wildlife.

Unique Experience: Experience true desert wilderness, with opportunities to see wildflowers, wildlife, and ancient fossils.

Amenities:
• Primitive campsites
• Scenic desert views

Activities:
• Hiking through desert trails
• Wildlife and wildflower viewing

Others Campgrounds

• Casini Ranch Family Campground
• Ponderosa RV Resort
• Paradise by the Sea RV Resort
• Ventura Ranch KOA
• Indian Flat Campground
• Coloma Resort
• Golden Shore RV Resort
• Mountain Gate RV Park
• Cava Robles RV Resort
• Frandy Campground

Others Boondocking

• Plumas National Forest (dispersed camping)
• Inyo National Forest (dispersed camping near Bishop)
• Tahoe National Forest (along Bowman Lake Road)
• Alabama Hills Recreation Area
• Carrizo Plain National Monument

Others National Park

• Sequoia National Park (Lodgepole Campground)
• Kings Canyon National Park (Azalea Campground)
• Yosemite National Park (Upper Pines Campground)

Alaska: The Last Frontier for RV Adventurers

There's nothing more captivating or wild than Alaska. I still remember the overwhelming sense of freedom I felt while driving my RV on roads that seem to lead to the edge of the world. If there's one state that makes you feel truly connected to nature, it's Alaska. Every turn reveals jaw-dropping vistas: towering mountains, majestic glaciers, endless forests, and that golden light that blankets everything during the long summer days.

The best season to explore Alaska in an RV is definitely **summer**, from June to August. During these months, the temperatures are mild, and the days are incredibly long, with the sun barely setting in some parts of the state. This gives you more time to uncover the wild beauty, fish in pristine rivers, or simply admire the untouched landscapes around you. On the other hand, **the season to avoid** is **winter**, from November to February, unless you're an experienced adventurer ready for the extreme. Freezing temperatures, snowstorms, and closed roads make this time of year very challenging for RV trips.

A trip to Alaska is synonymous with adventure. There are countless opportunities to stop and be amazed by nature's wonders. Campgrounds here aren't just rest stops; they're gateways to experiences that stay with you forever—like spotting grizzly bears fishing in the rivers, hearing the thunderous crack of glaciers calving, or witnessing the breathtaking northern lights on the colder nights toward the end of summer.

RVing through Alaska allows you to access remote locations, far off the beaten tourist path. And every stop, whether in a city like Anchorage or a remote wilderness area, makes you feel like you're part of something bigger—the Last Frontier.

Diamond M Ranch Resort

48500 Diamond M Ranch Rd, Kenai, AK 99611

(907) 283-9424 — $$

Campground Description:

Diamond M Ranch Resort combines a working ranch experience with modern RV amenities, offering a family-friendly atmosphere in the heart of Alaska's Kenai Peninsula. Perfect for fishing, hiking, and wildlife viewing.

Types of Sites Available:
- RV sites with full hookups
- Tent camping sites
- Cabins for rent

Amenities:
- Free Wi-Fi
- Restrooms and showers
- Laundry facilities
- Walking trails
- Fishing gear available

Activities:
- Fishing tours
- Hiking
- Community BBQs
- Exploring the Kenai River

Unique Experiences: Guests can experience life on a working ranch and enjoy world-class fishing on the Kenai River, along with breathtaking Alaskan sunsets.

Feedback: Perfect for families, couples, and adventure seekers. Friendly service, scenic views, and access to fishing make this a top choice.

Denali Grizzly Bear Resort

Mile 231.1 Parks Hwy, Denali National Park, AK 99755

(866) 583-2696 — $$

Campground Description:

Denali Grizzly Bear Resort offers a rustic Alaskan experience along the Nenana River, minutes from Denali National Park. Ideal for wildlife viewing and exploring Denali's vast wilderness.

Types of Sites Available:
- RV sites with full hookups
- Tent camping sites
- Cabins for rent

Amenities:
- General store
- Wi-Fi (in select areas)
- Shuttle service to Denali
- River access

Activities:
- Hiking in Denali
- Wildlife viewing
- Fishing on the Nenana River
- Shuttle tours to Denali

Unique Experiences: Enjoy riverfront camping with views of the Nenana River and easy access to Denali National Park. Evening campfires create a cozy atmosphere for sharing adventures.

Feedback: Ideal for nature lovers and families looking for a convenient base to explore Denali. Rustic charm with modern amenities.

Denali Rainbow Village RV Park & Motel

📍 Mile 238.6 Parks Hwy, Denali National Park, AK 99755

📞 (907) 683-7777 —— $$

Campground Description:

Just one mile from the entrance to Denali National Park, Denali Rainbow Village RV Park offers full-service RV sites, motel rooms, and easy access to local shops and restaurants.

Types of Sites Available:
- RV sites with full hookups
- Tent camping sites
- Motel rooms for rent

Amenities:
- Laundry facilities
- Free Wi-Fi
- Shuttle services
- Showers and restrooms

Activities:
- Hiking in Denali
- Rafting on the Nenana River
- Shopping and dining nearby
- Scenic drives

Unique Experiences: Stay close to Denali's natural wonders while enjoying modern conveniences. Perfect for booking tours or relaxing after a day of exploration.

Feedback: A great location for adventurers and families. The proximity to Denali National Park is unbeatable, making it a favorite for exploring the area.

Eagle's Rest RV Park & Cabins

📍 139 E Pioneer Dr, Valdez, AK 99686

📞 (907) 835-2373 —— $$

Campground Description:

Located in Valdez, Alaska, Eagle's Rest RV Park & Cabins offers stunning mountain views and access to outdoor activities like fishing, wildlife viewing, and glacier tours.

Types of Sites Available:
- RV sites with full hookups
- Tent camping sites
- Cabins for rent

Amenities:
- Laundry facilities
- Free Wi-Fi
- Restrooms and showers
- On-site store

Activities:
- Fishing trips
- Glacier tours
- Hiking
- Wildlife viewing

Unique Experiences: Wake up to views of mountains and glaciers. Enjoy glacier cruises and fishing expeditions, with easy access to the Alaskan wilderness.

Feedback: A favorite for adventurers seeking the wild beauty of Alaska. Excellent facilities and friendly staff enhance the experience in Valdez.

Nenana RV Park & Campground

Address: Milepost 304.5 Parks Hwy, Nenana, AK 99760

Campground Description:
Nenana RV Park offers a quiet, relaxed camping experience in Alaska's interior, perfect for travelers looking for a peaceful spot. Located along the Parks Highway, it's an ideal base for exploring nearby wilderness and rivers.

Unique Experience: Enjoy a quiet stay near the Nenana River with easy access to wildlife viewing and peaceful surroundings.

Amenities:
• Full RV hookups
• Camp store

Activities:
• Wildlife viewing
• Fishing on the Nenana River

Savage River Campground

sAddress: Denali Park Rd Mile 13, Denali National Park, AK 99755

Campground Description:
Located within Denali National Park, Savage River Campground offers stunning mountain views and close access to the Savage River for hiking and exploring. It's a perfect base for those wanting to experience the wild beauty of Denali.

Unique Experience: Camp in the heart of Denali National Park, surrounded by wildlife and awe-inspiring landscapes.

Amenities:
• Picnic tables and fire pits
• Shuttle service to park attractions

Activities:
• Hiking the Savage River Loop Trail
• Wildlife watching

Hatcher Pass RV Park

Address: 9000 N Palmer Fishhook Rd, Willow, AK 99688

Campground Description:
Hatcher Pass RV Park is a hidden gem in Alaska's Matanuska-Susitna Valley. Surrounded by mountains and lush landscapes, this campground offers breathtaking views and easy access to Hatcher Pass for outdoor activities.

Unique Experience: Camp with panoramic mountain views and access to hiking and gold panning in the Hatcher Pass area.

Amenities:
• RV sites with hookups
• Laundry facilities

Activities:
• Hiking in Hatcher Pass
• Exploring the historic Independence Mine

Riley Creek Campground

Address: Denali Park Rd Mile 0, Denali National Park, AK 99755

Campground Description:
Riley Creek Campground is the largest campground in Denali National Park and serves as the park's main entrance hub. It offers a range of amenities for campers while providing easy access to park trails and shuttle services.

Unique Experience: Stay at the gateway to Denali National Park with access to park shuttle services and stunning trails.

Amenities:
• Restrooms and showers
• Shuttle service

Activities:
• Exploring Denali's visitor center and hiking trails
• Ranger-led programs

Denali Highway

Address: Mile 0 Denali Hwy, Cantwell, AK 99729

Campground Description:

The Denali Highway offers vast opportunities for dispersed camping in the wilderness, providing campers with a rugged, off-the-grid experience. It's ideal for those seeking remote, open spaces surrounded by nature.

Unique Experience: Experience complete solitude and breathtaking Alaskan wilderness while camping along the remote Denali Highway.

Amenities:
• Primitive campsites
• Scenic vistas

Activities:
• Hiking and off-road exploring
• Wildlife watching

Kenai National Wildlife Refuge

Address: Skilak Lake Rd, Soldotna, AK 99669

Campground Description:

Kenai National Wildlife Refuge offers remote, primitive camping for nature lovers who want to escape into the wilderness. It's perfect for boondocking enthusiasts who enjoy fishing, wildlife viewing, and pristine lakes.

Unique Experience: Camp in the remote Kenai wilderness with abundant wildlife and scenic lakes for fishing and kayaking.

Amenities:
• Primitive campsites
• Boat launch access

Activities:
• Fishing in Skilak Lake
• Wildlife viewing and photography

Others Campgrounds

• Golden Nugget RV Park
• Glacier Nalu Campground
• Klondike RV Park & Cottages
• Palmer Creek RV Park
• Tok RV Village
• Hidden Lake Campground
• Eagle's Nest Campground
• Valdez Glacier Campground
• Clearwater State Recreation Site
• Big Bear Campground

Others Boondocking

• Turnagain Pass (Kenai Peninsula)
• McCarthy Road Pullouts
• Denali Highway (Milepost 121)
• Hatcher Pass (Willow, AK)
• Taylor Highway (Chicken, AK)

Others National Park

• Teklanika River Campground (Denali National Park)
• Wonder Lake Campground (Denali National Park)
• Sanctuary River Campground (Denali National Park)

Hawaii: The Tropical Dream

When you think of Hawaii, RVing might not be the first thing that comes to mind, but for the adventurous at heart, it's an experience like no other. Hawaii's lush landscapes, volcanic craters, and stunning coastlines make it one of the most unique places to explore by vehicle. While RVing in Hawaii comes with its own set of challenges—mainly because you'll need to rent an RV on the islands rather than bring your own—what you gain in return is the chance to see the beauty of this tropical paradise up close and on your own terms.

The best season to visit Hawaii is **year-round**, thanks to its warm tropical climate, but **spring and fall**, particularly **April to June** and **September to November**, are ideal times to avoid the peak tourist crowds and enjoy pleasant weather. The island temperatures remain fairly consistent, ranging from the mid-70s to mid-80s°F, making it perfect for exploring the beaches, rainforests, and volcanic landscapes. **Winter** can bring more rain to certain areas, especially on the windward sides of the islands, but it's also prime time for whale watching and catching the massive swells along the North Shore of Oahu. There's no specific season to avoid, but be prepared for more rain if you visit during the winter months.

Hawaii's islands—Oahu, Maui, Kauai, and the Big Island—each offer a unique flavor of adventure for RVers. Oahu is great for those looking for a mix of urban excitement and natural beauty, with campgrounds near world-famous beaches like Waikiki and the rugged North Shore. Maui's Haleakalā National Park, with its breathtaking volcanic craters, offers an out-of-this-world experience, while Kauai's lush valleys and dramatic cliffs, especially the Nā Pali Coast, are ideal for those seeking solitude and raw beauty. On the Big Island, you can experience everything from black sand beaches to active volcanoes, all while camping in the shadow of Mauna Loa and Mauna Kea.

RVing in Hawaii may require a bit of extra planning—there are fewer RV parks compared to the mainland, and rental options are more limited—but the rewards are unforgettable. Imagine waking up to the sound of waves crashing on the shore, with the scent of tropical flowers filling the air. Whether you're exploring hidden beaches, hiking to a waterfall, or watching a fiery sunset over the Pacific, RVing in Hawaii is an experience that brings you closer to the essence of these magical islands.

For RVers with a taste for adventure, Hawaii offers a unique opportunity to explore one of the most beautiful places on Earth in a way that few ever do. It's not your typical RV destination, but for those who take the leap, it's an unforgettable journey into paradise.

Bellows Field Beach Park

📍 220 Tinker Rd, Waimanalo, HI 96795

📞 (808) 259-8080　　　　—　　$$

Campground Description:

Beachside camping for military personnel on Oahu's beautiful windward coast, offering oceanfront tent sites and access to swimming, sunbathing, and beachcombing.

Types of Sites Available:
- Beachfront tent sites
- Group camping
- Rustic cabins

Amenities:
- Direct beach access
- Restrooms, showers, picnic areas
- Camp store, Wi-Fi, equipment rentals

Activities:
- Swimming, snorkeling, beachcombing
- Exploring nearby Waimanalo Beach
- Hiking in the surrounding mountains

Unique Experiences: A peaceful retreat with stunning beach and mountain views, reserved for military personnel and families.

Feedback: Praised for its serene location, beautiful beach, and well-maintained facilities.

Malaekahana Beach Campground

📍 56-335 Kamehameha Hwy, Kahuku, HI 96731

📞 (808) 674-7715　　　　—　　$$

Campground Description:

A peaceful, beachfront campground on Oahu's northeastern coast offering tent camping and rustic huts for a simple, nature-focused escape.

Types of Sites Available:
- Tent camping
- Plantation huts
- Vehicle campsites

Amenities:
- Beach access, restrooms, showers
- Picnic tables, BBQ grills, camp store
- Equipment rentals for water activities

Activities:
- Swimming, surfing, kayaking
- Exploring Goat Island and nearby Laie Point
- Relaxing in hammocks under coconut trees

Unique Experiences: A tranquil, uncrowded beach with access to natural beauty and nearby cultural attractions.

Feedback: Loved for its pristine beach, peaceful atmosphere, and friendly staff.

Ho'okena Beach Park

Campground Description:

Beachfront tent camping on the Big Island's west coast, offering calm waters for swimming, snorkeling, and dolphin watching in a peaceful, historic setting.

Types of Sites Available:
- Beachfront tent camping
- Group camping

Amenities:
- Restrooms, showers, picnic areas
- Snack bar, equipment rentals
- Cultural programs

Activities:
- Swimming, snorkeling, kayaking
- Dolphin and whale watching
- Cultural tours and programs

Unique Experiences: A rustic camping experience by the ocean with opportunities for cultural immersion and marine wildlife viewing.

Feedback: Praised for its serene, natural setting and cultural significance.

Hapuna Beach State Recreation Area

Old Puako Rd, Waimea, HI 96743

(808) 961-9540 — $$

Campground Description:

A popular beachside campground on the Big Island's Kohala Coast, offering access to one of Hawaii's top-rated beaches with pristine white sands and clear waters.

Types of Sites Available:
- Tent camping
- A-frame shelters

Amenities:
- Restrooms, showers, picnic areas
- Hiking trails, lifeguarded beach areas
- Free parking for campers

Activities:
- Swimming, snorkeling, sunbathing
- Hiking along the coastal trails
- Whale watching in the winter

Unique Experiences: Direct access to one of Hawaii's most beautiful beaches with hiking trails and seasonal whale watching.

Feedback: Highly praised for its beach access, scenic views, and well-maintained facilities.

Wai'ānapanapa State Park

Address: Waianapanapa, Hana, HI 96713

Campground Description:
Located on the Road to Hana, Wai'ānapanapa State Park offers stunning black sand beaches and coastal caves, providing a dramatic landscape for camping.
Unique Experience: Camp near a black sand beach, with access to lava caves and freshwater pools.

Amenities:
• Picnic tables
• Restrooms with showers

Activities:
• Hiking along coastal trails
• Exploring lava caves and tide pools

Whittington Beach Park

Address: 89-1751 Hawaii Belt Rd, Naalehu, HI 96772

Campground Description:
A lesser-known beach park on the Big Island, Whittington Beach Park offers a quiet, oceanfront camping experience away from the crowds.
Unique Experience: Enjoy peaceful camping near the water with the sound of waves and volcanic rock formations.

Amenities:
• Picnic areas
• Restrooms

Activities:
• Shoreline fishing
• Beachcombing

Hapuna Beach State Recreation Area

Address: Old Puako Rd, Waimea, HI 96743

Campground Description:
Hapuna Beach is famous for its wide white sand beach, offering campers one of the most beautiful spots on the Big Island.
Unique Experience: Camp near one of the best beaches in Hawaii, perfect for swimming and sunsets.

Amenities:
• Picnic pavilions
• Restrooms and showers

Activities:
• Swimming and snorkeling
• Sunbathing on the sandy shores

Kipahulu Campground (Haleakala National Park)

Address: Mile Marker 42 Hana Hwy, Hana, HI 96713

Campground Description:
Located within Haleakala National Park, Kipahulu Campground offers coastal camping near lush rainforests and waterfalls.
Unique Experience: Camp with views of the Pacific Ocean and enjoy easy access to the famous Waimoku Falls.

Amenities:
• Picnic tables
• Pit toilets

Activities:
• Hiking to Waimoku Falls
• Exploring the Pools of 'Ohe'o

Boondocking

Haleakala National Park
Address: 30,000 Haleakala Hwy, Kula, HI 96790

Campground Description:
Haleakala National Park offers remote boondocking options at high elevations, providing surreal views of volcanic landscapes and the Pacific Ocean.

Unique Experience: Camp near the summit of Haleakala Crater for an unforgettable sunrise above the clouds.

Amenities:
- Primitive campsites
- Pit toilets

Activities:
- Hiking through volcanic landscapes
- Stargazing in the clear night skies

Kipahulu Campground (Maui)
Address: Mile Marker 42 Hana Hwy, Hana, HI 96713

Campground Description:
This coastal boondocking spot in Maui offers a blend of rainforest and ocean views, ideal for off-grid camping near waterfalls and lush greenery.

Unique Experience: Camp under the stars, surrounded by the sounds of cascading waterfalls and ocean waves.

Amenities:
- Primitive campsites
- Picnic tables

Activities:
- Hiking and waterfall exploration
- Relaxing in a remote, natural setting

Others Campgrounds

- Anini Beach Park Campground
- Spencer Beach Park Campground
- Salt Pond Beach Park Campground
- Polihale State Park Campground
- Koke'e State Park Campground
- Kanaha Beach Park Campground
- Laupahoehoe Point Beach Park Campground
- Kalopa State Recreation Area Campground
- Palaau State Park Campground
- Kokee Campground

Others Boondocking

- Kehena Beach (Big Island)
- Polihua Beach (Lanai)
- Papakolea Green Sand Beach (Big Island)
- Honokohau Harbor (Big Island)
- Kaena Point (Oahu)

Others National Park

- Kalaupapa National Historical Park Campground

YOUR NEXT ADVENTURE BEGINS HERE

As we wrap up this guide, we want to thank you for joining us on this journey through the countless campgrounds, scenic spots, and hidden gems spread across the United States. Creating this book has been a passion project, born from our many years and miles of travel together. Each campground, from the cozy corners of state parks to the rugged stretches of boondocking terrain, has been chosen with care to bring you the best experiences and insights we could offer.

Now, before you close these pages, we encourage you to scan the QR code below. This is your key to a treasure trove of resources we've prepared exclusively for readers like you, with the same dedication that went into crafting this book. These bonuses aren't just an afterthought; they're designed to be practical, valuable tools for every RVer. From **detailed guides on selecting the right RV** for your needs to **RV cooking tips and recipes** that make life on the road easier, we've put together extras that we believe are just as essential as the campground listings themselves.

For those who are new to the RV lifestyle, the **introductory guide** included in the bonuses offers an approachable start to this fascinating world, breaking down the essentials you'll need to feel comfortable and confident on the road. And if you're a seasoned traveler, you'll still find **tools like our RV checklist and solar power guide** useful as you plan your next journey.

We hope these additional resources make your trips smoother, inspire new adventures, and enrich your experience as an RVer. Just as this book was created to guide you across states and regions, these bonuses are here to support you in all the moments in between.

So go ahead—scan the code, dive into the resources, and let the road take you where it may. Safe travels, and may every mile bring you closer to the next great story.

https://drive.google.com/drive/folders/1cBCcAIyD28dtAWPTKD9EmSsYEzJRdeqi?usp=sharing

If you have questions, suggestions, or want to share campground updates, don't hesitate to reach out!

We're happy to receive your feedback and enhance the RV travel experience for our entire community.

For any issues downloading the bonuses, please also contact us at **davisrvadventure@gmail.com**.

Made in the USA
Las Vegas, NV
29 March 2025

a63ad19f-91d2-45aa-8479-a61eac157c82R01